Contents

List of Figures

Post-Cinematic Theatre and Performance

Palgrave Studies in Performance and Technology

Series Editors: **Susan Broadhurst** and **Josephine Machon**

Books included in this cutting-edge series centre on global and embodied approaches to performance and technology. As well as focusing on digital performance and art, books in the series also include the theoretical and historical context relevant to these practices. The series offers fresh artistic and theoretical perspectives on this exciting and growing area of contemporary performance practice, and includes contributors from a wide range of international locations working within this varied discipline. Titles in the series will include edited collections and monographs on issues including (but not limited to): identity and live art; intimacy and engagement with technology; biotechnology and artistic practices; technology, architecture and performance; performance, gender and technology; and space and performance.

Titles include:

Susan Broadhurst and Josephine Machon (*editors*)
SENSUALITIES/TEXTUALITIES AND TECHNOLOGIES
Writings of the Body in 21st Century Performance

Susan Broadhurst and Josephine Machon (*editors*)
IDENTITY, PERFORMANCE AND TECHNOLOGY
Practices of Empowerment, Embodiment and Technicity

Maria Chatzichristodoulou and Rachel Zerihan (*editors*)
INTIMACY ACROSS VISCERAL AND DIGITAL PERFORMANCE

Aneta Mancewicz
INTERMEDIAL SHAKESPEARES ON EUROPEAN STAGES

Kara Reilly (*editor*)
THEATRE, PERFORMANCE AND ANALOGUE TECHNOLOGY
Historical Interfaces and Intermedialities

Piotr Woycicki
POST-CINEMATIC THEATRE AND PERFORMANCE

Palgrave Studies in Performance and Technology
Series Standing Order ISBN 978–0–230–29362–5 Hardback
978–0–230–29363–2 Paperback
(*outside North America only*)

You can receive future titles in this series as they are published by placing a standing order. Please contact your bookseller or, in case of difficulty, write to us at the address below with your name and address, the title of the series and the ISBN quoted above.

Customer Services Department, Macmillan Distribution Ltd, Houndmills, Basingstoke, Hampshire RG21 6XS, England

Post-Cinematic Theatre and Performance

Piotr Woycicki
University of Aberystwyth, UK

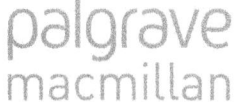

palgrave
macmillan

First published 2014 by
PALGRAVE MACMILLAN

Palgrave Macmillan in the UK is an imprint of Macmillan Publishers Limited, registered in England, company number 785998, of Houndmills, Basingstoke, Hampshire RG21 6XS.

Palgrave Macmillan in the US is a division of St Martin's Press LLC, 175 Fifth Avenue, New York, NY 10010.

Palgrave Macmillan is the global academic imprint of the above companies and has companies and representatives throughout the world.

Palgrave® and Macmillan® are registered trademarks in the United States, the United Kingdom, Europe and other countries.

ISBN 978–1–137–37548–3

This book is printed on paper suitable for recycling and made from fully managed and sustained forest sources. Logging, pulping and manufacturing processes are expected to conform to the environmental regulations of the country of origin.

A catalogue record for this book is available from the British Library.

Library of Congress Cataloging-in-Publication Data

Woycicki, Piotr, 1983-

Post-cinematic theatre and performance / Piotr Woycicki, University of Aberystwyth, UK.

pages cm. – (Palgrave studies in performance and technology)

Includes bibliographical references and index.
ISBN 978–1–137–37548–3
1. Motion pictures and theater.   2. Experimental films—History and criticism.   3. Experimental theater—History—21st century.   4. Motion pictures in the theater.   I. Title.
PN1995.25.W79 2014
791—dc23   2014018832

Typeset by MPS Limited, Chennai, India.

Series Editors' Preface

Susan Broadhurst was invited to be Series Editor of *Palgrave Studies in Performance and Technology* in 2009 and she invited Josephine Machon to be co-editor soon afterwards. Performance and technological resources, combined in various forms, constitute an increasingly popular area of artistic practice. In a relatively short time a proliferation of new technological applications have infiltrated and irrevocably altered everyday life. The consequences of this might not be unproblematic, but the ambitions of performance practitioners have been extended by the availability of such resources. The remit of this important series is to acknowledge the progressive and diverse approaches to various performances and artworks employing technology in their practices. The series was launched in 2010 at the Digital Resources Arts and Humanities Conference, hosted by Broadhurst and held at Brunel University, London. Books included in this cutting-edge series centre on embodied approaches to performance and technology globally. As well as focusing on digital performance and art, books in the series also include the theoretical and historical context relevant to these practices. The series offers fresh artistic and theoretical perspectives on this exciting and growing area of contemporary performance and arts practice, and includes contributors working within this varied discipline from a wide range of international locations. Titles in the series will include edited collections and monographs on issues including (but not limited to): identity and live art; intimacy and engagement with technology; biotechnology and artistic practices; technology, architecture and performance; performance, gender and technology; and space and performance.

Susan Broadhurst
Josephine Machon

Acknowledgements

I would like to thank all those who over the past few years have directly helped and supported this project offering generous feedback and providing invaluable materials and insights: Karen Juers-Munby, Andrew Quick, Carl Lavery, Gerry Harris, Imitating the Dog, Pete Brooks, Lancaster University and Aberystwyth University.

With regards to the figures reproduced in this book, I am pleased to acknowledge the following credits:

Richard-Max Tremblay for the photograph: Robert Lepage and the *Elsinore* set

Marie-Lan Nguyen for a photograph of *Laocoön*

Emmanuel Valette for a photograph from *The Andersen Project* by Robert Lepage

Station House Opera for a still of the running game in *Roadmetal Sweetbread*

Jan Poloczek for the photograph of the fantasy scene in *Roadmetal Sweetbread*

Christian Enger for the photograph from Station House Opera's *A Mare's Nest*

Mary Gearhart for the photograph from the Wooster Group's *House/Lights*

Paula Court for the photograph from the Wooster Group's *House/Lights*

Paula Court for the photographs from the Wooster Group's *Hamlet*

Stephen Cummiskey for the photograph of Julia Wieninger in *Wunschkonzert* by Franz Xaver Kroetz, Schauspiel Köln, 2008

Ed Waring and Imitating the Dog for the photograph of letterbox framing in *Hotel Methuselah*

Ed Waring and Imitating the Dog for the photograph of Amy's arrival at the Hotel in *Hotel Methuselah*

Ed Waring and Imitating the Dog for 'overhead' shot in *Hotel Methuselah*

Ed Waring and Imitating the Dog for the photograph of extreme close-up of Harry on front projection in *Hotel Methuselah*

Ed Waring and Imitating the Dog for the photograph of Amy and the Weird Woman walking down the corridor in *Hotel Methuselah*

Ed Waring and Imitating the Dog for the photograph of the bedroom scene in *Hotel Methuselah*

Ed Waring and Imitating the Dog for the photograph of the Weird Man and Harry in *Hotel Methuselah*

Steve Benford for the diagram concept of the mixed reality continuum

Zentropa Entertainments for the still of the enormous soundstage in Sweden where *Dogville* was filmed

Zentropa Entertainments for the still of the 'God shot' in *Dogville*

Zentropa Entertainments for the still of the houses without walls on Elm St in *Dogville*

Zentropa Entertainments for the still of the rape scene in *Dogville*

1
The Post-Cinematic Landscape

In recent years an increasing number of contemporary theatre works have employed a variety of mixed media and film techniques to enhance, but also potentially disturb, the perception of the worlds they create. The general term 'intermedial theatre' or 'multimedia theatre' may apply to these pieces, which range from multi-million-dollar mainstream Broadway shows and high profile opera stagings to radical avant-garde endeavours. Despite the variety of forms and aesthetics, as Freda Chapple and Chiel Kattenbelt suggest, the general form of intermedial theatre can be defined through one of its significant features, 'the incorporation of digital technology into theatre practice, and the presence of other media within theatre productions' (Chapple and Kattenbelt 2006b: 11). In that sense, intermedial theatre is essentially a hybrid art form encompassing theatre, film, live performance, computer generated virtual realities, communication technologies and so on. As a result, there is a blurring of generic boundaries at play which can crucially be associated with a 'self-conscious reflexivity that displays the devices of performance in performance' (Chapple and Kattenbelt 2006b: 11) – a process of re-perception and reconstruction through performance occurs (Chapple and Kattenbelt 2006b: 12). Thus there is more at stake here than technological innovation, since intermediality is not only a technological phenomenon but also concerns a hybridity of forms and conventions, resulting in styles that inspire different modes of perception. Therefore intermedial practices have the potential to radically change our perceptions of performance and interrogate their cultural and political foundations, even though not all necessarily seek to do so (for example, *Reel to Real* (2010), which will be discussed below).

This phenomenon has been accompanied by a wealth of scholarship on the subject of intermediality. Most notably, Chapple and Kattenbelt's

Intermediality in Theatre and Performance (2006), Steve Dixon's *Digital Performance* (2007), Greg Giesekam's *Staging the Screen* (2007), Nick Kaye's *Multi-Media Video Installation Performance* (2007), Jennifer Parker-Starbuck's *Cyborg Theatre: Corporeal/Technological Intersections in Multimedia Performance (Performance Interventions)* (2011) and Rosemary Klich and Edward Scheer's *Multimedia Performance* (2012) amongst others. These publications cover a very wide range of performance practices and critical approaches, yielding invaluable insights on the nature of intermediality which this book will draw upon. However, the focus here is on a subgroup of intermedial practices that I will call post-cinematic, and that critically addresses cinematic codes and conventions. In the light of the global influence of cinematic culture this focus can offer a valuable perspective on theatre's interinvolvement with film.[1] It also enables more specific insights to be gained by looking at the interinvolvement of theatre and film as a deconstruction of culturally dominant cinematic conventions. The chapters below explore the ways in which cinema operates within our contemporary culture, examining its effects on the audience's perceptual habits and expectations and asking what is politically, ethically and philosophically at stake in the deconstruction of these conventions. They also elaborate on the deconstructive intermedial strategies that are specifically sourced from and influenced by cinematic traditions.

Our notion of cinema – but also to an extent the broader cultural landscape – is heavily influenced by realist cinematic conventions. By means of perspectivist structuring and pleasure laden aesthetic forms, these conventions in turn calibrate our sensitivities and expectations and guide our perceptions, often inducing a passive mode of spectatorship, limiting audiences' ability to respond and making them prone to be affected by particular ideological perspectives and political agendas. Following Jean Baudrillard's argument from *Simulacra and Simulation*, one could even argue that popular cinema effectuates a deterrence of the real, where simulations precede and thus articulate in advance our perceptions of reality (Baudrillard 1994). In that sense, behind the aesthetic structures of cinema, there are political agendas determining how things should be perceived. Despite this lure, fixation and the spell of realism, we live in a post-cinematic age which can partly be characterised by a heightened awareness of cinematic modes of operation. However this awareness is not always stimulated and foregrounded, whereas post-cinematic theatre, I shall argue, has the capacity of doing that, essentially through its deconstructive intermedial strategies.

But can all intermedial theatre that uses film in cinematic ways automatically be defined as post-cinematic? Let us consider an intermedial piece called *Reel to Real* (2010), performed at the 2010 Edinburgh Festival. The piece was directed and choreographed by Lynne Taylor-Corbett and produced by the Broadway Asia International, LLC and the Beijing Huairou State Owned Assets Management Company, Beijing Rouyuan Cultural Media Co. Ltd, in order to celebrate the creation of their Film, Theatre and Multimedia Arts studio complex – a Chinese version of Hollywood. *Reel to Real* is an intermedial musical based around scenes from famous Hollywood musicals, which are loosely tied together by a simple story line. The story line follows the characters Jack and Jill whose father, head of a major Hollywood studio corporation, sends them on a journey around the world, full of 'quests' and twists and turns of plot, in order to find out which one of them will be the most worthy successor in his business. After their travels, having seen the Statue of Liberty, the Eiffel tower, Notre Dame and so on, having fought and had many arguments which reflected their rugged 'American' competitive individualism, Jack and Jill finally face the Great Wall of China. It is ultimately this great divide which brings them together and the father decides to make them both his successors, in the spirit of equality and cooperation. From an ideological and political perspective, the show was easily interpreted as promoting Chinese culture and the values of the Chinese political system, superficially set, as they were, in opposition to American culture and values; superficially and ironically since the current economic and political system of China is firmly anchored in its own version of Western capitalism. For instance, the Chinese producers of this multi-million-dollar venture made it clear that at least 20 per cent of the images and video material should promote Chinese tourist locations. The show did that quite explicitly and indeed the ideological 'reel' of the tourist advertisement would – in the case of the great majority of the audience – precede any 'real' experience of a trip to China. It is also an instance of cultural colonisation, ironically in this case, of Hollywood, appropriating Hollywood means and aesthetics. This show could easily be labelled as a cinematic intermedial piece, but not as a post-cinematic piece in the way I have defined it. This is because it essentially indulged in the dominant cinematic culture as opposed to developing a critical reflexive stance. In terms of intermedial aesthetics, for the most part the makers took great care to blend the film and live action and to offer a single cohesive perspective on the simplistic story. The musical clips were not addressed critically and apart from a few ironic jokes and parodies of stereotypical characters the show was essentially a celebratory medley of Hollywood musicals. For the most part, the choreography doubled the action on screen, making it virtually redundant. Film animations were mainly used as a method of enhancing scenes, as a virtual backdrop or wallpaper. Furthermore there was a 'concealed' (albeit blatantly obvious) political agenda behind the performance. Unlike the pieces which will be discussed below, *Reel to Real* did not deconstruct cinematic conventions in such a way as to emancipate the spectators to critically reflect on the way in which cinema can induce ideological perspectives and political agendas. Instead it provided a light, dazzling spectacle full of beautifully crafted, immersively cinematic stage effects.

But is it enough to offer such a critique? Is this spellbinding effect not a wider cultural phenomenon stemming from a century of realist cinema tradition? The conventions and aesthetic structures of realist cinema have become so culturally dominant and associated with all kinds of pleasures and harmonies that they must have re-calibrated our sensitivities but also modes of perception. These immersive, often affect-laden aesthetic journeys have become an incentive to concur with any argument a piece like that may propose and make the audience accord with whatever political agendas and ideological perspectives they offer. The case of *Reel to Real* speaks for itself, in the sense that it barely conceals a cultural/tourist promotion of China and that it could also be read as superficially and ironically evoking the superiority of Chinese 'communist' values over the individualist American capitalist mentality.

One could argue that there is nothing wrong with yielding to cinematic illusions that are reflective of a global cinematisation of culture. After all, it is only a bit of entertainment and we all need it after a hard day's work – the separation of work and entertainment obviously being part of the movie-going culture. But does yielding to this cultural dominance of cinema in ways that suspend critical thought not carry any dangers? What interests me here is what is politically and culturally at stake, and how post-cinematic theatre and film can interrogate and perhaps exhibit a form of resistance to this dominant cinematisation through deconstructive intermedial practice. The deconstructive nature of these works opens up possibilities for interpretation and foregrounds what Hans-Thies Lehmann describes as a 'politics of perception' (Lehmann 2006: 186). This is a politics that deals not with political content or 'messages' but rather with an awareness of the political and ideological factors underlying perception. It is a form of awareness and self-conscious reflexivity that arguably inspires a more active spectatorship but that is usually lost, concealed and discriminated against within the design of a mainstream realist cinematic experience.

The overall structure of this project is as follows. This introductory chapter will mainly comprise of an articulation of post-cinematic theatre as a subset of intermedial practices and an elaboration on Lehmann's notion of the 'politics of perception', also referred to as an aesthetics of 'response-ability' (Lehmann 2006: 186) (as translated by Karen Jürs-Munby: *Verantwortung* in the original). The first section will trace the background and some of the cultural influences surrounding post-cinematic theatre. It will contend that we live in a culture that is progressively saturated with cinematic forms and conventions and that the notion of post-cinema, which defines post-cinematic theatre, is a cultural reaction to this cinematisation both in art practice and theory, one that is marked by a shift towards a heightened awareness of cinematic modes of operation and their influences on cultural perceptions. Despite the plethora and variety of film forms that emerged in the twentieth century, contemporary cinema culture on the whole remains dominated by aesthetics and conventions rooted in classical realist cinema stemming from early mainstream Hollywood and Soviet montage traditions. Thus post-cinema will be defined as a contemporary critical and reflexive trend in mainly avant-garde culture, aimed at interrogating and deconstructing dominant cinematic conventions and the expectations associated with them. This discussion benefits from the introduction of some critical theories, mainly from film studies' 'post-theory', that have critiqued these developments in mainstream cinema and analysed their effects on the way ideology and social relations were and are being constructed through cinematic works.

The next section of the chapter elaborates on some of the general aesthetic strategies that are essentially concerned with the deconstruction of realist cinematic conventions. This section will introduce an overview of post-cinematic aesthetics, hence locating post-cinematic theatre in the broader post-cinematic artistic landscape. It will also draw a parallel between post-cinematic theatre and Lehmann's concept of postdramatic theatre, since both are concerned with a reaction against culturally and institutionally dominant conventions and aesthetics. These affinities will become useful and relevant during the analysis of the specific case studies and will provide interesting insights for the discussions that will follow. The third section introduces and defines the concept of the 'politics of perception', in order to clarify the nature of the political resistance that the post-cinematic pieces in question offer. The final section takes a brief look at the history of critical discourses that dealt with the intermediality of film and theatre, ranging from the early debates to more contemporary approaches.

The case studies chapters deal with post-cinematic works from the late 1980s to the present day and argue that these pieces exhibit a cultural and political resistance to realist cinematic conventions, emancipating the audience by offering them a broader spectrum of perceptual choices. I will look closely at the following post-cinematic theatre pieces: Robert Lepage's *Elsinore* and *The Andersen Project*, Station House Opera's *Roadmetal Sweetbread* and *A Mare's Nest* and the Wooster Group's *House/Lights* and *Hamlet*, Katie Mitchell's *Wunschkonzert*, Imitating the Dog's *Hotel Methuselah* and Duncan Speakman's cinematic sound walk *As If It Were The Last Time*. All of them are fairly recent post-cinematic pieces, and they exhibit the post-cinematic trend of deconstructing cinematic culture, whilst at the same time being heavily influenced by it. They also deal with various aspects of the 'cinematic apparatus' and employ an array of different intermedial strategies, interinvolving film and theatre to challenge the audience's perceptions and expectations associated with cinema. The final chapter deals not with a piece of theatre but with a film, Lars von Trier's *Dogville*, which could be categorised as a Brechtian,[2] post-cinematic film. Like the theatre pieces *Dogville* uses an intermedial strategy of interinvolvement of theatrical and filmic aesthetics to deconstruct and challenge realist expectations. Even though *Dogville* is not a theatre piece it draws upon theatre's deconstructive political potential. Hence the theatrical aesthetic used in the film is not naturalistic but Brechtian, one that is historically associated with the notion of challenging political perceptions.

An array of post-structuralist approaches comes into play in the analysis of the ways in which intermedial strategies in post-cinematic theatre deconstruct cinematic conventions. Here, these will include theories by Jean-François Lyotard, Emmanuel Lévinas, Gilles Deleuze, Jacques Rancière and Jacques Derrida, each of which can be related to specific case studies. The value of post-structuralist theory here lies in the fact that to a great extent the perceptual experiences of realist cinema are organised through discursive conventions and aesthetic *structures*. Thus these post-structuralist theories will be used to articulate what is perceptually at stake in the aesthetics of disorientation, undecidability, multiplicity and aporias that emerge in the post-cinematic pieces. They will be also used to explore what is at stake in this deconstruction of cinematic conventions from different angles: political agendas, ethical perceptions, perspectivist approaches to narratives, moral frameworks, each of which will be dealt with specifically in the case studies.

The shows discussed are all ones with which I am familiar and inevitably my interpretations of audiences' and spectators' experiences will reflect the perspective of my own experiences. This is obviously a subjective and speculative approach, yet it will serve the argument since it is concerned with demonstrating different *possibilities* of reading and interpretation resulting from deconstruction effects as opposed to claiming determinate audience experiences. However there will always be a degree of subjectivity and speculation because cinematic culture affects everyone differently, and while a lot of its influences on the way we perceive culture and our expectations associated with it are to an extent shared, there will always be variances of response even to the most conventional of films. Thus my argumentative methodology will be primarily concerned with a spectrum of perceptual freedom and the claim that post-cinematic pieces essentially broaden this spectrum for an audience, in contradistinction and possibly in reaction to realist cinematic conventions which work towards narrowing this spectrum down.

Chapter 2 looks at Robert Lepage's *Elsinore* (1996) and *The Andersen Project* (2006). The point of departure for the discussion is Sergei Eisenstein's theory of classical film montage and cinematic metaphor. In particular his notion of the image of movement and his critique of Edward Muybridge's famous movement studies, which Lepage deliberately references in *Elsinore* in order to effectuate a deconstruction of cinematic montage. To supplement the theoretical approach Colin MacCabe's (1985) discursive critique of Eisenstein helps us to explore the ways in which the post-cinematic aesthetic of *Elsinore* jars the possibility of an ideologically cohesive cinematic meta-discourse, thus stimulating the audience to become more active in the process of meaning making, exemplifying Lehmann's aesthetic of 'response-ability' or 'politics of perception'. *The Andersen Project* is discussed in the light of the notion of the mediaphoric body, in relation to Eisenstein's interpretation of the Laocoön. *The Andersen Project* presents us with mediaphors of 'impossible' bodies, where the tensions between the different constituents of these pseudo-metaphors (mediaphors) deconstruct the 'integral' nature of classical metaphors as postulated by Eisenstein.

The third chapter looks at Station House Opera's *Roadmetal Sweetbread* and *A Mare's Nest*. Jean-François Lyotard's critique of mainstream realist cinema in his essay 'Acinema' offers the theoretical context, where he argues that through 'pleasure'-bound montage aesthetics and representations realist cinema effectuates a capitalist philosophy of reproducing ideological constructs. However, these post-cinematic pieces have the potential to go beyond 'pleasure'-bound representations, by playing upon the tension between *pleasure* and what Lyotard defines as *jouissance*. This experience of *jouissance* can have a key role in deconstructing the formulaic 'pleasures' of realist film and revealing enjoyment beyond the standard social and cultural ramifications implicit in it.

By foregrounding this tension between *pleasure* and *jouissance*, and shifting the emphasis towards the pole of *jouissance*, it can be argued that the case studies in this chapter negotiate the 'politics of perception' behind representations of pleasure in film culture. More specifically this is the case with the deconstruction of the perception of heteronormative pleasures in Station House Opera's *Roadmetal Sweetbread*. In *A Mare's Nest*, to an extent the audience itself performs and embodies what could be called the 'cinematic apparatus', making the piece an exploration of the *jouissance* of a wandering perception. By allowing this freedom to the audience, the piece explores enjoyment beyond a more fixed and structured perspectivist spectator position.

Chapter 4 extends the arguments of the previous chapter and looks at the work of the Wooster Group, *House/Lights* (1996) and *Hamlet* (2009). *House/Lights*, like much of the Wooster Group's work, is based on numerous intertexts. In this case, the key texts are Gertrude Stein's opera *Doctor Faustus Lights the Lights* (1938) and *Olga's House of Shame* (1964), a horror film about perverse tortures and a crime syndicate underworld. The analysis in this chapter begins with Stein's methodologies for theatrical staging, and continues with a discussion of the staging of *Olga's House of Shame* (1964). It looks specifically at the relation between the notion of the 'imaginary body of film', the impossible reality of a movie, and the attempt to stage and physically embody this cinematic illusion. The deconstructed nature of the piece allows for a simultaneity of perceptions of the protagonist, ranging from victim to villain, from object of desire to tortured subject. This complication is a result of the post-cinematic nature of the piece and foregrounds a 'politics of perception' that frees the spectator to take a more active part in the framing and montage of the world of the piece. Discussion of the Wooster Group's *Hamlet* (2009), based on Richard Burton's famous filmed Broadway production of Hamlet from 1964, centres on the way in which this piece functions as post-cinematic 'karaoke', a staging of the spectators' experience and 'libidinal journey' through the original Burton film.

Chapter 5 takes a different angle on the 'politics of perception' in exploring the 'ethics of perception' in Katie Mitchell's staging of Franz Xavier Kroetz's *Wunschkonzert* (2009). This enables an exploration of the ethical considerations that are taken into account in constructing filmic and cinematic representations but that are usually 'concealed' in mainstream realist constructs. I will also explore the ethical dimension of revealing and staging this process theatrically. The specific concern is with the ethical issues behind representing and eliciting identification with a story about suicide. From a representational perspective, it could be said that the *Wunschkonzert* brings forward questions about how suicide ought to be perceived and represented. This may have political implications, as in the case of the high suicide rates in Eastern Germany, which were routinely covered up during the communist regime.[3] However, ethical interrogation in the *Wunschkonzert* is not so much concerned with specific representations (though these inevitably spring to mind) as it is with the very forms of representation and consequently the forms of perception of these issues and the perceptual choices that an audience is offered by the intermedial aesthetics of the piece. There is an ethics of perception at play within the choices offered, which becomes foregrounded by the piece. In this chapter it is the work of philosopher Emmanuel Lévinas that will be brought to the exploration of the ethics behind these potential perceptual choices. In turn this will provoke questions about the relationship between ethics and morality, affective engagement and critical engagement, but also between the notion of goodness and perception of truth.

The sixth chapter looks at Imitating the Dog's *Hotel Methuselah* (2005) and the disorienting aspects of the processes underlying post-cinematic performance, which stimulate the audience to reconstruct a narrative from the disconnected elements conveyed by the spectacle. Lyotard's metaphor of the 'disorienting landscape' will be used to analyse the ways in which the formal interplay of cinema and theatre question representations of war trauma. *Hotel Methuselah* was performed at a period of heated debates and media accusations of political apathy surrounding the Iraq war. In many ways *Hotel Methuselah* could be said to provoke the spectators to be more active and reflexive of how they perceive the issue of war in the media and cinema, and the political implications of their perceptions. By freeing the spectator through these formal strategies the piece negotiated a 'politics of perception' in relation to its war themes and the dominance of realist cinema in the construction of historical narratives.

Chapter 7 looks at Duncan Speakman's *As If It Were The Last Time.* The analysis works through the prism of Peter Greenaway's (2010) four 'tyrannies' of realist cinema in order to explore how the post-cinematic aesthetics of this particular soundwalk re-fashion and deconstruct culturally dominant conventions of realist cinema. It will be argued that this kind of audio-theatre offers a categorically different degree of participation and audience emancipation from the other pieces, whilst still embedding itself heavily within cinematic culture. The intermedial theory in Chapter 7 mainly stems from Gabriella Giannachi's and Steve Benford's research on 'mixed-reality performances', supported by site-specific performance theory and, where appropriate, Michel Chion's concept of 'acousmatization'[4] in order to explore the 'politics of perception' arising from the piece's post-cinematic aesthetic. The relationship between the 'politics of perception' and neo-situationist philosophy, namely Guy Debord's concept of *dérive*, offers insights into the site-specific soundwalk character of the piece.

The final chapter looks at Lars von Trier's film *Dogville* (2003) in relation to the 'politics of perception' involving moral judgements. The obvious difference between this chapter and the earlier chapters is that this concerns an intermedial film (a theatricalised, Brechtian film) and not an intermedial piece of theatre. The chapter's focus is not the political fable of *Dogville* as such but the intermedial aesthetics through which the fable is conveyed. It will be argued that these aesthetics deconstruct and challenge the expectations of realist cinema conventions and by doing so create a space of moral ambiguities and interpretative freedom. Thus the 'interinvolvement' of theatrical and cinematic modes of representation in *Dogville* will be looked at from the angle of moral judgements that potentially come into play when negotiating perceptual choices. Jacques Derrida's theory of aporias concerning moral judgements and the notion of justice will be used to demonstrate what is politically at stake in making these perceptual choices.

All of the case studies in the book are seminal examples of post-cinematic theatre and performance works which can help to define the field. They construct a spectrum that enables exploration of different degrees of interinvolvement of theatre and film. At one end of the spectrum, Duncan Speakman's/Circumstance's *As If It Were The Last Time* is a cinematic audio walk that does not use film at all. Instead it creates a cinematic experience through a mixture of soundtrack, storytelling, a guided tour and site-generic performance. At the other end of the spectrum lies a Brechtian-film, *Dogville*, which in contradistinction to Speakman's piece has no 'live' theatrical or 'live' performance element, even though theatrical conventions and theatrical perceptual habits play a defining role in its composition. In between there are pieces that use mediated film on stage in order to augment theatrical space and expand on theatre's expressive possibilities. These are pieces such as *A Mare's Nest* by Station House Opera and *House/Lights* by the Wooster Group. Then there are case studies where mediated film is more dominant and it is the 'live' performance that potentially augments and supplements filmic space, as is the case with Robert Lepage's *The Andersen Project*, Imitating the Dog's *Hotel Methuselah* or Katie Mitchell's *Wunschkonzert*. This range of pieces and the different degrees of interinvolvement of theatre and film that they display in turn offer a wide range of insights into ways in which deconstructions of cinema in theatre and performance can be theorised. Explorations and deconstructions of cinema in theatre and performance have developed a long history, which will be addressed later in this chapter. However it is worth remarking at this point that there is a vast and growing landscape of contemporary performance that is post-cinematic. Some of these – other than the ones analysed in detail in this book – continue to expand the post-cinematic field in new directions.

A lot of interesting recent work in the field of post-cinematic performance has been done by film director Peter Greenaway. Working in Holland and in collaboration with many Dutch artists, his post-cinematic work engages with an exploration of intermedial approaches to the deconstruction of cinema. For example, *4 Triennale* (2007) explored various unconventional forms of screen framings and ways of projecting cinematic images. This work challenged expectations relating to the framing of cinematic images within the panoramic frame. *Venaria Reale* (2007) was a cinematic installation based on classical paintings and portraiture and telling a series of disconnected narratives about characters living in a Renaissance hunting lodge. The piece reflected Greenaway's interest in challenging expectations of linear narrative progression in cinema that, he argues, are the result of the long-standing influence of nineteenth-century novel narrative structures on realist film montage. *Tulse Luper VJ Performance* (2009) explored the cinematic potential of VJ-ing and *A Survivor from Warsaw* (2008) saw a form of 'live' cinema projected on to multiple screens and montaged to Arnold Schoenberg's music. This 'live' deconstruction of the relationship between music and image explored the potential of liberating cinematic imagery from pre-montaged, 'fixed' aesthetic frameworks but also explored the cinematic image through the realm of digital manipulation.

In terms of digital performance, works such as *Model 5* (1994) by Kurt Hentschläger and Ulf Laingheinrich challenge viewers' perceptions of time and spatiality in relation to facial expression in close-ups. Performance artist Akemi Takeya's face is filmed in close-up and subjected to a digital manipulation procedure called 'granular synthesis' which distorts and intensifies her facial movements, making them unnaturally fast and abrupt. Jeffrey Jones suggests: 'The often seemingly aggressive audiovisual installations shake the viewer out of the stupor of habitual consumption and, in the best traditions of the avant-garde, bring about an unusual, even shocking, level of experimental intensity' (Shaw in Klich and Scheer 2012: 186). The celluloid ghost of an actor's face is being deconstructed here by subjecting it to extreme intensities of speed and sound volume. This creates potentially terrifying chimeric impressions which effectively create 'impossible' articulation, a facial expression that is only achieved through digital synthesis, becoming a deconstruction of the organic cinematic close-up.

CREW is a Belgium collective under the direction of Eric Jones that explores immersive cinema, mainly focusing on the virtual reality apparatus and one-man audience experiences. As Kurt Vanhoutte and Nele Wynatts explain:

> CREW triggers the theatrical imagination of design and production, text and sound. The artistic outcome tends to be hybrid; with the technological live art of CREW troubling installed categories of theatricality leading to immersive embodied environments that challenge common notions of (tele)presence, spectatorship, interactivity and narration.
>
> (Vanhoutte in Bay-Cheng et al. 2010: 69)

Their works include pieces such as *Crash* (2004), *U_raging standstill* (2006–07), *EUX* (2008) and *Centrifuga* (2013) amongst others. These are often concerned with the dichotomies of live and virtual presence, exploring the ways in which spectators can engage and interact with virtual avatars and narratives inspired by cinematic culture.

Another interesting collective in the context of interactive post-cinematic work is the iCinema part of the Centre of Interactive Cinema Research at the University of New South Wales, Australia. Their work includes pieces such as *Conversations* (2004–06), *Eavesdrop* (2004) and most recently *Scenarios* (2011). A distinct feature of their work is the use of interactive cycloramas, stereoscopic movies and virtual reality to create environments in which spectators can interact and manipulate cinematic spectacles. For instance in *Eavesdrop* spectators stand in the middle of a 360 degree cyclorama where a landscape of characters, their conversations and dramatic scenarios unfold simultaneously. Every character's conversation is concerned with a moral dilemma:

> [a] woman discusses her attempts to find identity through cosmetic surgery; an old couple discuss their preferred method of suicide; a middle-aged man suffers the pangs of unrequited love; a radio broadcaster interviews an activist about ethics, choice and revolution; a young man tries to convince his girlfriend to leave their small-town suburb for the promise of the city; while two other young men drink, smoke, and mourn their lost potential.
>
> (Klich and Scheer 2012: 60)

Using a console in the middle of the cyclorama, spectators could choose to zoom in and zoom out on these scenes, allowing them to choose and frame their perception at will. Director David Pledgers explained it on their website as follows:

> Special to this space is the ability to enter into the private, interior landscapes of each of the characters. These interior landscapes convey a compressed sense of the emotional states the characters are experiencing. Get too close to any of the characters and the spectator will be bumped into this interior life without warning. In this way, *Eavesdrop* is intended to work on three layers: the interior landscapes of the characters, their public narratives, and the engagement with the spectator through the simple interactive medium of zoom and pan functions on a platform-module that the user employs to navigate the space.
>
> (iCinema 2013)

Thus *Eavesdrop* breaks from the traditional notion of a passive cinema audience, instead positioning the spectators within an interactive format where they can make decisions on how they wish to structure their own experience of the film image.

These practitioners and the pieces that they devise explore new directions in post-cinematic performance in terms of aesthetics, technological implementation, cultural and political contexts. In such an expansive field, laden with hybrid performance works that incorporate a vast array of stylistics, technologies, cultural and political contexts and performative modes, the task of carving out a definition of the post-cinematic is challenging. Let us begin then by considering the cultural context of post-cinema in general.

1.1   Post-cinema as a cultural phenomena

We live in a culture that is saturated with cinematic modes of representation that also constitute forms of perception, modes of framing and perceiving the world around us, and what one might call expectations of a 'cinematic gaze'. It is easy to bring to mind examples from all manner of cultural works. For instance, the visual structures of web pages, aesthetic cinematic influences on photography, the editing of publicity and advertisements, the aesthetics and thematics of poster design, popular literature like *The Da Vinci Code* and even the way people tend to structure storytelling in daily life are but a few examples of the way cinematic tropes and conventions influence and shape the forms of our culture and the expectations we may have when perceiving them. Half a century ago, when referring to cinema, Béla Balázs claimed 'that the mentality of the people, and particularly of the urban population, is to a great extent the product of this art, an art that is at the same time a vast industry' (Balázs 1959: 202). For Balázs the development of cinema as an art form was paralleled by the development of the public's ability to understand the then 'new form-language' (Balázs 1972: 34) of film. Along similar lines of argument Herbert Blau, in his essay on theatre and cinema, quotes Marx's *Grundrisse*, conveying the notion of dominant cinematic aesthetics:

> In all forms of society, there is one specific kind of production which predominates over the rest, whose relations thus assign rank and influence to the others. It is a general illumination which bathes all the other colours and modifies their particularity. It is a particular ether which determines the specific gravity of every being which has materialised within it.
>
> (Blau 1982: 121)

Even though Blau and Balázs may seem somewhat outdated in the era of the internet, especially when Blau puts cinema at the top of a Marxist hierarchical pyramid, their statements still hold true. I believe that to this very day the development of cinema is irrevocably linked with the development of the cultural perceptions influenced by it. In the age of oral culture it was myths, legends and their respective lyrical forms that shaped the conventions through which people told the stories of their lives, reconstructed histories, established social and political relations and through that defined their identities. Cinema can thus be seen as a powerful contemporary cultural phenomenon that has 'replaced' all of these previous forms. The mainstream cultural phenomenon of cinema consists of a set of forms and conventions through which our society defines itself across various media. Consequently this dominant zeitgeist is literally 'ghosting' much of our cultural production, triggering cultural and artistic critical reactions which could be termed as post-cinematic.

But in order to better understand what is culturally at stake in post-cinematic theatre we should consider the broader notion of 'post-cinema'. Post-cinema is a contested – and fairly recent – term referring to a cultural trend that encompasses a wide range of artworks and disciplines that interrogate and challenge our perceptions of dominant cinematic conventions. It is also often associated with the terms post-classical film or post-classical cinema. Specifically, post-classical film is a reaction against classical realist conventions – which is also a big part of post-cinematic art. But post-cinema in itself refers to a wider cultural phenomenon of cinema that is not bound to the medium of film. Hence post-cinematic art often resorts to 'intermedial' practice, which usually combines the use of film (because traditionally that was the main medium of cinema) and another medium. It is also clear that post-cinema explores the margins of cinematic perceptions and is located somewhat outside of, or in opposition to, the mainstream, hence it can be broadly categorised as an avant-garde trend. Thus post-cinema can be exemplified by a variety of hybrid art forms such as contemporary intermedial theatre, but also computer games, DVDs, virtual realities, installation work, websites and happenings. Their characteristics often emphasise non-linear narrative forms, audience interactivity, the witnessing of the process of production of cinematic images or an experience of aesthetics of flux, to give but a few examples. One example of this ample and growing field of work would be the Brazilian Live Cinema project which encompasses a spectrum of live performances from VJ-ing to live re-editing of Hollywood classics (http://www.live cinema.com.br). Other examples would be independent sector projects such as Simon Pumell's *Bodysong* (2003) and practice-based research projects in the video art sector by Lev Manovich and Adrian Miles. Furthermore, there are mainstream works that exhibit a post-cinematic aesthetic, such as the DVD version of Chris Nolan's *Memento* (2001), where the spectator can choose different camera angles as they watch the film, hence montaging their own experience.

As noted above, affinities with post-cinematic aesthetics can be found in works dating as far back as the advent of cinema. But to a great extent this affinity is the result of retrospective analysis because post-cinema is not so much an aesthetic, stylistic phenomenon as one that concerns a cultural critical re-framing of cinema. So when does this cultural shift towards a heightened and critically reflexive stance towards cinema emerge? The 'post' prefix of post-cinema can be looked at from two perspectives. One view is simply that as with most 'post' terms it represents a historic shift that comes after the cultural dominance of cinema has ended, in the same way perhaps that post-modernity follows modernity. This also implies that it comes after cinema has reached some kind of limit, though this is a rather simplistic, chronological view. The other perspective, and the one that will be addressed here, is to articulate post-cinema as a cultural trend that is a reaction to cinema's ongoing cultural dominance. Lyotard defined the age of the post-modern as the age of reactions against notions of modernity, and in particular the age of 'incredulity towards metanarratives' (Lyotard: 1979: xxiv). According to this broad analogy, post-cinema can be defined as exemplifying 'incredulity' towards the great narratives of classical realist film, but also as stretching that incredulity to cinematic conventions and forms through which these narratives were constructed, forms that are increasingly dominant in our contemporary culture.

It is easy to see a link in this rise in heightened awareness of cinematic conventions with the proliferation of television in the 1970s and 1980s, as a result of which cinemas ceased to be the dominant carriers of the medium of film in Western culture. The cinema was replaced by cosy television and later home video culture. When a new medium emerges on the cultural scene, audiences tend to become more aware, reflexive and critical of the old medium and its operations – a notion that can also be applied to post-cinema. When cinema was slowly replaced by television the audiences became increasingly aware and reflexive of its modes of operation as a result of a cultural reframing and 'remediation' of cinematic conventions.[5] Arguing along similar lines, in his essay 'A Cinema Exploded', Michael Clayfield tries to define the moment that post-cinema began, quoting Peter Greenaway in the 2003 Variety Cinema Militants Lecture, 'Toward a Re-invention of Cinema', who suggested that cinema died with the introduction of the remote control. Greenaway suggested that 'throwing away [established cinematic language] in anticipation of a new cycle of "aesthetic-technologies" was inevitable' (Greenaway quoted in Clayfield 2005: n.p.). Clayfield uses this anecdote about the impact of the remote control on the experience of film to highlight the fact that the emancipation of the spectator through televisual culture was decisive in making the audience develop a more critical stance towards cinema over which they now had seemingly more control. This is an insightful anecdote since it shows how a technological advance might inspire a significant change of perception, in this case the perception of aesthetic and structural aspects of cinematic experiences, and thus a certain cultural re-framing of cinema.[6]

But television and home video culture were not the only factors influencing this growth in heightened awareness of cinematic conventions. Defying predictions, the popularity of cinema is growing to this very day. The medium of film – formerly more or less exclusive to cinema – became absorbed by television and eventually remediated through the aesthetics and representational modes of other platforms. Hence, perhaps ironically, the popularity and cultural dominance of cinematic tropes and conventions grew as a result of remediation. This in turn inspired avant-garde art practices and theories to exhibit a reaction to this cultural dominance of cinema – a reaction that has cultural, aesthetic and political implications. It is no coincidence that these post-cinematic art forms, including theatre, use intermedial strategies to do so, since the very dominance of cinema as a cultural phenomena is to a great extent a result of remediation and in the same sense so is the post-cinematic reaction.

So far I have argued that the post-cinematic trend in art, which includes post-cinematic theatre, concerns intermedial reactions against dominant cinematic conventions resulting from a cultural shift. However cinema and the cinematic are very broad terms that can be understood in many ways. The different chapters in this book will deal with specific intermedial pieces and their post-cinematic approaches and hence incorporate different takes on cinema that are specific to each of the case studies. It is important at this point, however, to articulate in more detail what will be generally referred to as dominant cinematic conventions. There is no unified concept of cinema as such; hence the immediate question is how can we articulate a notion of the 'cinematic' to which post-cinematic theatre would respond? And what has become of that notion of cinema by the time post-cinema emerges as a new form of artistic response? Cinema has had many definitions since it appeared as an art form. These range – among many others – from the cognitive approaches of Hugo Münsterberg, to the elaborate theory of montage by Sergei Eisenstein, to the unassailable theory of realism of André Bazin, to post-structuralist readings by Gilles Deleuze, psychoanalytic readings by critics such as Christian Metz and the 'vision machine' of Peter Greenaway. All of these approaches have different particularities and many will be dealt with and referred to specifically in respective chapters of this book. Plainly it is difficult simply to generalise what cinema is. Nonetheless it is worth noting that all these theoretical approaches share a commonality in that they effectively deal with cinema's illusionism. This illusionist aspect is often referred to as realism, or classical realist film and it is broadly understood to come out of 'mainstream' filmmaking.

The paradox at the heart of illusionism in cinema is that nothing moves in the cinematic image. The illusion of movement underpinning cinematic experience is stimulated by the dark void between two still frames, an effect resulting from the 'after image' that appears on the retina as a response to the instantly disappearing previous frame. This central paradox of the illusionist spectacle, the 'doubt or mistrust of apparent continuity, or the refusal to disavow what one knows about illusionism in order to believe in its impression' (Rees 1999: 5) is what has constituted cinema's power as industrial product and cultural myth. It is important to distinguish here between film and cinema. Film is essentially the medium of cinema, its main material, whilst cinema is an art form and a cultural phenomenon that also has an institutional aspect. For instance mainstream Hollywood cinema is institutionalised by the different studios and film companies that contribute to its cultural production. The emergent cultural phenomenon of cinema could have gone in many directions, not necessarily in the classical realist direction it took through mainstream Hollywood and Soviet cinema. One instance of that would be German expressionism. Even though there always has been a cinematic avant-garde, for the most part when people refer to cinematic conventions or cinema in general they are referring to classical realism. It is also worth adding at this point that this notion of a realist cinema based on illusion developed through a process of discrimination and selectivity of representations of reality. If one were to follow theories of Soviet cinema montage, films were essentially designed to stimulate an 'image of movement' in the spectator's mind, an image that was beyond the actual depictions represented in particular shots and resulted from an aesthetically harmonised montage sequence. This notion of cinematic experience as essentially imaginary, representing an aesthetically harmonised image of reality that is removed from 'real' experience, became the subject of a long history of critical discourses ranging from early film theory through media theory to post-theory and discourses on intermediality. It is also a source of artistic exploration for post-cinematic theatre. Thus it will be useful to briefly introduce some of these critical discourses, which will become points of reference for the case studies in the chapters that follow.

From its early beginnings film was seen as medium with the potential to change the way reality was perceived. If realist cinema can be seen as a map in a Baudrillardian sense, one that constantly 'precedes the territory [...] the desert of the real itself' (Baudrillard 1994: 1) and thus the experience of the 'real', then the history of realist cinema is the history of the effacement of the 'real'. When film emerged as a new medium, long before any conventions or specific aesthetics had become established, questions were being raised about its technological constitution and the techniques by which it attempted to mediate and convey reality. Over time people became familiar with the perception of film, and its specific cinematic conventions and aesthetic formalities became transparent. An assumption is often made that this tendency to perceive the medium in a more transparent, non-critical way is desirable for the mass audience. There seems to be a progression or a desire in the development of every medium to attain a sense of transparency, or an appearance of 'truth'. This could be seen in the developments of perspective aesthetics in painting during the Renaissance period, of ultra naturalism in theatre at the end of the nineteenth century and of realist filmmaking in the inter-war period. Different media offer different possibilities of attaining the illusion of reality. In the case of film an early expression of enthusiasm in that respect came from Georg Lukács. 'Everything is true and real, everything is at the same time equally true and real' (Lukács in Kuchenbuch 2006: 170). With this bold statement in his 1913 essay, 'Gedanken zu einer Ästhetik des Kinos', Georg Lukács made a point about the unifying, homogenising nature of the silver screen's surface. Likewise in his seminal essay, 'The Silent Photoplay' (1916), Hugo Münsterberg articulated the immense potential of film to evoke an imaginary reality through the discontinuities of montage. He set this potentiality in opposition to theatre, which at the time had a dominant role in conveying realist representations. Münsterberg's argument reflects the early twentieth-century view that film and cinema were increasingly being perceived as technically more adequate and efficient in creating realist representations. He claimed that in cinema:

> The pictorial reflection of the world is not bound by the rigid mechanisms of time. Our mind is here and there, our mind turns to the present and then to the past [...] This fountain like spray of pictures in film has completely overcome the causal world. [...] The theatre would not have even the technical means to give such an impression, but if it had, it would have no right to make use of them.
> (Münsterberg 2002: 134)

Thus the discontinuous nature of cinematic 'syntax' led theorists such as Lukács, Münsterberg and Prague structuralist Mukarovsky to postulate cinema as a specifically transparent art form with a capacity to unify disparate events, forlorn landscapes and archaic time spans – three unities reconciled and undisturbed by the lack of presence of the 'real' actor or object.

This notion that cinema can objectify, make salient and discrete the plethora and excessiveness of the 'real' world was further expanded by the Soviet filmmaker and theoretician Sergei Eisenstein. It is he who makes the bold claim that there is no movement in cinema. All 'movement' in cinema is an illusion resulting from a sequence of static images displayed at a uniform frame rate; this is the fundamental unit of the 'image of movement'. This microscopic montage not only indicates that the substance of film, the image of movement, exists in the imagination (in the darkness between successive frames) but essentially identifies movement in cinema as a vector. The vector is understood here as a force that prompts the spectator to complete the image in their mind. The discontinuous precepts offered by the film would thus stimulate a reconstruction of an event in the spectator's mind, like the disturbing revolt of the working masses on Bloody Sunday in Eisenstein's film *Battleship Potemkin* (1925). To watch a movie is far more than to experience a succession of still images, it is to construct an imaginary world in the mind which will be stimulated by the myriad of aesthetic choices made by the filmmaker. These range from shot composition, *mise-en-cadre*,[7] lighting, accelerations, decelerations, bringing out significant gestures through acting, camera movement and the linkage between the shot sequences down to broader arrangements of scenes within the whole body of film, cross-cutting, narrative lapses and the orchestration with the soundtrack.

It is not surprising then, that these analytical approaches were also articulating cinema's potential to 'educate' the masses – in a very calculable way. This was because they were not mere descriptions of the structurality of movies but also comprised of an analysis of how film aesthetics stimulated the cognitive and mental processes of the spectator.[8] Critics like Walter Benjamin 'stressed the mind-forming qualities of film construction and the respective film reception inducing a mental state in the observer' (Kuchenbuch 2006: 173) or in Münsterberg's words, 'the pictures are not taken for art's sake: the aim is to serve the spread of knowledge' (Münsterberg 2002: 64). Thus the positioning of cinema as the art form of the knowable and programmable was a consequence of an in-depth investigation of its aesthetic specificity.

Consequently cinema became a 'map' for ways of perceiving reality. It became a map for perceiving social relations, history, cultures – but most importantly, it became an affective map, reconfiguring our identifications, aesthetic sensibilities and ethical sentiments towards the concepts which it represents. Many theorists have critically approached this alluring capacity of cinema to create images of reality that might possibly even replace the viewer's own perception of reality. Whenever a new media technology is introduced that will allow artists to manipulate perception with seemingly greater control and prowess, two reciprocal questions can be asked. First, is cinema 'a means to an end', a wonderful kaleidoscope of moving pictures that we can wilfully arrange to explore and evoke experiences inaccessible otherwise? And second, in return for this, does it also manipulate us in ways of which we may not be immediately conscious? As with wearing a mask but also being worn by it, or the Nietzschean abyss,[9] theorists such as Marshall McLuhan posited that there is a 'phantom menace' within the very forms through which knowledge can be mediated that conditions the way we come to perceive it.

McLuhan is often criticised for prioritising technology when investigating what is at stake in media such as film. He boldly claims that there is no 'content', instead there is a medium remediated by another. According to McLuhan '[the] content of a movie is a novel or a play or an opera. The effect of the movie form is not related to its program content. The "content" of writing or print is speech, but the reader is almost entirely unaware either of print or of speech' (McLuhan 1975: 18). He argues that:

> The 'content' of a medium is like the juicy piece of meat carried by the burglar to distract the watchdog of the mind. The effect of the medium is made strong and intense just because it is given another medium as 'content'.
>
> (McLuhan 1975: 18)

The 'watchdog of the mind' is the conscious perception, whilst the 'effect', an instant of immediacy, is the gullibility and naivety with which one's mind can absorb incoming sensations. McLuhan postulates that a medium's technology allows for a specific organisation of 'sense perception'. The invisibility, and thus the transparency of the medium's technology are postulated by McLuhan as a threat to Western civilisation. He sees Western society as being totally unaware of the effects of media technology:

> The effects of technology do not occur at the level of opinions or concepts, but alter sense ratios or patterns of perception steadily and without resistance. The serious artist is the only person able to encounter technology with impunity, just because he is an expert aware of the changes in sense perception.
>
> (McLuhan 1975: 18)

Even though here McLuhan talks about print and media in general, his theory can be easily related to the progressive cultural dominance of realist cinema. Cinema has been seen as a vehicle for propaganda and, as shown in the theories above, has influenced the 'organisation of sense perception' – in other words, aesthetics. When critically considering McLuhan's theory it is questionable how far readers are 'unaware' of the print as he puts it, and thus of the technology of the media. Supposedly McLuhan is a reader who is aware. However this problematic by no means invalidates his theory, I would simply claim that certain artworks can stimulate 'moments' of unawareness by concealing their inner workings through which they construct representations. Films are a very good example of this. Along similar lines Kattenbelt argues that the media have 'replaced' our experience of reality, where 'our mediatised culture has become a hyper-reality, that is to say a world of signs that are more real than the objects, to which they seem to refer' (Kattenbelt 2006: 38). He introduces Theodor Adorno's remark: 'The more complete the world as representation, the more inscrutable the representation as ideology' (Adorno quoted in Kattenbelt 2006: 38). As far as cinema is concerned, this notion of a 'hidden' ideology, an invisible ramification that organises meaning, has become a popular consideration. One only has to quote the famous example of Jean Baudrillard's *Orders of Simulacra* to argue for an extent to which *simulation* has preceded the experience and construction of reality. In this context Baudrillard goes even further, arguing in his book *The Vital Illusion* (2000), in the chapter titled 'The Murder of the Real', that the progressive virtualisation of communication in our society, which is also influenced by cinema, effaces the possibility of our experiencing the 'real'. He claims that:

> By shifting to a virtual world, we go beyond alienation, into a state of radical deprivation of the Other, or indeed of any otherness, alterity, or negativity. We move into a world where everything that exists only as idea, dream, fantasy, utopia will be eradicated, because it will immediately be realized, operationalized. Events, real events, will not even have time to take place. Everything will be preceded by its virtual realization.
>
> (Baudrillard 2000: 66)

This reflection upon a 'readymade' virtual universe that precedes the experience of the real applies to the ways in which realist cinema's grasp over the mentality and perceptions of its audiences has been problematised. After all, cinematic conventions reconfigure our aesthetic sensibilities and ways of perceiving and understanding social relations, while representing them. It also suggests that this progressive virtualisation both veils a reality and conceals different perceptions and ways of looking at political and ideological constructs. Therefore according to

McLuhan it is the role of the 'serious artists', the 'more aware' artists, to break this spell and offer different cultural perceptions, making audiences more critically aware of how forms through which knowledge is conveyed construct ideological and political worldviews. Post-cinematic theatre can thus be located within the context of cultural criticism of cinema's modes of operation and an ambition to provide its audience with a freer perceptual experience. In that sense it becomes a form of cultural resistance against the illusion-laden cinematic culture but also one that challenges its ideological and political implications, namely by foregrounding a 'politics of perception'. This brings us to some of the 'post-theory' critics. These theorists contest the developments of classical realism in mainstream cinema and question their effects on the way ideology and social relations were/and are being constructed through cinematic works. Keeping in mind that post-cinematic theatre demands a critical stance, I would like to briefly look at some of the critical film theories that began to articulate a need to break with what were perceived at the time as dominant forms of cinematic representation and their illusionistic nature, and began to question and ponder upon the possibilities of emancipating the spectator's agency in responding to these forms.

In many ways these theories problematise realism and try to answer some of the key questions with which this book will be concerned. Questions such as: What are the problems of passive spectatorship instigated by realist cinema? Should these forms of popular entertainment which are so prolific, relaxing and widely appreciated be problematised at all? What is politically and ideologically at stake in yielding to the pleasures and beautiful aesthetics of these realist illusions? What is the artistic potential for post-cinematic theatre to explore this problematic? In their book *Post-Theory: Reconstructing Film Studies*, David Bordwell and Noel Carroll anthologise a collection of essays that seek to redefine cinema and postulate alternative modes of spectators' engagement with film. In the 1970s theorists such as Jean-Louis Baudry, Colin MacCabe and Christian Metz began to re-articulate what is at stake in the perception of film, but also to consider how cinema could go beyond its 'boundaries' and redefine audience engagement with the medium.

One of the key cinematic concepts that film theory from the 1970s onwards began to address was that movies, especially Hollywood productions, had to create unified and coherent representations of reality. Thus their arguments focused on various aspects of filmmaking in relation to notions of unity: be it a unified perspective, a coherent subject, a privileged discursive position, seamless montage or cinematographic operations. The attitudes and stances taken by different theorists towards these aspects of cinema varied considerably. Christian Metz came up with the 'mirror screen' concept to articulate what is substantially specific about the cinematic experience. In his celebrated work, *The Imaginary Signifier* (1982), Metz tried to articulate the difference between cinema and other cultural products. In order to do so he explored two psychoanalytic concepts, the Lacanian 'mirror stage' and Freud's concept of the fetish. The gist of his argument was that the film screen acts as a mirror of the spectator's reality, an image that the spectator knows is not true but chooses to believe in and identify with nonetheless. The other important point was that unlike with a real mirror the spectator cannot affect the image on screen; hence the identification process is, by definition, more passive. By claiming that films have an unconscious hold over their audiences, despite their knowledge and the possibility of critical reflection, Metz raised an important question about the spectator's agency and the possibility of negotiating it during the experience of cinema. Even though these questions were being addressed towards cinema culture specifically they are also important when looking at a post-cinematic theatre that uses intermedial strategies to break and deconstruct the spell of the cinematic and recalibrate this potentially fetishist dynamic Metz was arguing for.

Jean-Louis Baudry and others took a Marxist stance and perceived the aesthetics of realism, which are designed to create a sense of perspectivist unity, as a method for constructing ideological representations. In his article, 'Ideological Effects of the Basic Cinematographic Apparatus',[10] Baudry argued that Hollywood films make invisible the methods of production by which they create an illusion of reality. As a result they deliver *ideological* representations of social and economic relationships between the represented subjects. What he defined as the 'cinematic apparatus' was mainly associated with classical realist conventions, which he argued achieved an ideological construction by eliminating all possible differences and points of view in favour of one unified ideological stance. Colin MacCabe in his essay 'Realism and the Cinema: Notes on Some Brechtian Theses' (1974) argued along similar lines. His definition of classical realist films was based on the notion of a hierarchy of discourses, stemming from the narrative structures of nineteenth-century novels, and the existence of a privileged discourse which unfolds throughout a movie. What both Baudry and MacCabe wanted was a change in the way movies were structured, a different type of film altogether; one that MacCabe called a 'revolutionary film' that would enable a 'possibility of a different activity [...] the displacement of the subject within ideology – a different constitution of the subject'

(MacCabe 1985: 51). Stephen Heath developed this concept more closely in his essay 'Lessons from Brecht'. Heath distinguishes two concepts that could be used to theorise the difference between classical realist film and revolutionary film: separation and distanciation. According to Heath spectators can freely take pleasure in experiencing the illusion because they are outside the reality of film; hence their sense of identity and personal integrity remains 'unaffected'. He then claims that 'the essential denial of work, production, the refusal to grasp the positions of subject and object within that process' (Heath 1992: 235) are faults in realist cinema which the phenomenon of separation helps to cover up. Along similar lines Jean-François Lyotard in his essay 'Acinema' (Lyotard 1987) negotiated the possibilities for a cinema that would be free from narrative forms, aesthetic rules and classical 'pleasures', whose constant imposition and 'return' in the process of filmmaking within the mainstream he identified with a soulless, ideologically driven need to generate profit (value) in a capitalist society.

Heath's recommendation was that revolutionary films should attempt to employ distanciation as opposed to separation. The notion of distanciation is borrowed from Brecht. The idea was to place the spectator within the realm of production, inspiring a more active mode of spectatorship wherein viewers would partake in the production of meaning. Thus Heath draws a distinction between films that attempt to fix the spectator in a specific interpretation and films that sustain spectators in an active position by means of distanciation. The notion of going beyond the illusionary frame or mirror of cinema to expose the inner workings of the cinematic apparatus is clearly apparent in post-cinematic theatre and also in a post-cinematic film such as *Dogville*, which would easily fall under the category of a revolutionary film, particularly because of its Brechtian aesthetic.

All this criticism reflected a preoccupation with the ways in which cinema was affecting cultural perceptions and somehow becoming a substitute for 'real' experiences. These theories, which deconstructed cinema's cultural dominance, arguably become a point of inspiration for post-cinematic theatre. They also exemplify the cultural shift of post-cinema towards a more critical and reflexive awareness of how cinema affects and shapes our perceptions, indicating some of the political and ideological traps and thus the potential dangers of uncritically yielding to cinematic illusions.

Arguably a lot of the aspects of classical realism criticised by these theorists, such as the notion of a privileged discourse, seamless montage, harmonic aesthetics and unified subject positions, are sources of pleasure for spectators within our cinematised culture. Hence the allure and appeal of a cinematic show such as *Reel to Real*, which might as well be called *Reel to Reel*. This cinematic allure in turn produces a series of cultural expectations that become a potential subject of deconstruction and interrogation for post-cinematic theatre. For instance some of the case studies I will be looking at, such as Station House Opera's *A Mare's Nest*, challenge the expectation of a privileged discourse and an optimal perspectivist experience of the show through their intermedial staging. Post-theory arguments and those of critics such as McLuhan tend to postulate that cinema is a dominant cultural form whose spell is so powerful that is leaves very little room for alternative perceptions. Bolter and Grusin challenge the notion of almost perfect transparency by postulating that media (including film in cinema) become essentially self-referential in their pursuit of transparency. In their work *Remediation* (1999) they propose a model that separates the experience of media into two polarities which they define as 'immediacy' and 'hypermediacy':

> If the logic of immediacy leads one either to erase or to render automatic the act of representation, the logic of hypermediacy acknowledges multiple acts of representation and makes them visible. Where immediacy suggests a unified visual space, contemporary hypermediacy offers a heterogeneous space, in which representation is conceived of not as a window on the world, but rather as windowed itself – with windows that open on to other representations or other media.
>
> (Bolter and Grusin 1999: 33)

They argue that spectators are always shifting between the experiences of immediacy and hypermediacy, at times being seduced by the illusion and at times stepping back and being aware of its mediated character. The essential point of Bolter and Grusin's argument is that this experience of shifting between immediacy and hypermediacy is 'central to the Western tradition: the desire to be immediately present to oneself' (Bolter and Grusin 1999: 236). The double logic of remediation, that of immediacy and hypermediacy, is an important part of mediatised culture and, by extension, of the cinematic culture. Arguably, post-cinematic theatre and film has the potential to evoke and amplify this double logic of an immersive cinematic experience (immediacy) and self-referential reflexivity (hypermediacy), whereas in more mainstream cinematic works (whether film or theatre) the potential for hypermediacy or self-conscious reflexivity is concealed or deliberately erased in favour of immediacy, and the residue of hypermedial potential obliterated, for instance by a psychic mechanism of the fetish, as Metz would argue. In this sense Bolter and Grusin also help to locate hypermediacy, which is central to post-cinematic pieces, as a tendency arising from Western culture. It is within this cultural trend of hypermediacy, a heightened awareness of how dominant conventions such as those of cinema influence our perceptions and sensibilities, that post-cinematic theatre is located.

1.2   Aesthetics

This section offers an overview of the aesthetics of post-cinematic theatre and their deconstructive nature in relation to cinematic conventions. When approaching the topic of the aesthetics of post-cinematic theatre it is difficult to generalise since – like most hybrid art forms – it has affinities pertaining to cinema, theatre, installation art and digital culture in general. Some of the aesthetic influences intermedial avant-garde theatre and performance may have had on the more contemporary post-cinematic pieces have been outlined above; however, these are specific to particular pieces and will be explored in detail in the case study chapters. Here, we will consider aesthetic tendencies and strategies that seem to be quite prolific and essentially associated with the deconstruction of cinematic conventions in order to give a basic idea of what a post-cinematic aesthetic experience consists of. A parallel between post-cinematic theatre and postdramatic theatre will enable an excavation of similarities of deconstructive strategies since both trends deal with a re-framing and an interrogation of culturally dominant art forms. These affinities will also serve as a point of reference throughout the book.

Mathew Clayfield outlines some of the characteristics of post-cinematic art, mainly focusing on installations, DVD experience and video art,[11] which is not strictly intermedial theatre, but nonetheless enables an insight into the gist of post-cinematic aesthetics in general. According to Clayfield the key characteristics of the post-cinematic form are: 'non-linear granularity and the possibility for interactive audience participation' (Clayfield 2005).[12] These characteristics rest on a polarity between two modes of perception. According to Clayfield, movies can be perceived in two ways: 'holistically' or 'atomistically'. The former comprises of 'a more or less cohesive formal system or emotional experience' where the movie is perceived as a 'sole discursive entity'. The latter is a mode of perceiving the movie 'as a series of smaller constituent elements'. These constituents – for example, sequences, scenes, shots and frames – become 'a collection of potentially discursive entities' (ibid.).

This approach is dependent on the focus a spectator chooses to adopt, whether they choose to focus on the whole and at all times reintegrate its constituent parts, *pars par toto*, or perceive the elements as potentially autonomous. The post-cinematic experience is somewhere between the holistic end-product and the excessive, 'not yet organised', material. This definition has strong affinities with the cultural phenomenon of 'hypermediacy' discussed in the previous section. It also suggests that post-cinematic aesthetic strategies foreground this polarity of perceptual choices. The other key aspect of post-cinematic works is that they are intermedial. They usually involve the interinvolvement of film and some other medium. This is certainly the case with post-cinematic theatre which uses the interinvolvement of film and theatre to deconstruct cinematic conventions thus opening up and foregrounding the perceptual and interpretative freedoms that Clayfield talks about.

An insightful perspective on the deconstructive aesthetic strategies of post-cinematic theatre can be gained by looking at some of the commonalities it shares with what Lehmann defined as postdramatic theatre. Postdramatic theatre is a no less problematic term than post-cinematic theatre. It can be addressed as an epochal term encapsulating avant-garde theatre of the 1970s onwards, otherwise broadly characterised as 'postmodern theatre', or it can be addressed as a response to the notion of dramatic theatre, a way of answering aesthetic questions that arise from trying to go beyond the horizon of what is established as the dramatic paradigm. In that sense a lot of intermedial theatre – from the 1970s onwards – including post-cinematic theatre can be categorised as postdramatic or at least as exemplifying some aspects of that trend. The forms of postdramatic theatre seek to deconstruct and interrogate traditional notions of drama and especially the role of character and narrative as the pivotal elements of theatrical experience. This tendency to deconstruct dominant aesthetics – and the accompanying tendency to challenge and reflect upon the modes of perceiving a work of art and its constituent material – is arguably the main connection between the postdramatic and the post-cinematic theatre. Also both postdramatic and post-cinematic theatre are *dependent* on their 'post-' prefix. This dependency is complex. The notion of post-drama could be read as presupposing and requiring a prior experience of drama. Similarly post-cinematic theatre can be interpreted as presupposing an experience of (mainstream) cinematic illusion, an experience that in its turn presupposes certain expectations.[13]

Thus postdramatic theatre, according to Lehmann, is not free from the ghosts of representation and narrative. On the contrary it is a reiterative and dynamic concept relating to a theatre that seeks compromises with the established traditional forms of the past. Similarly the relationship of post-cinematic theatre to realist cinema rests on a dynamic reiteration, because the post-cinematic effect rests on a heightened awareness of culturally dominant cinematic conventions and the expectations associated with them. It is important to state that both are also potentially based upon a fascination with the aesthetics of illusion, representation and narrative that they set out to critique, interrogate or, conversely, enhance.

In the chapter titled 'Panorama of Postdramatic Theatre' Lehmann (2006) provides a list of stylistic traits of postdramatic theatre. This is by no means a checklist, he claims, but represents categories of what could potentially be the 'sign usage' of postdramatic theatre. When he refers to 'signs' he not merely means identifiable signifiers attached to specific signifieds producing signification, but 'virtually all elements of the theatre' (Lehmann 2006: 82). In order to establish affinities between the postdramatic theatre and post-cinematic theatre, it is worth evaluating some of the categories proposed by Lehmann.

An illuminating affinity between the postdramatic and the post-cinematic theatre is what Lehmann defines as the 'retreat of synthesis' (Lehmann 2006: 82). For Lehmann the strength of 'great' forms and aesthetic genres such as drama lies in their potential of 'articulating [a] collective experience' (Lehmann 2006: 83). Postdramatic theatre challenges this notion of commonality and seeks to provide a potentially more solipsistic experience through a 'theatrical realization of freedom – freedom from subjection to hierarchies, freedom from the demand for coherency' (Lehmann 2006: 83). These aspects are particularly prominent in the work of Robert Wilson or Tadeusz Kantor, where the synthesis of different elements of the theatrical spectacle such as set, props, physical action and spoken text no longer aims to provide a traditional dramatic narrative-based perspective. This allows spectators more freedom to frame their own experience. Lehmann claims that the 'retreat of synthesis is a matter of the freedom to react arbitrarily, or rather involuntarily and idiosyncratically'. The 'perturbing strategy of the withdrawal of synthesis means the offer of a community of heterogeneous and particular imaginations' as opposed to a collective spectator response implied within a holistic structure (ibid.).

This approach has affinities with post-cinematic pieces which often seek to deconstruct the possibility of narrative synthesis offered by classical film montage. This can be achieved by exposing the spectator to a more open, multiple and unstable perception of partial structures as opposed to an 'organic' whole. A good example of this would be the work of John Jesurun whose *Rider without a Horse* demonstrates the possibilities of montage as no longer subservient to a narrative or an organic perception of the film world. Following on from this, Lehmann claims that synthesis is sacrificed in favour of 'intensive moments' that are 'no longer organized according to prescribed models of dramatic coherence or comprehensive symbolic references and does not realize synthesis' (ibid.). Similarly one of the features apparent in post-cinematic theatre is the foregrounding and emphasis on energies and intensities of 'cinematic moments', whilst narrative structures as subject matter of the piece are relegated to the background. This idea will re-emerge in more detail in the chapters on acinematic montage in the work of the Wooster Group and Station House Opera.

This takes the discussion to the affinity between the performance text and the screened film text. Lehmann claims that the relationship between the 'perception of performance text' (the final performance to be seen and potentially 'read' by the audience) and its constituents, the 'linguistic text' (the script of a play for example) and the 'text of the staging and mise en scene' (as in lighting, *mise-en-scène*, actor's physical and vocal performances, set design and so on) has changed. The 'performance text' or texture that is the effect of the transition from the script to the 'text of the staging' no longer maintains the emphasis on the end product in postdramatic theatre. The emphasis on these different levels has shifted, has been 'turned upside down' (Lehmann 2006: 85). As a result, the 'performance text' becomes 'more presence than representation, more shared than communicated experience, more process than product, more manifestation than signification, more energetic impulse than information' (ibid.). Post-cinematic theatre carries similar traits. In post-cinema, the completed product, the outcome of pre-production (screenplay, storyboards, set designs, research and so on), production (actors' performances, camera performance, *mise-en-scène* of the studio space translating to the *mise-en-cadre* of film, lighting, animatronics, scenography and the like) and post-production (montage, editing, music, image treatment, visual effect) is no longer the main vehicle of signification conditioning audience response. Like narrative synthesis it retreats into the background. The theatricalisation of the filming process is thus brought to the foreground. This is very clear in the work of the Wooster Group, for example in *House/Lights* or *To You the Birdie*. It is also present in the work of Katie Mitchell, for example in *Wunschkonzert* and *The Waves*. Furthermore, films that carry strong post-cinematic features such as *Dogville* illustrate this aspect and affinity with the postdramatic as well, as will be discussed in Chapter 8.

Two other insightful stylistic affinities are to do with the concepts of parataxis and simultaneity. According to Lehmann, in postdramatic theatre parataxis or non-hierarchy concerns a non-hierarchical use of signs that contradicts 'the established hierarchy, at the top of which we find language, diction and gesture and in which visual qualities such as the experience of an architectonic space [...] figure as subordinate' (Lehmann 2006: 86). This leads to an even spread of attention where the production of meaning by the spectator can be postponed. For example, a lighting effect or a seemingly disconnected physical action can momentarily dominate the spectator's attention and make them forget the spoken text. This liberation of techniques which are usually a *support* for the production of meaning is also found in post-cinematic performance. This is very visible in the works of the Wooster Group and Imitating the Dog.

Linked to this is the notion of simultaneity. Specific moments or events that traditionally could be read as central carriers of meaning are no longer privileged. Post-cinematic theatre relates to this with multiple actions being performed at multiple times and spaces, potentially simultaneously mediated through live action and film. This 'abandonment of totality' (Lehmann 2006: 88) allows the audience to engage in a freer and potentially choice-driven response and structuring of the material. Works of Station House Opera such as *Roadmetal Sweetbread* and *A Mare's Nest* are good examples of this.

Furthermore, the play with the density of visual signs and consequently the notion of plethora where 'conventional form' is abandoned in order to realise an exploration of the limits of form – 'the wasteland of unsizeable extension and labyrinthine chaotic accumulation' (Lehmann 2006: 90) – also has an important stylistic role in post-cinematic theatre. In 'Acinema', Lyotard hints at two formal extremes of either immobilisation or excessive mobility as potential directions for exploration in contemporary cinema, in order to avoid what he calls 'libidinal normalization' (Lyotard 1989: 175). Thus the preoccupation with form as a normalising, harmonising, homeostatic factor is shared with post-cinema here, as are the aspirations to create more heterogeneous, perceptually challenging spectacles.

Lehmann also addresses the notion of physicality and corporeal presence in postdramatic theatre, which again plays an important role in post-cinematic theatre. He claims that:

[d]espite all efforts to capture the expressive potential of the body in a logic, grammar or rhetoric, the aura of physical presence remains

the point of theatre where the disappearance, the fading of all signification occurs – in favour of a fascination beyond meaning, of an
actor's 'presence', of charisma or 'vibrancy'.

(Lehmann 2006: 95)

The body in post-cinematic theatre transgresses norms that would normally render it a site of the production of meaning. Essentially there
is a separation of the body from language. In post-cinematic theatre a
separation of the corporeal body on stage from its filmic representation
(constituted within the potentially meaning-laden film material) can
occur quite literally, as for example when we don't see the heads of the
actors in *Hotel Methuselah.*

The notion of an 'irruption of the real' (Lehmann 2006: 99) is also
very pertinent to post-cinematic theatre and perhaps one of its key features. Traditionally theatre assumes a 'closed fictive cosmos, a "diegetic
universe", that can be called thus even though it is produced by means
of mimesis' (Lehmann 2006: 100). The traditional play exists in a
'framed' reality 'governed 'by its own laws and by an internal coherence of its elements' (ibid.). Similarly in realist cinema the audience is
asked to immerse themselves within a 'framed' fictional reality which
potentially mirrors their own. Theatre, however, has an additional extra
material reality, the reality of the physical space and its constituent elements, which does not form part of the 'illusory' reality of the play's
world. Even though, in traditional theatre the expectation is that this
extra material reality will be ignored by the spectator, classical realist film has even less extra material reality to be ignored. After all the
extra material reality of cinematic experience is diminished by the fact
that lights go off in the auditorium and the cinema is soundproof. The
fact that moving images on screen are actually still images giving the
impression of movement and that they are made up of halogen compound molecules is easier to ignore than the fact that a chair on stage is
not a mountain. In Station House Opera's *A Mare's Nest* the menace of
metal chains falling from the ceiling often breaks the illusion of filmic
reality within the piece, reminding the audience of the materiality and
physicality of theatre in a violent manner.

1.3   Politics of perception

Lehmann argues that we live and witness the 'Society of the Spectacle' as
described by Guy Debord (1995). The continual presentation of images
within the media – be they catastrophes, wars, victories – means that as

viewers we are always on the outside, isolated from the 'real' place of production of these images. This according to Lehmann creates 'a radical distance for passive viewing: the bond between perception and action, receiving message and "answerability", is dissolved. We find ourselves in a spectacle in which we can only look on...' (Lehmann 2006: 184). Even though he mainly concentrates on electronic images conveyed through televisual means, this argument can be extended to cinematic fiction. This is because Lehmann is mainly concerned with the 'mechanics' of perception, and the technicalities of the media through which the viewers are invited to be passive. By isolating the viewers from the place of production of images, arguably mainstream realist film can also induce a passivity into the viewer's experience by using technical means to occult the viewer's sense that 'participation in language also makes them, the receivers, responsible for the message' (Lehmann 2006: 185). There is a sense of comfort and cosiness at stake within the screened image. According to Lehmann theatre cannot 'oppose an effective alternative to the massive superiority of these structures' (Lehmann 2006: 185). It cannot compete with the powerful way in which media and by extension cinema can 'shape' or induce perceptions of reality by posing a 'political thesis or antithesis' (ibid.). However, Lehmann claims that the political engagement of theatre 'does not consist in the topics but in the forms of perception' (Lehmann 2006: 184). He proposes that this problem can be addressed in the following way:

> Theatre can respond to this only with a *politics of perception*, which could at the same time be called an *aesthetic of responsibility (or response-ability)*. Instead of the deceptively comforting duality of here and there, inside and outside, it can move the mutual implication of actors and spectators in the theatrical production of images into the centre and thus make visible the broken thread between personal experience and perception. Such an experience would be not only aesthetic but therein at the same time ethico-political.
>
> (Lehmann 2006: 186)

The central idea here is, thus, that where the dominant mass media, including cinema, can be viewed as offering an experience of perception of politics, a representation of a political debate surrounding issues, theatre, on the contrary, offers a politics of perception. This is an important difference since it means that the 'politics of perception' is primarily concerned with form and the way in which formal aspects of the piece affect the perception of its content.

Joe Kelleher in his book *Theatre & Politics* (2009) makes a similar argument that there is much more to politics in theatre than the act of representing it and engaging with representations. In many ways he claims that an essential component of politics in theatre is for the audience to question their role and engagement with what they see – in short to question the basis of their perceptions of theatrical events. And it is in this act of grasping and witnessing the production of the image by the spectator that a potential political agency lies. 'In grasping hold of the act that produces an image', Kelleher claims, 'we put ourselves in a position to do something about what we see, to conceive new laws for instance; in short, to do politics' (Kelleher 2009: 14). This is not only a theatrical concern, it has been postulated by post-theorists such as Baudry, Metz, Heath and MacCabe that the 'mainstream' cinema, originating from the classical realist tradition, has often sought to create a detachment of the film spectator from the realm of production of images. In turn, the broken thread between the spectator and 'real' experience would be replaced with an illusionary representation, a fictional double that for many post-theorists, notably Baudry, working on theoretical assumptions put forward by Althusser carried strong ideological and political implications. For these theorists the main conclusion was that the 'cinematic apparatus' had the potential and the tendency to implicate the spectator within its ideological representations and create a cohesive image of social, political and economic relations. This often constructed the spectator as passive and cinema as manipulative. The challenge for contemporary film was then to undo and possibly reverse this relationship, by making the spectator part of the process of production of representation thus emancipating their agency. In essence this could be defined as an attempt to shift from the 'perception of politics' to the 'politics of perception'. A shift from an ideologically and politically framed representation to a position where the spectator could reflect upon their own process of framing representations of reality.

Most political plays and films which simply offer representations and commentaries of political events are capable of inducing political thinking and potentially political action. However what Kelleher, Lehmann and post-theory writers are concerned with is bringing to the fore the representational mechanisms that stimulate the very perceptions of political events.

1.4   Discourses on intermediality

The notion of looking at the intermediality of film and theatre from the perspective of their interinvolvement has only recently gained momentum within critical discourses. Historically, for the most part, this relationship has been theorised as one of opposition. The initial debates on intermediality or what could be described as the pre-intermediality debates, as Chapple and Kattenbelt argues, were located within film theory especially the 'classical film theories' (Chapple and Kattenbelt 2006b: 13). The early French and Russian debates on the principles of film aesthetics, with key theoreticians and practitioners such as Eisenstein, 'helped to legitimise film as a "new art"' (ibid.) that could potentially take over the role of representational theatre. This in turn initiated a debate about the differences between film and theatre, setting the two art forms in aesthetic and ontological opposition. With his statement, 'Everything is true and real, everything is at the same time equally true and real' (in Kuchenbuch 2006: 170), Georg Lukács made a point about the unifying, homogeneous nature of the cinema screen. This potential to build a transparent and homogeneous imaginary world was then contrasted with the opaqueness of theatrical presence: 'the theatre is a realm of uncovered souls and of fate' (ibid.). As Thomas Kuchenbuch claims, this 'brief intervention [...] began a tradition of theoretical discussion about theatre and film that would set the two media apart in stark opposition to each other' (ibid.). As we have seen Hugo Münsterberg argued along similar lines in his seminal essay, 'The Silent Photoplay' (1916; see Münsterberg 2002),[14] pointing out an essential difference between the discontinuities of cinematic time and space and the continuity of the physical reality of theatrical time as influencing the aesthetic choices in the two arts. Susan Sontag has also commented on this distinction in her famous essay, 'Film and Theatre' (1966):

> If an irreducible distinction between theatre and cinema does exist, it may be this. Theatre is confined to a logical or *continuous* use of space. Cinema (through editing, that is, through the change of shot – which is the basic unit of film construction) has access to an alogical or *discontinuous* use of space.
>
> (Sontag 2006: 141)

Similarly Béla Balázs in his essay on theatrical representation, 'Zur Kunstphilosophie des Films' (1938) postulated a totality of theatrical experience in opposition to the fragmented nature of space and time in film. What Balázs seems to introduce is also the dimension of spectatorship itself. The anonymous witness of the cinematic experience is contrasted here with a spectator present within the same spatial totality of the theatrical setup. Balázs argues that the fixed position and perspective of the spectators in theatre allows them to make choices as to what and how they wish to perceive. Although theatre directors often use a considerable array of techniques to 'direct' their audience's attention (gestures, lighting, blocking, stage composition), the effect is less oriented than in film. Also a distinction is made in that a theatrical audience is more aware of themselves and their collective reactions as an audience and hence less anonymous. Balázs's arguments can easily be problematised both ways here, but in themselves they reveal an attempt to think through the differences in the ontology of spectatorship in both arts. The conclusion of his argument was to point out a contrast between, on the one hand, the necessary transparency and effacement of a technical awareness of the means of film (at least during the act of spectatorship), and, on the other, the relative opacity and resistance to illusion that is offered by the here and now corporeality of theatrical performance.

All of these distinctions between theatre and film, in particular those concerning the effects of ontological differences between the two media, have been problematised in recent years. With the emergence and abundance of hybrid, intermedial art forms and the expansion and refashioning of different media the theoretical focus has shifted from the effects of the differences between theatre and film to notions of intermediality, hypermediation and remediation which often assume an interinvolvement of the two media. For instance the more contemporary intermedial debates, such as the work of Bolter and Grusin's *Remediation* (1999) and Philip Auslander's *Liveness* (1999), oppose the more essentialist arguments of the past by arguing that in contemporary culture the differences between media are becoming effaced as different media constantly incorporate and refashion each other. However it is impossible to escape the fact that distinctions such as those discussed above remain ingrained within our culture and affect the way film and theatre are perceived. At times this may have the effect of blurring these distinctions, as in the case of *Hotel Methuselah*, at other times differences are emphasised and film and theatre are set in dialectic opposition, as in the case of *House/Lights* or *Wunschkonzert*.

It is also important to draw attention to the ongoing debate concerning the status and significance of the materiality of media. This notion of materiality is important here since most of the post-cinematic pieces discussed in the following chapters stage film, the one exception being *Dogville*. Since most of the theoretical approaches that consider materiality oppose or somehow complement and/or depart from Auslander, I will first briefly introduce the gist of his argument. Auslander's main argument consisted of the rejection of an ontological difference between the live and the mediatised, claiming that it is essentially historically and culturally contingent. In his book *Liveness* he evaluated two approaches to theorising the relationship between live and mediatised performance. One is an exploration based on ontological and technological oppositions between live and mediated performance and the other is an exploration of 'that relationship as historical and contingent' (Auslander 1999: 51). He subsequently argues that ontological and technological differences no longer offer a clear distinction between the two media and that from the standpoint of cultural economy 'mediatised representations [...] dominate the cultural landscape' (Auslander 1999: 37). His methodology is to address performance as a product of a cultural economy, where both film/television and theatre are treated as commodities and any ontological distinction is in fact ideological: 'the relationship between live performance and mediatised as oppositional are not neutrally descriptive; rather, they reflect an ideology central to contemporary performance studies' (Auslander 1999: 42).

Auslander's book stirred wide controversy in theatre studies and he has often been accused of ignoring a range of contemporary performance works that would have substantiated the ontological argument. Freda Chapple and Chiel Kattenbelt have also criticised his standpoint, claiming that it does not adequately address the 'understanding of the materiality of media and their codes' (Chapple and Kattenbelt 2006b: 16). For instance, Chiel Kattenbelt made an interesting argument about theatre being a 'hypermedium'. He argued that theatre cannot be classified as a medium since it has no specific technology of its own. It cannot record nor absorb other media like film, television or digital video can. Those media 'can remediate other media, which implies in the end a refashioning' (Kattenbelt 2006: 37). Theatre by contrast becomes a hypermedium where 'components of a live performance, film, television and video recordings are not only screened, but also and at the same time staged' (ibid.). In essence their arguments do not oppose those of Auslander but rather point out the need to consider the materiality of the staged media as an insightful aspect of how intermedial practices affect our cultural perceptions.

This focus on the materiality of the media and the intricacies of staging such materiality in theatre is also shared by other theorists, among them Peter Boenisch. Boenisch argues that films, like most virtual media, can remediate other media but that theatre can remediate remediation, by confronting 'its spectators with the ever changing workings of perception' (Boenisch 2006: 113). A lot of early film remediated theatre (as in the case of German expressionist films of the 1920s) and/or was heavily based upon the thematics and syntaxical structures of literature (as in the case of Eisenstein's films and early Soviet cinema in general). Film can of course film theatre, painting, photographs and even film itself but all of these media will ultimately become subject to the medium of film and be processed through its specific technology. Thus film can only offer an aestheticisation of other media, unlike theatre which has the potential for what Boenisch defines as *ai*sthetic effects as opposed to aesthetic. This is what Peter Boenisch argues is the difference between aesthetics and aisthetics:

> We must go beyond theatre's alleged aesthetic originalities (the beautiful and the sublime) to scent that microscopic, yet ever so obvious effect. It is no technical, no mechanical, nor a digital effect – but an aisthetic one, which does not transform nor physically affect the actor, photo, or video-tape, as their mediation by means of a camera, scanner, or TV screen did. This trace of theatrical mediation is produced in the observers' perception alone: the actor on stage is no longer the actor, but the actor exposed on stage. That photo becomes a photo placed on stage and strangely different from the very same photo hanging stored back-stage before the show...
>
> (Boenisch 2006: 114)

The blurred distinctions between different media suggested by Auslander are contested when the theoretical focus shifts on to intermedial strategies, as Kattenbelt and Boenisch demonstrate.

Both of these lines of argument can be insightful when approaching intermedial strategies in post-cinematic pieces because they cover the historical and cultural aspects of film and theatre and also their specific materialities. The problem remains, however, that many theorists dealing with intermediality of film and theatre tend to refer to film in very general terms. This is especially the case with some of the older arguments that refer to film as synonymous with cinema. This book will look at intermediality through the notion of post-cinema and consider the difference between film as a medium and cinema as a cultural construct. Hence throughout this book close attention will be paid to cinema culture as a set of codes, practices, languages and conventions and the ways in which these interact within an intermedial setting. This will offer a more specific lens for analysis of the case studies than the more general intermedial approaches outlined above.

2
Décalage and Mediaphors in Robert Lepage's *Elsinore* and *The Andersen Project*

This chapter will look at the 'politics of perception' in Robert Lepage's *Elsinore* and *The Andersen Project* with a particular focus on the concepts of 'décalage' and 'mediaphors', which can be argued to function jointly as a deconstructive aesthetic prompting the audience to assume a more reflexive and *writerly* role in the construction of meaning. The theoretical point of departure for this discussion is Sergei Eisenstein's theory of classical film montage and cinematic metaphor. The main focus will be on his notion of the image of movement and his critique of Edward Muybridge's famous movement studies, which Lepage deliberately references in *Elsinore* in order to play with the expectations of cinematic montage. Colin MacCabe's discursive critique of Eisenstein supplements this approach in order to explore how the interinvolvement of film and theatre in *Elsinore* jars the possibility of an ideologically cohesive cinematic meta-discourse, thus stimulating the audience to become more active in the process of meaning-making and exemplifying what Lehmann calls the aesthetic of 'response-ability' or 'politics of perception'. In the case of *The Andersen Project*, the chapter will look at the notion of the mediaphoric body in relation to Eisenstein's interpretation of the Laocoön. *The Andersen Project* presents us with mediaphors of 'impossible' bodies, where the tensions between the different constituents of these pseudo-metaphors (mediaphors) deconstruct the integral nature of classical metaphors as postulated by Eisenstein.

Robert Lepage has been described as a unique theatre maker, exploring the boundaries of theatricality through highly stylised and visual intermedial performance. His originality not only lies in his artistic and technological innovations but also in the way in which he blends personal and geographical dimensions into his work and positions himself as an outsider. He comes across as a multifaceted character in the contemporary arts landscape. As Christopher Innes points out, he is 'a gay artist in a predominantly heterosexual culture, as a Francophone separatist and a Quebecois voice in an Anglo-dominated nation, and in opposition even to that voice speaking largely from outside the Province' (Innes 2005: 124). Throughout his career, Lepage has presented himself as a multitalented performer, director, lighting-engineer, lead actor, auteur and dramaturge. This carefully constructed image is of course a marketing tool, sometimes self-consciously played out, as was in the case of *Elsinore*, a piece which was pitched as a one-man interpretation of Shakespeare's *Hamlet*. Furthermore most of Lepage's productions use a mixture of cinematic film projections, live video feeds and complex machinery which in some ways act as 'an extension of his own or his performers' bodies' (ibid.) and add to the multidisciplinary character of his work.

The emphasis on the theatre as a machine, echoed in the name of his company Ex Machina, is prevalent in most of his productions and engenders an emphasis on a quasi-Brechtian reflexivity of the inner workings of a theatrical spectacle and a performative exposure of the process of construction of theatrical imagery. Thus, technology, and in particular film, plays an important part in his work and defines the dramaturgical emphasis of his theatre, a dramaturgy which puts technology at the centre of spectatorial attention. Christopher Innes comments that the aim of Ex Machina:

> is to explore new ways of devising pieces by bringing creative technicians, including video artists and engineers together with actors, musicians and directors from widely different places and traditions. In this post-industrial, post-national, post-human formula Lepage has become the poster-artist for aggressive post-modernism.
>
> (Ibid.: 125)

Even though Lepage uses a myriad of technological devices to propel his *mise-en-scène*, ranging from robotic sets (*Zulu Time*, 1999) to large transport trucks on a highway (*Romeo and Juliet*, 1989), and a large variety of media, such as interactive computer animation, 3D renderings, CD-ROM, holograms and internet feeds, his main interest and fascination seems to lie with film, and more specifically, with a cinematic way of telling stories.

Many commentators have pointed out Lepage's fascination with film, which results in what can be described as cinematic theatre, a hybrid of cinematic and theatrical forms. Some critics seem to oppose this approach and see it as a form of circus trickery adding more confusion than clarity to what they perceive the end product should be. One of the heaviest criticisms of this sort concerned *Elsinore*, a piece that makes extensive use of film technology and is very transformative of theatrical tradition. For instance, Peter Marks of the *New York Times* wrote of *Elsinore* as 'an uninterrupted succession of stage stunts, some as clever as the best moments in "Seven Streams," others as hokey as the pseudo-solemn theatrics of David Copperfield' (Marks in Lavender 2001: 103). Other commentators simply posed questions, such as 'Why not just make a movie instead?', encapsulating this line of criticism. As an interpretation of *Hamlet, Elsinore* immediately situates itself within an epic theatrical tradition. The strength of some of the criticism directed at this piece might have been a register of broader discontent in relation to the intermedial and technological treatment of Shakespeare's classic. Tamsen Wolff in a performance review of *Elsinore* for the *Theatre Journal* commented on the piece in the following way:

> Director Robert Lepage's technologically busy distillation of *Hamlet* is a frequently dazzling succession of visual stunts. [Peter] Darling, playing all the characters but assisted by hidden cameras, microphones, projections, and a body double, gives a workmanlike performance. Unfortunately, no matter how capably he clambers about on his flexible jungle gym of walls and floors, he is scrambling as fruitlessly as a caged hamster on a wheel. This is not a one-man show that aims to explore either an actor's virtuosity or the original text, but a magic show designed to display one conjurer's mastery of illusions.
>
> (Wolff 1998: 238)

It would certainly be possible to infer from this that Lepage's exploration of the text through an intermedial-technological aesthetic somehow did not do justice to the original text. It also implies that Shakespeare's text should have been the central focal point of the production. This is despite the fact that the very title – *Elsinore* – suggests a shift of focus away from the traditional 'dramatic' aesthetics and structural trappings of the play to the architecture of Elsinore, where technology and machinery become the focal theatrical exponents. Neither does Peter Darling's 'workmanlike' performance seem to comply with standards of theatrical virtuosity; and much in the spirit of Aristotle's metaphor of the 'untamed animal' (Aristotle in Lehmann 2006: 40) – a criticism he makes of malformed dramaturgies – Darling is compared to a fidgety 'hamster on a wheel'.

Other criticism takes a similar line. John Heilpern from the *New York Observer* comments: 'the prince's indecisive intellectual core is well known, and the director's interpretation confines Hamlet to the neurotic. There are times, too, when this raging, one-dimensional Hamlet is lost in the shadowy, dangerous turrets of Elsinore, drowning in technology' (Heilpern 1997: n.p.). Richard Christiansen from the *Chicago Tribune* called it a 'technological stunt'. Christiansen also remarked the fragmented nature of the piece, writing that 'it is probably best to take this unique show simply as a series of exceedingly inventive and clever riffs on the "Hamlet" theme.' He concludes: 'This is "Hamlet" for the short-attention-span generation' (Christiansen 1996: n.p.).

At the root of much of this criticism are questions about the value and purpose of using technology and film media in the piece, and a perception of its fragmented, arguably postdramatic aesthetics, as an unnecessary burden. The refusal to acknowledge value in the deconstructive nature of the show may in some cases be a cultural or political choice pertaining to a value system that upholds that there are specific and acceptable ways of staging *Hamlet* which should not be violated.

Much of the criticism also seems to miss the inevitability that any production of *Hamlet* will be haunted by the 'ghosts' of its past performances (pardon the pun) and that theatre makers will often feel obliged to respond in some way to the representations and stagings that came before. It is also true that some of the most significant 'ghosts' of *Hamlet* would have come out of cinema, which has a lengthy tradition of representing the play. The cinematic ghosts of *Hamlet* are an important cultural heritage, which influences the way that Hamlet is perceived, read and staged. This cinematic haunting is even true of 'pure' theatrical productions. No wonder, then, that Lepage with his particular interest in cinema as a methodology for scenic construction decided to make the cinematic a central aspect of this show.

I would like to challenge these preconceived notions of how *Hamlet* should be staged and argue instead that rather than being superfluous, misguided and unnecessary, the interinvolvement of film and theatre in *Elsinore* has the potential to question and challenge cultural expectations associated with cinematic representations of *Hamlet* by creating a décalage. To define it by contrast, décalage in Lepage's terminology is the opposite of métissage, which is a form of hybridity, a mixing and crossbreeding of art forms 'on both a cultural and aesthetic level' (Pluta 2010: 192). Lepage himself described it as 'the crossing of the languages of theatre and cinematography as "two forms of expression that will be merged together"' (ibid.). Thus, métissage can be broadly defined as a way of blending different scenic elements, such as live performances, film projections, text, music, set, lighting and props into a cohesive aesthetic superstructure, an aesthetic totality often inspired by the holistic qualities of cinematic illusions. By contrast to this form of blending, décalage can be defined as the 'strange impression of [...] disparity' (Hébert and Perelli-Contos 2001: 19) between these scenic elements; a disparity that arises out of the 'impossibility' of achieving such a cohesion in a live theatrical event. In a sense décalage is the failure of Lepage's cine-theatrical machine to achieve a métissage. The explicitness of this failure is what seems to have sparked many of the negative critical responses to *Elsinore,* but décalage essentially effectuates the deconstruction of cinematic aesthetics in his work and prompts the sense of spectatorial 'reflexivity' on how cinematic culture influences perceptual expectations of theatrical works.

Lepage has produced a number of one-man interpretations of Shakespeare and these earlier productions make extensive use of different types of technologies and scenographical arrangements. For instance, he has staged *A Midsummer Night's Dream* in a giant 'mud-bath', *The Tempest* in a rehearsal room, *Coriolanus* through a letter-box framing, *Romeo and Juliet* in trucks on a highway and *Macbeth* through an extensive use of shadow puppetry. Andy Lavender claims that one of the ambitions common to these adaptations is to challenge and reconfigure the notion of spectatorship:

> 'Looking at the stage' is turned into a reflexive pleasure, since what's on the stage is arranged to emphasize its surprising, unorthodox, unexpected relation to actual proportions, spatial relationships and to the spectator herself. *Elsinore* has the same ambition: Shakespeare to be *seen differently.*
>
> (Lavender 2001: 103)

What is special and unique about *Elsinore* is its substantial use of film projections, movie conventions and references to cinema culture throughout. The general scenographical concept was as follows. Like *Needles and Opium,* an earlier one-man show by Lepage on the life of Jean Cocteau, *Elsinore* had a moving screen as its central scenographical feature. Film was projected onto a central panel, which the company called the 'monolith' (Figure 2.1 shows Robert Lepage and the set of *Elsinore*). This was a circular platform held in place by a pneumatic apparatus which could make it turn and rotate in different directions: horizontal, vertically skewed at a specific angle and so on. This added

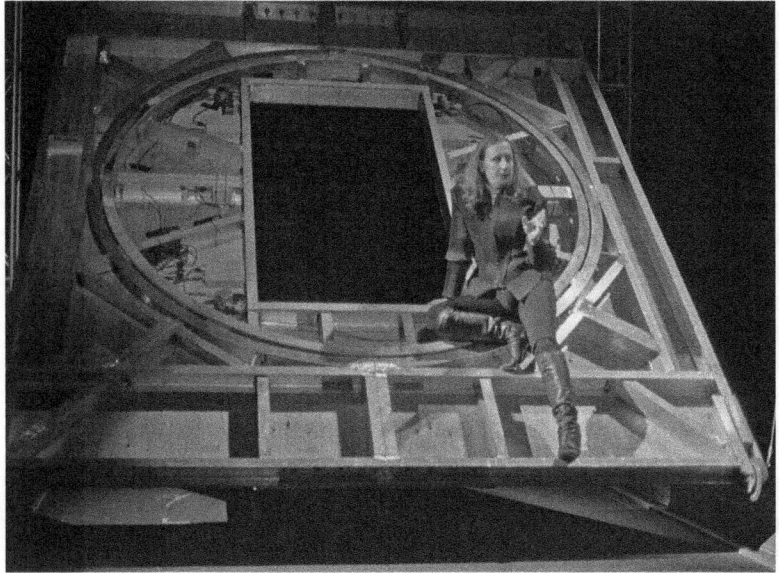

Figure 2.1   Robert Lepage and the *Elsinore* set. Photo © Richard-Max Tremblay

considerable flexibility in terms of the way it could be used to represent roof, floor and walls of the castle once images were projected onto it. There was also a door in the centre which could stand in for gates, a grave yard, a throne and so on. The set also had a screen on either side for additional projections and a mini camera attached to a sword was used during the final duel. This intermedial configuration utilising film projection screens is very well suited to deconstructing cinematic aesthetics as it allows for the exploration of diverse post-cinematic effects: simultaneity of multiple perspectives, the exposition and staging of the process of film production, juxtaposition of live feeds and pre-recorded material, temporal and spatial fragmentations, montage parataxis and so on. Thus, to a great extent *Elsinore* can be described as a 'cine-theatrical' machine in a perpetual state of métissage and décalage, dynamically composing and decomposing cinematic images.

Classical realist film montage

Before taking a closer look at *Elsinore's* post-cinematic aesthetics, it will be useful to discuss what is aesthetically at stake within classical montage theory and for that purpose Eisenstein's theory of montage proves a viable starting point. His theories will also become a point of reference when discussing the intermedial deconstruction of cinematic conventions in the later chapters. To this day Eisenstein is considered the father of classical montage in cinema and his theories continue to have widespread influence in filmmaking practice all over the world. Thus, his theories hold significant sway over the methodologies of contemporary mainstream cinema and the way it influences our modes of perception. In many ways they also reflect what expectations of cinematic experience lie at the heart of our cinematised culture and thus are important to the understanding of culturally dominant cinematic conventions.

The image of movement

For Eisenstein montage is the key methodology for the creation of the film world. According to Eisenstein, the image that arises out of montage is different in degree to the images depicted and illustrated within each successive shot. Eisenstein claims that the key structural principle of montage is rooted in the spectator's ability to synthesise successive discontinuous shots into an 'image of movement' (Eisenstein 1991: 123). The imagined world of a film, he argues, is created by the juxtaposition of discontinuous fragmented shots. He sees it as a perceptual phenomenon arising from two functions: '[o]ne of them involv[ing] visual depiction, the other an attitude to what is depicted, or rather to a succession of pictures in a montage sequence. The first lies entirely in the film, the second in the perception of the spectator' (ibid.: 122). He illustrates this with an example of a shot sequence of a galloping horse: '[g]alloping hooves, the rushing head of a horse, a horse's rump disappearing into the distance. Those three pictures. Only when they are combined in the mind does there arise a visual *sensation* of a galloping horse' (ibid.: 123). The gaps and discontinuities between various shots prompt the spectator to fill in what is absent, and thus recreate the event in their imagination. The gap is understood here as an insufficiency, a mystery, the opposite of excess or overflow.[1]

Another good example of this would be an attempt to represent something more abstract, such as midnight. The face of a clock can tell us that midnight is approaching, but in itself it does not create an image of midnight with all the possible associations and perceptions that an author may wish to evoke. While this broader image of midnight cannot be directly depicted, it can nonetheless arise out of montage as an image of movement. Eisenstein illustrates this with an example from

Maupassant's *Bel-Ami*, where the protagonist Georges Duroy, 'is sitting in a cab waiting for Suzanne, who has agreed to elope with him at midnight' (ibid.: 303). The passage evokes the image of midnight through a successive montage of depiction of clocks and midnight strokes. The storyboard shown in Figure 2.2 illustrates this (this story board has been reconstructed and interpreted by me based on Eisenstein's descriptions).

The twelve strokes of midnight, depicted in different shots, fuse into an image of midnight that is distinctly different and of a different order to any of the individual elements of the sequence. Classical cinema needs montage to recreate an event and requires an aesthetic system – a way of organising and structuring sensorial data that can stimulate *meaning* and *reading*. The gaps prompt the audience to reconstitute an 'imaginary whole'. In short, classical realist filmmaking consists of organising an insufficiency of images in order to stimulate a reconstruction of an event in the spectator's mind. Discontinuity works by creating gaps, which result from reduction and elimination in the process of translating the *mise-en-scène* into *mise-en-cadre*. This notion is very relevant to post-cinematic pieces, such as *Elsinore*, which through their deconstructive aesthetics hint at the potential to recuperate the 'real' that is lost during this elimination process, hence *resisting* these types of classical aesthetic operations.

MacCabe's critique

How can the décalage in *Elsinore* function as a deconstruction of this cinematic concept? What is perceptually at stake in this deconstruction? In order to answer these questions it will be useful to look at Colin MacCabe's critique of Eisenstein's concept of the 'image of movement'. MacCabe begins his critique by referring to Eisenstein's example of the 'mourning widow'. In his essay 'Word and Image' in *The Film Sense* Eisenstein proposes a story of a widow mourning as an example of the operations of montage:

> A woman in widow's weeds was weeping upon a grave. 'Console yourself, madam' said a sympathetic stranger. 'Heaven's mercies are infinite. There is another man somewhere, beside your husband, with whom you can still be happy.' 'There was,' she sobbed – 'there was, but this is his grave.'
>
> (Eisenstein in MacCabe 1985: 40)

Eisenstein uses this to explain the effect of montage. Both the images of the woman and the mourning dress are depictions, direct 'objective

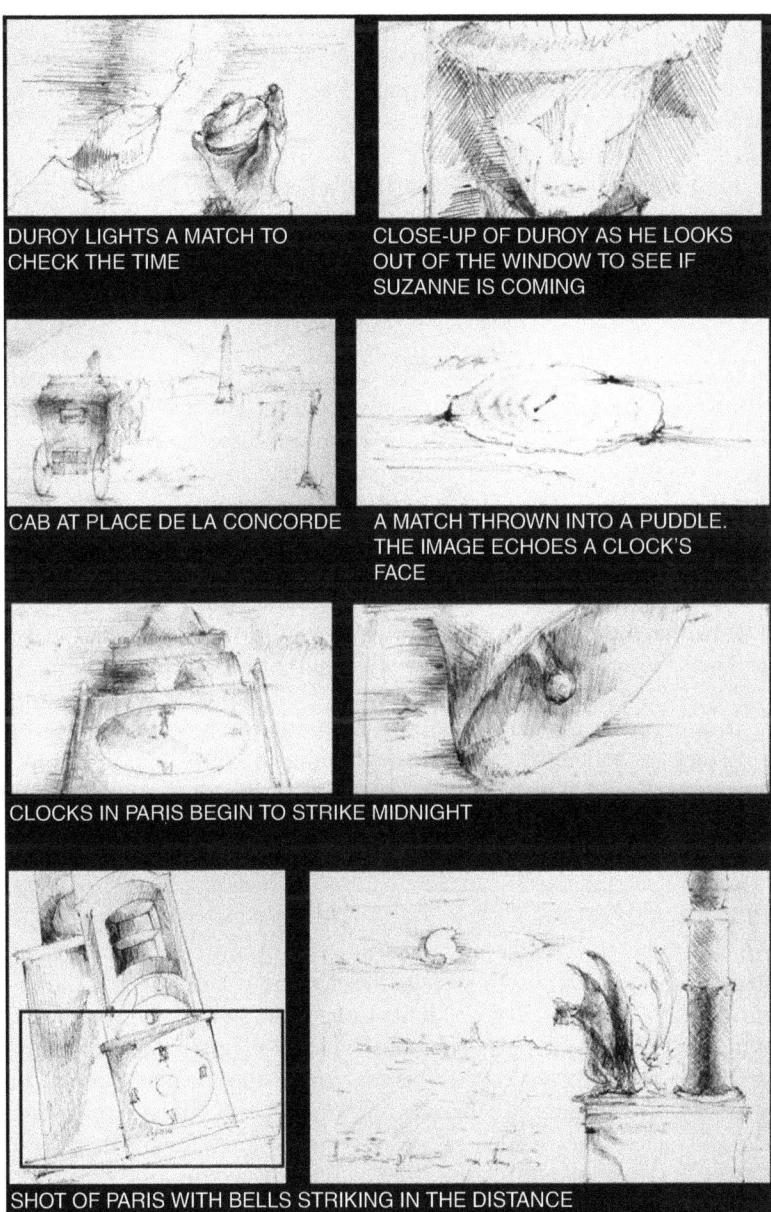

Figure 2.2 Storyboards based on Eisenstein's descriptions. Piotr Woycicki

representations' (MacCabe 1985: 40). The image of the widow, however, is a representation of a different order which arises out of its constituent elements. MacCabe criticises Eisenstein for focusing too much on the aesthetics of montage.

> Montage is thus, for Eisenstein, in this passage, the manipulation of definite representations to produce images in the mind of the spectator. [...] Eisenstein would have montage linking onto representation but not in any sense challenge it.

(Ibid.: 41)

In his analysis of the realist text MacCabe argues that even though realist texts juxtapose different perspectives and points of view, the result does not critique or render opaque the meta-discourse which frames all these different discursive positions. He argues that: '[w]hereas other discourses within the text are considered as material which is open to re-interpretation, the narrative discourse simply allows reality to appear and denies its own status as articulation' (ibid.: 36). Following the example given by Eisenstein he argues that classical realist montage is essentially designed to create this transparent meta-discourse. He critiques Eisenstein's methodology by arguing that:

> It is essential to realise that this account leaves both subject and object unchallenged and that the montage becomes a kind of super representation which is more effective at demonstrating the real qualities of the object through the links it can form within the [subject's imagination].

(ibid.: 42)

For MacCabe this dominant meta-discursive position can be deconstructed by exposing a set of contradictions within representation. However, these contradictions have to be exposed in such a way as to avoid the *transparency* of the meta-discourse. Instead the meta-discourse should be rendered *opaque*. After giving an account of how that can be achieved in literature he attempts to transpose this strategy to cinema and postulates for what he calls a subversive film – a film that could subvert its own meta-discourse. He postulates that this kind of subversion could be carried out by 'articulating reality through an investigation of the different forms of language' (ibid.: 50) in order to expose a set of contradictions, like the 'ineliminable contradictions of the sexes, the eternal struggle between Desire and Law, between articulation and position' (ibid.). This kind of cinema would also have to draw attention to the process of the production of images, the very process of filming and framing discourses within the film text. He suggests Brecht's *Kuhle Wampe* and Godard's *Tout Va Bien* as exemplifying these subversive features.

Thus, for MacCabe what is necessary in order to subvert the dominant discourse is an 'investigation of different forms of language', the exposition of contradictions and the articulation of the process of production of images. To what extent this subversive strategy is achievable for film on its own, for instance without the hypermedial framing of theatre, is problematic. Let us now focus on some of the aspects of this subversive strategy outlined by MacCabe and take a look at how they feature in the post-cinematic aesthetics of *Elsinore*.

From the outset the audience is exposed to a very visual form of storytelling, which in many ways engenders and suggests a cinematic stylistic and mode of organisation of dramatic material. As Lavender points out the prologue is strikingly cinematic:

A story board of the Prologue might appear as follows:

(1) Spotlights on edge of stage surrounded empty throne.
(2) Spotlights on Hamlet on throne.
(3) Hamlet stands on the edge of the precipice.
(4) Ghost appears in the middle of everything.
(5) King and Queen on throne (raised in mid-air).
(6) Hamlet on throne (returned to floor).

(Lavender 2001: 122)

However, the way in which this 'cinematic' sequence materialises on stage is far more disorienting and fragmentary than the above outline might suggest. The piece opens with the famous 'To be or not to be speech' echoing the voice-over prologue of Olivier's film version of *Hamlet* (1949). The action quickly progresses to the scene where Hamlet meets the Ghost. What is immediately striking about the production is that all the characters are played by one performer, originally Lepage, but in later productions Peter Darling. Darling plays Hamlet, performing physically in the space, whilst the Ghost is a negative film projection, a pre-recorded version of Darling's performance. When the Ghost describes the murder, the two side panels show a pre-filmed version of the poisoning scene. One screen shows close-ups of the poison vial whilst the other, echoing a German expressionist stylistic, shows

Darling as the poisoner climbing a giant ear and pouring poison into its opening. The casting of Darling in multiple roles, as simultaneously Hamlet, the Ghost and Claudius could suggest a reading that Hamlet's identity is a multiplicity and he is staging his drama in his own mind. However, this reading is complicated by the cinematic qualities of the film elements and by their relationship to the live action. Do the – pre-recorded – filmed sequences belong to the past? Are they flashbacks, Hamlet's fantasies, his hypotheses of what has happened to his father? Or are they a representation of what has truly happened? Is the film supposed to be read as the imaginary space of Hamlet's psyche? Is Darling's mediated presence on film supposed to be read as Hamlet performing (imagining these scenes) or is this simply part of the one-man theatrical convention? From a cinematic standpoint the implicit perceptual leap from the depictions on screen to the second-order imaginary image, 'the image of movement', is being deconstructed. The courtroom scene follows and is characterised by a similar sense of deconstruction. The monolith rotates in vertical space and Darling is now seated in its aperture, which denotes the throne in the court room. Both Gertrude and Claudius are played by Darling, his voice is electronically modified live in order to fit the characters. As the scene ends Darling changes his posture, from that of the elegant authoritative Queen to a subdued, melancholic Hamlet. Again the audience is faced with a décalage of filmed and staged fragments, projected onto the screens and enacted through the complex intermedial machinery on stage. It is not impossible to piece together a sense of narrative or to come up with a metaphorical interpretation of this intermedial collage, but the fragmentary nature of this sequence complicates any attempt at forming a direct interpretation in the manner postulated by Eisenstein.

With its technically explicit staging, Lepage seems to favour an aesthetic that favours disorientation rather than narrative clarity. With all the moving screens, explicit exposition of technical aspects, such as the movements of the monolith, the side panel film projections and live voice manipulation, the emphasis seems to lie more on the apparatus through which the spectacle is being constructed than on the dramatic content. In his critique MacCabe has pointed out that one way of deconstructing the 'image of movement' and the meta-discursive position associated with it is by inducing a reflexive mode of spectatorship in the audience. This can be achieved by exposing the process of the production of images which underlie cinematic production. According to MacCabe for Eisenstein the process of filmmaking is a transition from the *mise-en-scène* to the *mise-en-cadre*. The discontinuities, when montaged, can elicit an imaginary unity of the film world in the spectator's mind – as in the depiction of the image of midnight. By staging these discontinuities and drawing attention to them, *Elsinore*'s décalage constantly thwarts the possibility of experiencing a unified image of movement. This is not to say that instances of métissage do not occur in this scene. But the overall intermedial aesthetic is unstable and oscillates between a movement towards a unified composition (métissage) on the one hand and its decomposition (décalage) on the other.

According to MacCabe, once the reflexive mode has been established a further deconstruction of the meta-discourse can be achieved by creating a set of contradictions between the different discursive positions in the text. In the case of *Elsinore* the use of one actor to play all the roles complicates the possibility of a unified sense of identity. The different discursive positions of all the characters become confounded, which in effect creates a further sense of discursive instability. The spectator is not asked to evaluate the different discourses from a set implicit meta-discursive position but rather is faced with irresolvable questions as to how all these discursive perspectives relate to each other. For instance, are Claudius and Gertrude one and the same person in Hamlet's mind or are they just univocal? Is the ghost as projection a 'flashback' or a visual effect of an apparition? What role does technology play in terms of manipulating these various discourses? Could the various characterisations be interpreted as quotes within the dominant discourse? If so is there a dominant discourse at all? This deconstructive stance follows Lehmann's notion of the 'politics of perception', in that postdramatic theatre is more about conveying the forms of perception as opposed to the content of perceptions. The décalage complicates the possibility of assuming the position of a dominant discourse here, instead Lepage's 'cine-theatrical machine' challenges the audience to reflect upon the very processes that induce perceptual constructs and perceptual expectations.

Later scenes continue this deconstructive momentum. Lepage has added a scene where Hamlet visits Ophelia's chambers and engages in an ambiguous act of cross-dressing. Darling slips in through the 'window' opening of the monolith and onto Ophelia's bed. He then picks up her nightgown, smells it, re-arranges it in various ways and into various shapes until it forms a body like figure of Ophelia. He takes his shirt off and puts on Ophelia's nightgown. He then tries different things, such as putting on Ophelia's make-up, brushing his hair, fixing some earrings and slowly loosening the nightgown around his shoulders in a sexualised manner (Lavender 2001: 124). Then Darling bursts into the soliloquy that normally follows the Players' performance of the 'Mouse-Trap': 'Is it not monstrous that this player here, / But in a fiction...'. This fragment functions as a flashback (analepsis) to a certain extent, although its status as a flashback is never quite made clear. Darling stops halfway through and goes into Ophelia's song in Act 4 Scene 5 (the 'mad' Ophelia song), which is a scene that features later in the play. This could be read as a flash-forward (prolepsis), of the scene to come. However, he then lapses back into Hamlet, turns once more into Ophelia to finish off the song and then again to Hamlet. With that he finally finishes this complicated scene, rousing himself into a state of vengeance (ibid.).

Lavender has commented that the cross-dressing might be read as a 'male fantasy of dressing as a woman' (ibid.: 125), a fetishistic desire of the male to dominate the objectified female body. However, it may also be a 'glimpse of Ophelia herself' (ibid.). The scene potentially presents us with both an image of Hamlet and of Ophelia, through the complex interplay between the two characterisations. The discursive forms adopted in the scene could be read as instances of role-play, analepsis, prolepsis or even Ophelia watching Hamlet from the side depending on which perspective the spectator chooses to adopt. Once again the 'performative' aspects of the scene generate what MacCabe defined as a contradiction. The fetishism of Ophelia does not have to be a minor quote within a dominant discourse, which in this case could be a glimpse into Hamlet's world of role-play fantasies, but a contradictory, un-decidable perspective of Ophelia's character herself. The materiality of performance does not merely translate into a particular representation but falls back on itself, allowing for a different representation in which we see the character of Ophelia herself.

This deconstruction is particularly interesting if we locate it in relation to past cinematic representations of Ophelia. For instance in Olivier's film, Jean Simmons portrays Ophelia as oppressed and fragile, a shy creature dominated by all the male characters in the play. Lepage 'flirts' with that same dominant male perspective but then changes it into something else, implying a new Ophelia, existing beyond the frame of fetishistic fantasy that seems to be suggested at the beginning of the scene. Once again the viewer is faced with multiple perspectives and possible readings, which depend on the spectator's own active 'montage' choices. Any expectations of a cinematic montage are deconstructed by the fluidity of the performative aspects of this scene. In classical realist montage a fragmented yet organised sequence of images is designed to create a unified discursive perspective. The forms through which such perspectives are delivered are usually made transparent. This can induce a specific discursive position, as in the case of Olivier's film *Hamlet*. However, here a specific discursive position is not being induced but rather the audience experiences an aesthetics of flux. The different suggested stylistics, such as flashback, forward cuts, point of view changes, are all collapsed on the material body of the performer, which in turn makes these forms of perception *opaque*. It becomes the 'response-ability' of the spectator to choose how they wish to perceive the scene, and the way the scene has been designed induces and allows for this kind of reflexive approach.

Cinematic metaphor

The second Eisensteinian concept I would like to look at in relation to décalage in *Elsinore* is the concept of the cinematic metaphor. This begins with the question of what constitutes a metaphorical construction for Eisenstein who differentiates metaphor from metonymy in cinema. To illustrate this concept let us look at a simple montage sequence that consists of a juxtaposition of two shots. Metonymy in this case is a juxtaposition of two specific shots that generate a concept which arises as an image of a higher order, an order beyond the two depictions displayed. For example a close-up of a character's face followed by a desolate landscape to create a notion of a psychological state. A metaphor can also arise out of a juxtaposition of two images but it requires the co-existence of two elements. One is the specific element which constitutes the substance of each shot and the other is a generalising element which gives the whole montage sequence a sense of 'unity'. In order for this to occur the two shots need to have the same visual harmonics. The existence of these harmonics is what differentiates metaphor from metonymy. Let us look at a simple concrete example concerning shot composition. Again this is a scene I storyboarded from one of Eisenstein's descriptions, which gives an example from his film *Battleship Potemkin*. This is a juxtaposition of two shots: Shot 1: the legs of an agent of the revolution, cut to Shot 2: The factory (Figure 2.3).

The metaphor might suggest that the progress of the Soviet Union rests upon the revolutionaries. What makes this sequence metaphorical for Eisenstein is the shot composition of two images that carry similar visual harmonics. Compositionally the legs in the puddle resonate with the chimneys and the clouds of smoke of the factory. A metonymy would look more like the shot sequence 3 and 4 which is merely a juxtaposition of two images without a substantial harmonic aesthetic binding

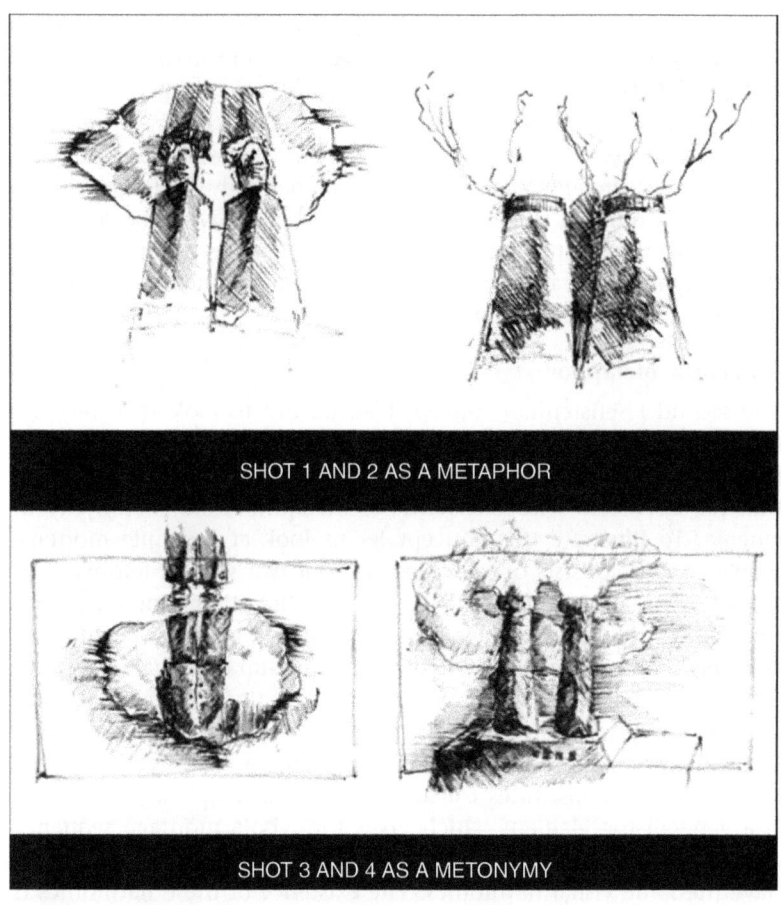

SHOT 1 AND 2 AS A METAPHOR

SHOT 3 AND 4 AS A METONYMY

Figure 2.3 Metaphor and metonymy – storyboards based on Eisenstein's descriptions. Piotr Woycicki

the two images together. This is a simple example and obviously there are more complex ways of crafting metaphors which incorporate the rhythm of editing, music, the actor's gestures, lighting, camera movement and so on and are more extended in time. An example of a more extended metaphor from *Battleship Potemkin* would be the culminating scene where the images of the ship's crew, accompanied by a rhythmic atonal soundtrack, are juxtaposed with images of the revolving ship's engine from which a metaphor arises, that of the ship and its crew as the beating heart of the revolution. What is important in the notion of a classical metaphor in general is that it not only binds two distinct images into a harmonic whole and by doing so gives a degree of aesthetic pleasure to the spectator, but that its aesthetic structure supports a message and an argument that may carry an ideological and political agenda. The allure of this beautiful aesthetic may inspire the spectator to agree and 'go along' with that argument as opposed to stimulating a critical reflection. This notion is obviously very problematic as perceptual attitudes are complex and will vary depending on the individual. It is impossible to tell how an audience member will experience a given image. The point here, however, is the design of an aesthetic set-up, which regulates inscriptions and potentially carries with it an inscribed political/ideological agenda.

When looking at décalage as a deconstruction of cinematic metaphors in *Elsinore* an interesting example is the metaphor of the castle of Elsinore itself. The castle has often been interpreted and used as a metaphor to represent Hamlet's state of mind. Examples of productions that paid special attention to scenography in that respect are Edward Craig's Moscow Arts staging of *Hamlet* in 1915 and Lawrence Olivier's 1949 film.

Olivier made extensive use of set design and camera work in order to represent the castle as a sequence of psychological spaces reflective of Hamlet's subjective attitudes towards characters and localities and in which internal conflicts are played out. In his essay 'Claims' he states that:

> Roger Furse's 'mise-en-scène' for the film liberates the play's language and actions from deadening literalness and reinforces the psychological nature of the drama. The vague Kafkaesque castle, with its large rooms, pillars, corridors, and archways, its misty ramparts and tortuously winding staircases, its bleak stone walls and ominous areas of impenetrable shadow, is suggestive of the mind's labyrinths.
> (Olivier quoted in Davies 1988: 57)

Olivier achieves these effects through standard classical realist montage and composed shots utilising unusual depth of field, which allows for different components of the image to juxtapose and resonate with each other. Arguably a Freudian interpretation of this extended metaphor is in place, where the battlements become the stage space of the *super ego*, the court room that of the *ego* and Gertrude's bedroom the space of the *id*. In Lepage's *Elsinore* the set is similarly strongly metaphorical. In 'Puppets and Machines of the Mind: Robert Lepage and the Modernist Heritage', Christopher Innes compares Lepage's scenographical designs to those of Edward Craig, and observes the propensity of the set in *Elsinore* to exemplify a metaphor of Hamlet. He claims that 'as the machine-movement of Elsinore suggests, Lepage's geography is in fact psychological' (Innes 2005: 133). Innes's description of the different potential psychological spaces into which the Lepagian machine-set can morph suggests an affinity with Olivier's and Furse's psychologically-charged designs and thematic spaces for the film set of *Hamlet* (1949):

> In the centre of the acting area stands a circular frame with a square central opening. This revolved horizontally like a great wheel or vertically as a spinning coin – presenting Gertrude's bed when flat, a window or door when upright, a web in which all the characters are caught, with a throne suspended in its centre for Lepage as Claudius, or with white lace stretched across it, through which Lepage puts his arms and head to appear as Ophelia.
>
> (Ibid.: 132)

However, Lepage's set does not constitute a coherent metaphorical construct. Instead it is an unstable metaphor. The different physical spaces (components) of the set are not clearly mapped onto psychological spaces of the play as was the case with Olivier's extended metaphor. The whole aesthetic of this cine-machine, with all the different screens, panels and film projections, is in a state of perpetual flux in which any instances of psychological geography, as Innes suggests, are more or less fortuitous and invariably ambiguous, depending for meaning on the spectator's perceptual choices – their individual 'politics of perception'. It could be argued for example that the chaotic nature of the revolving set with all the multiplicity of its components acts as a metaphor of Hamlet's madness – but the set's constant movements resist its 'settling' on any specific representation. Instead it is a deconstructed set in perpetual flux, where all the inner workings and machinery of the theatre are constantly exposed. Again we are faced with an oscillation between the dynamics of métissage and décalage. This quasi-Brechtian aesthetic exposes the process of production. It does not offer a coherent meta-discourse, a unified camera's 'eye/I', but rather a dispersed mechanical structure, a cine-theatre machine that 'draws' the spectator's attention to the forms through which meanings in cinema are produced.

Laocoön

Finally I would like to look at the notion of imaginary unity in classical realist montage. In thinking about unity Eisenstein asks: what are the conditions and limitations of a work of art composed out of fragments to maintain its unity? If there were none, then any random film abstraction would produce a similar effect. Eisenstein was interested in investigating the limits or the extent to which elements of a work of art could be discontinuous but still maintain a subjective unified perspective. He explored this notion in his essay on the Laocoön (Figure 2.4).

Eisenstein argues that the postures of the figures in the classical statue of Laocoön and his sons represent an impossibility, because all the different contortions of the bodies, the expressions and gestures would never occur within an instant; such a scene could not be captured in a photograph. The statue in effect consists of montaged elements from a longer sequence that have been brought together to form an *image of*

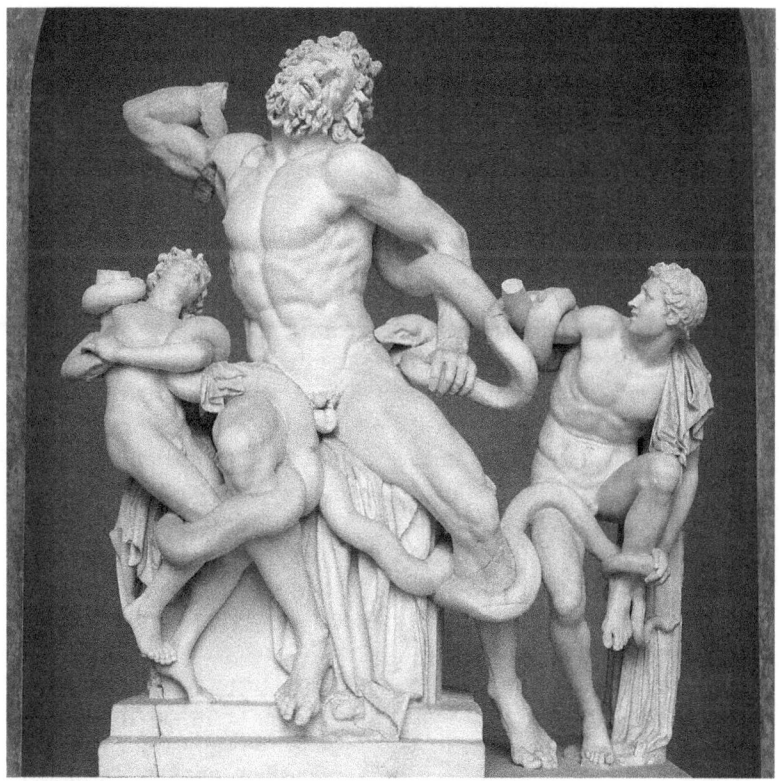

Figure 2.4   Laocoön, c. 40–20BC. Photo © Marie-Lan Nguyen / Wikimedia Commons

movement (not animation). So when one looks at the statue an impression of movement is created when all the discontinuous elements coalesce on the body of Laocoön.

Eisenstein makes a similar claim about the way in which horses' legs are depicted in Renaissance paintings. Frequently, the way in which the legs are positioned adds up to anatomical impossibility because each leg comes from a different phase of animation. Most artists cannot 'snapshot' a horse's movement, they have to focus on fragments that come from different temporal instances. Once these fragments are put together they form a whole that is a composite of different moments.[2] As a result the artwork conveys an image of movement. The sense of movement is the result of the merging of the phases into one in the spectators' imagination. To illustrate this concept I devised a photomontage of Edward Muybridge's famous horse gallop sequence (Figure 2.5).

Eisenstein contrasts the organic tendencies of Renaissance artists with Cubism, which is about the simultaneous juxtaposition of different perspectives of a subject without intending to unify them into one entity. Eisenstein claims that cinematic montage should seek ways of unifying multiple perspectives into one, extending the classical tradition as opposed to being inspired by 'cubist mismatch'. Hence, when attempting to deconstruct cinematic conventions, post-cinematic pieces often resort to exposing a multiplicity of perspectives and exploring the 'impossibility' of embodying the illusionary constructs of realist montage.

In *Elsinore* this deconstruction is far from subtle and is epitomised in a scene in which Lepage directly references Muybridge. Melancholy, Hamlet describes the world as a 'foul and pestilent congregation of vapours'; he is on stage standing in the aperture of the monolith. Behind there is a projected image of the cosmos and Hamlet is spun around on a revolving platform centre stage, an image evocative of the cinematic convention of the 360° tracking shot. What follows is the famous speech: 'What a piece of work is man! How noble in reason! How infinite in faculties! In form and moving how express and admirable!' The side panels show a projection of a naked man running in various temporal phases, which is a direct reference to Muybridge's proto-filmic experiments with stop-frame photography. Following this projection, Lepage projects the image of Leonardo da Vinci's Vitruvian man onto the main panel.

One way of looking at this scene is by considering it as a postmodern citation: 'We might see this as a productively ironic citation of the epitomes of Renaissance and post-Enlightenment study of the human

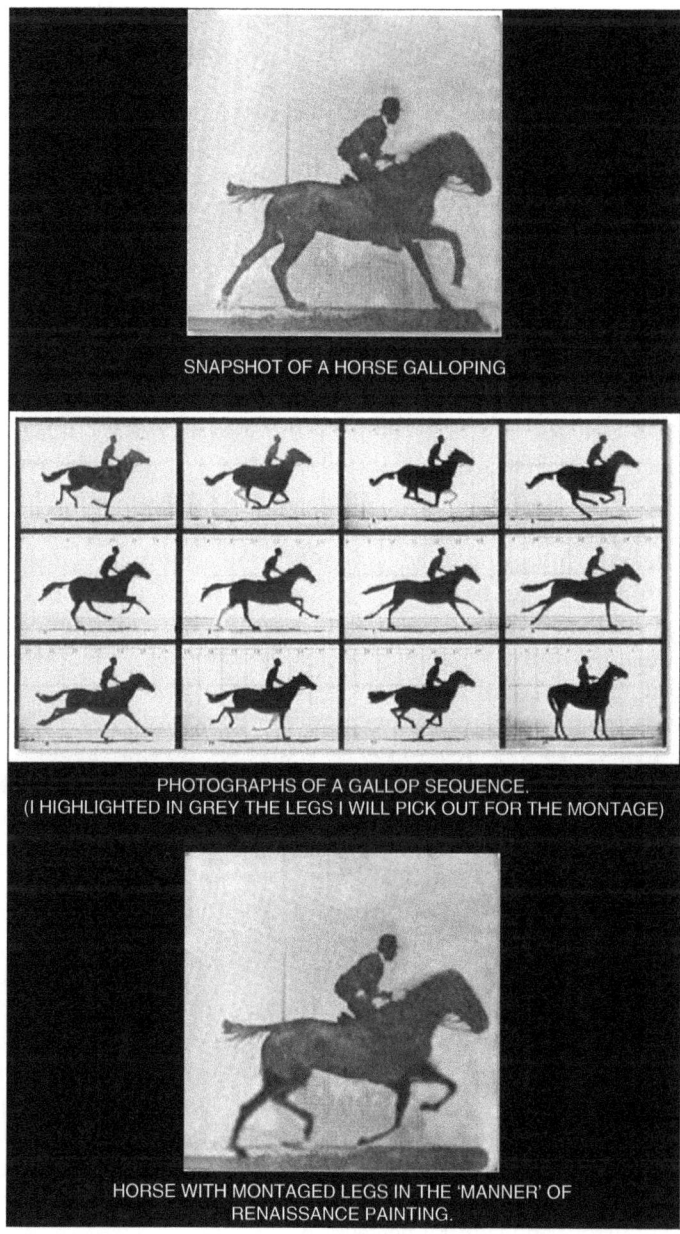

Figure 2.5 Photomontage of Edward Muybridge's horse gallop sequence. Piotr Woycicki

"form and moving"; or it may seem a rather obvious steering of the audience's response to the speech' (Giesekam 2007: 231). I think that this reference to Muybridge epitomises what is perceptually at stake in classical montage philosophy precisely because it deconstructs the experience of the 'image of movement' and the sense of 'organic unity' associated with it as theorised by Eisenstein. Whether Lepage's choice of this reference has anything to do with Eisenstein's theorisation of montage or not is difficult to tell but nonetheless, from a formal aesthetic point of view, it makes an important statement. Significantly, he includes this image in the programme for the show.

According to Eisenstein, cinematic montage is what creates an illusion of movement, an 'image of movement'. The actual fragments of figures and imagery depicted in the various shots (the raw material of montage) coalesce in the spectator's mind into an organic image, an 'imaginary unity'. Thus, the key stimulating factor in classical cinematic montage is the management of 'gaps', the in-between spaces of those fragments. As was argued above, this organic image is of a different order than the images depicted on film. So as to achieve this 'imaginary unity', the filmmaker has to find ways of organising the various fragmented depictions in such a way as to create an illusion of organicity. It is, thus, through a carefully arranged depiction of these fragments that a unified image of movement is achieved. What Muybridge did, in his proto-cinematic experiments, was to depict as many phases of movement of a given figure as was technically possible at the time, representing the results simultaneously on a timeline. In doing so to some extent he eliminated the 'gaps'; exposing the different movement phases as opposed to leaving them for the imagination of the spectator to compile and unify.

Lepage's décalage of the movements of the human figure resonates with Lehmann's notion of 'simultaneity'. By addressing Muybridge's concept, Lepage is saying something very profound about how classical realist cinema constructs imaginary worlds. Perhaps the reference to Vitruvian man can be read as ironic here. Man no longer stands strong as the centre of the universe but is uncoupled, spinning on moveable platforms amongst projections of fragmentary images. Thus, the pre-Enlightenment invocation: 'What a piece of work is man!' could be translated into 'What has cinema made of man?' – a question eliciting critical reflection of how cinematic forms transform our notions of identity, history and cultural perception.

What is important here is to appreciate that this self-reflective deconstructive stance is achieved primarily in relation to *forms* of representations, less so in relation to *content* or specific meanings and representations per se. Thus, by looking at the aesthetics of deconstruction in *Elsinore* from a post-cinematic perspective, it can be argued that what is at stake in *Elsinore* is a meditation on the cinematic *forms* and *mechanisms* which underlie representation and inspire particular forms of perception. Before moving to the analysis of *The Andersen Project* I will elaborate further on what is at stake in the 'politics of perception' in *Elsinore*.

Politics of perception

Historically many cinematic and theatrical productions of *Hamlet* have had strong discursive stances and political agendas associated with them. These discursive positions and their political meanings were reflective of the specific historical and cultural contexts in which they were made.

For instance, in Olivier's 1948 film Ophelia is portrayed as a fragile, helpless girl who is manipulated by her father, brother and Hamlet himself. Many of her lines have been cut – literally taking the character's voice away – and Jean Simmons's vocal performance palette often resorts to almost animal like squeaks and cries in spaces left by the removal of spoken dialogue. The overall impression is that she is weak, inarticulate, childlike and dominated by the male characters. This submissive portrayal of Ophelia can be explained in terms of the historical context in which the film was produced. During the Second World War, women took up the jobs left vacant by men who were in the forces, for instance working in factories. When the war was over, political and social pressure demanded a return to a conservative model of family roles where women were expected to stay at home and engage with housework. This was reinforced by the appearance of new kitchen appliances and electronic commodities whose sale would greatly benefit from a re-popularisation of the conservative female role. In the light of these changes it can be argued that Olivier's version of Ophelia as submissive and passive reflected the cultural shift in gender politics.

A different example comes from Kenneth Branagh's 1996 *Hamlet* where a mirror hallway stages the famous soliloquy in a scene that can be read as reiterating Michel Foucault's invocation of the panopticon as metaphor, since the mirrors are used by Claudius to spy on Hamlet. During the late 1990s there were many debates surrounding the extensive introduction of CCTV technology into British public life. Branagh's interpretation can be read as resonating with these public debates concerning the politics of individual freedom.

Lepage's *Elsinore* suggests the possibilities of such readings or rather cross-references some past representations by means of a postmodern 'bricolage'. There is no attempt to convey any specific political message; instead Lepage gives us a play of *forms* through which messages can be conveyed. In that sense his interrogation of the cinematic forms of representation, a deliberate avoidance of a meta-discursive position and a reluctance to disclose meaning could be read as a 'typical' postmodern, post-cinematic attitude. If we apply Lehmann's notion of the 'politics of perception' it becomes more evident that the piece plays with modes of seeing but also addresses some of the past cinematic renderings of *Hamlet* which coalesce and mix within the décalage created on stage. Lepage also addresses iconic representations of humanity, such as in the case of the Vitruvian man and Muybridge and his photographic experimentation. It becomes the spectator's 'response-ability' to construct their own interpretation. They can choose how the gender politics of Hamlet's cross-dressing should be perceived. By contrast, in Olivier's film representations have been 'fixed' and realist montage has been used to organise and arrange specific discursive positions. The opaqueness of the theatre machine which deconstructs the cinematic in Elsinore foregrounds the very process of perception and the potential political factors influencing it. What is essential to note here, however, is that Lepage's methodology does not simply make superficial reference to these tropes as some have argued, but rather addresses the forms and aesthetic structures through which the 'content' is conveyed. The piece is post-cinematic to the extent to which it deconstructs cinematic forms of perception through which *Hamlet* and its mythology have been represented.

The Andersen Project

The Andersen Project (2005) is particularly interesting in the context of post-cinematic aesthetics since it exemplifies a deconstructive stance towards cinematic metaphors. This deconstruction is achieved by means of a décalage of the actor's presence on stage, a process that has been termed by Izabela Pluta as 'mediaphorisation' (Pluta 2010: 191); or, more specifically, the creation of the 'mediaphoric body' (ibid.). Thus, it will be interesting to analyse the piece from the perspective of the differences between a 'cinematic metaphor' and a 'mediaphor'.

The Andersen Project is Lepage's fifth solo work. Once again he is director and actor, playing the protagonist and all the other characters as in the first version of *Elsinore*. Also as in *Elsinore* and most of Lepage's other solo works the actor 'appears as an operator of the stage' (ibid.), mediating and controlling transitions between the different aspects of the intermedial spectacle (set changes, projections, lighting and so on).

The script was written and devised by Peder Bjurman and Marie Gignac and emerged from a series of trials, rehearsals and discussions (ibid.). The plot was structured around three interwoven threads. The first concerned a journey by Hans Christian Andersen to Paris and was based on a factual account. The second thread consisted of two tales by Andersen, *The Dryad* (1868) and *The Shadow* (1847). The third thread was a (fictional) narrative set in the present and built around two characters, 'Arnaud de la Guimbretière, the director of the Garnier Opera, and Frédéric Lapointe, a Canadian composer invited by the Garnier to write a libretto (ultimately never completed) based on Andersen's writings' (Pluta 2010: 192).

As in *Elsinore* the threads and characters were interwoven and Lepage found different ways of juxtaposing both scenes and characters in order to produce a form of mixing and crossbreeding between different art forms and mediums in the theatrical spectacle – métissage. He employed a vast array of scenic techniques, ranging from shadow puppetry and marionettes to cinematographical effects such as shot composition techniques used to juxtapose live and pre-recorded material, projected live feed simultaneity in order to augment the performer's presence and what could be termed as a form of performative rotoscopy (which will be discussed below).

This analysis will focus on a key post-cinematic aspect of *The Andersen Project*, which is the deconstruction of the actor's presence. The emphasis is thus on the concept of the 'mediaphoric body' inherent in the staging of *The Andersen Project* and the way in which it can be seen as a deconstruction of 'cinematic metaphor', which historically has been a dominant design pattern in much of realist mainstream cinema. Before taking a closer look at the piece it will be important to define and contrasts the two concepts of a 'cinematic metaphor' and the 'mediaphoric body' or 'mediaphor'.

Cinematic metaphor

To Eisenstein, metaphors represented aesthetic superstructures that comprised of different images, sounds and rhythms bound together in a harmonious whole in order to convey meaning. The aim behind this aesthetic superstructure was to manufacture identification with characters and their storylines and to communicate a potential ideology (which, in the case of his works, usually amounted to communist/Soviet propaganda). Cinema history is replete with examples of metaphors, but perhaps it is worth noting another iconic example just to further exemplify their structure. In Stanley Kubrick's *2001: A Space Odyssey* (1968) there is a famous jump-cut between two scenes. After the ape has bashed the bones to the glorious sounds of the prologue from Richard Strauss's *Thus Spoke Zarathustra*, he/she throws the bone up into the sky. The bone rotates and twists in slow motion in mid-air, against a bright blue sky, until the last chord of the dramatic C-major dominant played on the organ fades away into silence. A few seconds later, once the bone has rotated to a correct position, the shot cuts to a spaceship making its way towards the camera. The spaceship has a cylindrical shape and a greyish texture, visually echoing the appearance of the bone. It is also positioned in a way that corresponds to the bone's shape and rotation from the previous shot. The metaphorical interpretation of this can be quite straightforward, especially if one considers Kubrick's cynical agendas: a prehistoric tool is directly compared to a futuristic tool. Despite the advances in technology and human intellect, in some respects the creators of the civilisation of tomorrow do not differ much from the raging, aggressive primitive apes of the past, and technology – advanced or primitive – will ultimately serve the purpose of self-annihilation. Obviously, this is my interpretation but the aesthetic structure works to support such a discursive position.

As with the examples of metaphors in Eisenstein's films discussed earlier there are a few things to be said about the structure of Kubrick's sequence here. First, it compares disparate objects. As in most metaphors it connects and merges two seemingly unrelated concepts. Second, there is a transport from one object to another. The juxtaposition stimulates the spectator to find a logical connection which would justify the juxtaposition. This is exemplified by the rationale I have given although other interpretations will work just as well. Third and most importantly there is a harmonic coherence binding the two objects. This is present on an aesthetic level. The way the two juxtaposed objects are filmed and portrayed is not random, but done in such a way that they fit together. This harmony is an important incentive to stimulate the need for a logical explanation. This notion works on the presupposition that if something 'feels' right aesthetically there must be a logical explanation (and interpretation) underlying it. For Eisenstein the key challenge of crafting a classical metaphor lies in finding the right amount of disparity between the two objects in question in order to ensure aesthetic congruity. This was a research question for Eisenstein and a way of differentiating between 'good' and 'bad' metaphors and cinematic practice. While the above examples fall under the category of 'good' metaphors the concept of the 'mediaphor' is an example of a 'bad' metaphor *par excellence* – a metaphor with inherent, unresolved tensions.

Mediaphors and the mediaphoric body

Intermedial performances are full of metaphors and metaphorical structures. There are various ways of constructing and designing them, but of particular interest and proper to intermedial theatre is what could be called the 'mediaphor'. Izabela Pluta's definition of the 'mediaphoric body' is useful in understanding the broader term of a mediaphor and its relationship to a cinematic metaphor:

> From an etymological perspective, this concept [the mediaphoric body] incorporates three elements of a different order, both concrete and conceptual: the living, the media-related and the metaphorical. The actor in flesh and blood represents the first element. The media-related element is introduced on the stage (so might be thought extra-theatrical), and its components might range from the projected image to the device (such as the screen or camera). The third element, of a conceptual order, represents a semiological figure (the metaphor), and is linked to a semiological process of metaphorisation).
>
> (Pluta 2010: 193)

Thus the 'mediaphoric body' is a construct made up of an actor's physical presence on stage, an 'extra theatrical'[3] technology, which for the most part in the case of *The Andersen Project* is the use of film projection, and the conceptual dimension – that is, the meaning it conveys in semiological terms and the imaginary image it forms. This concept can be extended to the notion of a mediaphor where it does not have to be a 'body' per se but any other object transformed through intermedial technologies in a similar way. So in what ways is this concept different to the notion of a cinematic metaphor outlined by Eisenstein? After all cinema uses actor's bodies and other objects, frames them, fragments them and reassembles them by means of technology in order to create metaphorical concepts – images of movement that are of a different order and exist beyond the actual 'depictions' on screen.

The difference lies in the emphasis on the forms of perception. Metaphors blend disparate concepts together in ways that are analogous and carry a sense of aesthetic harmony. A mediaphor has a metaphorical aspect to it, its third element, but it also contains an explicit presentation of the forms through which a given image or representation is being constructed. Classical cinematic metaphors are constructed in such a way as to engender almost seamless aesthetic links between the juxtaposed concepts. The art is, thus, to create an almost imperceptible connection and to draw the spectator into what often is a conceptually tensile juxtaposition (as, for example, the aesthetically seamless yet conceptually jarring example of Kubrick's bone–spaceship). This linkage is often reliant on the transparent use of a medium. Mediaphors draw attention towards the disparity between the different media involved in the construction of the image. By explicitly staging and emphasising the forms of perception proper to cinematic culture, *The Andersen Project* deconstructs cinematic metaphors by means of mediaphorisation and foregrounds the 'politics of perception' behind these classical realist forms of representational structuring.

A good example of this is the first scene of the show in which Lepage, as Frederic Lapointe, explains to the audience that the show they are just about to see has been cancelled.

My name is Frederic Lapointe and thanks to the generosity of the Canadian Arts Council, and the Letters Council of Quebec, and the Office of French-Canadian exchanges, I had the privilege in recent weeks to work as a writer in residence here at the very prestigious National Opera in France. But unfortunately, today I am facing the difficult task of telling you that the first performance of La Boheme, scheduled for tonight, has been cancelled due to circumstances beyond our control. You see, following the arrest of this morning of Rachid El Youssef Walassi the union leaders decided to declare a strike, and in solidarity with them, all other caretakers at the Palais Garnier chose to do so as well. What do you expect; we are in France after all... And France is France...

(Lepage 2007: 14)

Lepage, playing the protagonist, is projected in close-up onto the screen, with a superimposed background of the auditorium. We also see Lepage standing with his back to the audience and facing his own close-up. So we have the three elements of a mediaphor, the live presence of the actor, his mediated image and the resulting metaphor of a character. The 'strange impression of [...] disparity or (décalage)' (Hébert and Perelli-Contos 2001: 19) is what deconstructs the cinematic image. There are three particular aspects of post-cinematic décalage in this scene: the décalage of the close-up itself, the décalage of the relationship between the close-up and the *mise-en-scène* and the voice-over (see Figure 2.6).

There is a sense of transparency in the way that cinema close-ups communicate meaning. They are often construed as providing access to a character's emotions and perceptions. They convey the character's way of seeing the world and are posited as sites of affect.[4] By turning his back to the audience, Lepage deliberately interrupts this affective relationship by the interpolation of the live portrayal of the protagonist – a particular visual caesura. As spectators we cannot see what the protagonist is seeing. The interruption of affective charge is brought into stark juxtaposition with the screened image that allows for this identification.

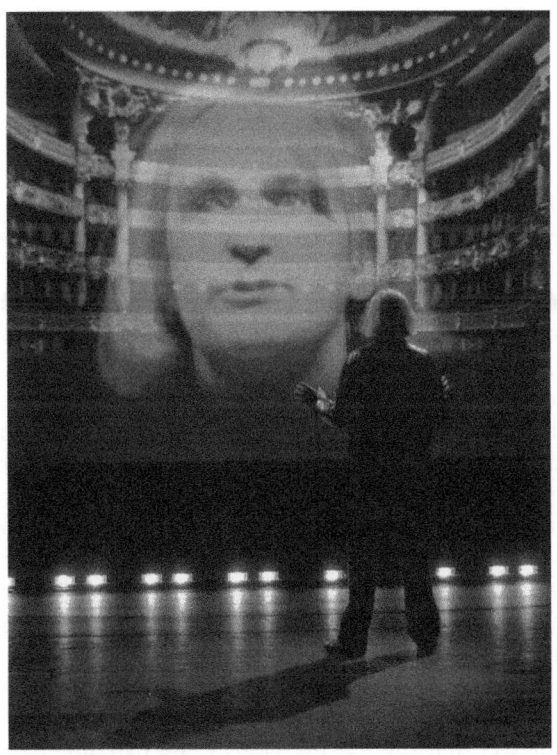

Figure 2.6   The Andersen Project by Robert Lepage. Photo © Emmanuel Valette, 2006

Close-ups in cinema are partial objects. In Lacanian terms they engender a sense of lack and elicit a desire for completeness. They are depictions of faces detached from the body of an actor, and as such prompt the spectator to imagine the rest of the figure in order to create an organic image. In this scene in *The Andersen Project* the spectators see two figures that do not correspond; the close-up is huge and the body on stage is small. As a result there is a 'simultaneity' (Lehmann 2006) of exposition and excess of information generated in the scene. Whereas in cinema the discontinuity of the images prompts the spectator to reconstruct an organic, gestalt image in an attempt to re-establish an imaginary continuity, here there is continuity in the persistent live figure of Lepage on stage, and it is the excess generated by the two simultaneous renderings of his presence that creates a sense of discontinuity – a décalage.

The second point relates to the deconstruction of the relationship between the close-up face and the surroundings. Again this involves the juxtaposition of the virtual image with the live figure of Lepage on stage, but it also involves the auditorium in which the piece is performed. The real auditorium works here as a mirror reflection of the virtual one. This not only blurs the boundaries between the screen and the stage, the cinematic and the theatrical, but also implicates the audience in the 'performance text' of the piece. In contrast to a traditional movie theatre where the audience sits in a darkened space and is construed as anonymous, here the placement of the audience emphasises their presence both in relation to the spectacle and other audience members. This effect is further reinforced by scenes in which actors emerge from the screen and appear in the actual auditorium or vice versa. For instance, during one of the instalments of the *Dryad* story the character of the Dryad wanders around Paris exploring various art exhibitions. Halfway through the scene she decides to leave the screen and the actress playing the Dryad materialises on stage and goes to sit amongst the audience, admiring the exhibition on screen from the auditorium. These magical moments not only dazzle and blur the audience's perceptions of cinematic and theatrical space but also help to create what Lehmann terms the 'performance text'. By emphasising the placement of the audience in the actuality of the theatrical event, Lehman argues that postdramatic theatre inspires a stance of critical reflexivity by making audience members complicit within the process of meaning-making. In other words the spectators become self-critically aware of the fact that they, as individuals, are partially 'response-able' for the creation of meaning. Instances like these also foreground the spatio-political context of the scene.

Thirdly, this scene demonstrates an interesting décalage of the voice-over. This décalage could be described as a particular inverse of the cinematic phenomena of *acousmêtre*. Michel Chion defines *acousmêtre* as a term derived from *acousmatic* and *être*, being. Acousmatic is a term 'pertaining to sound one hears without seeing its source. Radio and telephone are acousmatic media. In film, an off-screen sound is acousmatic' (Chion 1990: 221). *Acousmêtre* is an 'acousmatic character whose relationship to the screen involves a specific kind of ambiguity and oscillation' (ibid.: 129). This character is neither inside nor outside of the film. Chion elaborates:

> It is not inside, because the image of the voice's source – the body, the mouth – is not included. Nor is it outside, since it is not clearly positioned off-screen in an imaginary 'wing', like a master of ceremonies or a witness, and it is implicated in the action, constantly about to be part of it.
>
> (Ibid.)

He gives a few examples of these types of characters: 'the master criminal of Lang's *Testament of Dr. Mabuse,* the mother in Hitchcock's *Psycho,* and the fake Wizard of Oz in the MGM film by that name' (ibid.). The *acousmêtre* has three main powers that fiction films usually attribute to it. It has the power to see everything, the power of omniscience and the power of omnipotence. It also has the power of ubiquity; it can be anywhere it wants to be. Because there are no limits to these powers the *acousmêtre* often comes across as a disturbing presence. The power to see everything is closely associated with the primary identification with the camera. A popular example of this would be the phone caller in Wes Craven's *Scream.* What is interesting is the way in which this power can be taken away once the source of the voice is revealed. Chion claims that the best way to undermine the power of the voice is to reveal the face of the character (Chion 1990: 130). This is the case in *Scream,* when the mysterious 'omnipotent killer' turns out to be a duo of troubled teenagers, who are revealed by eventually losing the 'infamous' mask. This linking of the voice with its source is called 'de-acousmatization' (ibid.: 130).

In the case of Lepage's staging we are dealing with an inverse of the *acousmêtre.* This is because the source of the voice is located both inside and outside the film world. It is inside the film with the talking head on the screen. It is outside the film because Lepage is on stage. The voice is also simultaneously connected and disconnected to its source: 'the face'. It is connected to the face because we can see the close-up head talking and it is disconnected from Lepage because he has his back turned towards us and we do not actually see him talk. This complex intermedial aesthetic creates an oscillation between the effects of acousmatisation and de-acousmatisation. The emphasis will lie on the way an audience member will choose to perceive this speech. As a result the effect may oscillate between a mysterious, omnipresent master of ceremonies, engendering the classical characteristics of a cinematic *acousmêtre,* or a de-acousmatised character whose juxtaposition undermines this very omnipresent power of the *acousmêtre.* Again, the scene also carries out a décalage of cinematic rhetoric by addressing this unusual and complex effect of the *acousmêtre.*

By using a mediaphor to deconstruct this cinematic metaphor, *The Andersen Project* asks its spectators to reflect on the captivating power of the cinematic construct. The 'politics of perception' are being foregrounded here since, considering the content of the speech, the scene draws attention to the question of how far cinematic constructs and representations can be trusted. Close-ups with their inherent potential for creating an affective charge can often serve as part of an aesthetic of manipulation. Here the close-up not only emphasises what is being said (an introduction to the show itself) but asks the audience to reflect on the factors that constitute their perceptual choices in relation to how the cinematic construct operates.

Performative rotoscopy represents another interesting way in which mediaphoric aesthetics are used in this piece to deconstruct cinematic metaphor. Rotoscopy[5] in contemporary visual effects is the practice of manually mapping one image or film clip onto another. It involves creating a matte (a superimposition of an image) in order to composite it over a background. Lepage used a specially designed concave screen for this production. The concave shape enabled the actors to walk into the screen space, achieving a greater sense of merging between the live actor and the virtual projection. One of the scenes depicts the parallel journeys of Andersen and Lapointe. Projected backgrounds are used to convey a passage through time. Nineteenth-century streets in Paris dissolve into train journeys, passing fields, rushing clouds; cutting through different time frames of narrative progression. The time of Andersen's journey visually blends with the journey of Lapointe. This sense of 'immersion' is achieved both through the digital editing of the film and through a 'practically pantomimic, effect' (Pluta 2010: 195). Lepage on stage attempts to blend his physical presence with the onscreen animation, mapping his figure onto the world of film in a manner which is evocative of rotoscopy in a performative sense. He 'enters the space in front of the screen and sits down on the suitcases that have been placed there. He removes the costume of the historical figure (Andersen) and puts on the clothes of the contemporary protagonist (Fréderic the composer)' (ibid.). During this scene Lepage maps himself visually onto the onscreen imagery creating a sense of oscillation between the immersive illusion and the self-reflexive staging. Again, the audience is faced with a dynamic oscillation between the métissage and the décalage. Where cinematic metaphors aim for a seamless blend of images – in particular when rotoscopy is used for such effects in a way that carefully conceals the technicalities of the image constructions – here Lepage breaks the 'cinematic fourth wall' by stepping out of the screen. His theatrical use of cross-dressing and the exposition of the process of dressing up as different characters deconstruct the concept of classical rotoscopy in a performative way. The aim here seems not to be to achieve a rotoscopic effect but rather to expose the mechanics of cinematic image constructions by 'performing' rotoscopy.

Conclusion

When critiquing the mechanisms of representation in general and the way they can form culturally dominant political and historical inscriptions, Lyotard refers to the concept of the 'theatre machine' as a formal mechanism designed to generate representations. Even though Lyotard's metaphor is indicative of a very traditionalist way of looking at theatre and its inner workings, it is a useful concept when approaching the operations of the more postmodern 'theatre machine' in Lepage's work, or rather Lepage's deliberate exposition and inversion of the logic inherent in Lyotard's concept. Lyotard's concept of the 'theatre machine' is as follows: Lyotard sees theatre as consisting of three limits. The first limit is the building itself. It is a place where 'the "real world" is outside, the theatre is inside. Walking into the theatre means walking into a different sort of space' (Bennigton 1988: 10). The second limit is the separation of the audience from the stage. In traditional theatres this division is demarcated by the proscenium arch or the orchestra pit. Finally, there is the third limit, the hidden 'theatre machinery'. This 'machinery' does not only consist of stage mechanisms, such as smoke machines, stage hands, lighting, sound equipment, but also the directorial, organisational and dramaturgical choices made during the production. For Lyotard this machinery is essentially invisible, hidden away from the spectator. When considering the potential of dismantling these representational mechanisms and revealing the forms which constitute them, Lyotard talks about the role of the historian. The role of the historian he claims is that of an analyst, someone who will uncover the 'invisible' mechanisms that construct historical and political inscriptions.

> The historian is supposed to undo all the machinery and machination, and restore what was excluded, having knocked down the walls of the theatre. And yet it is obvious that the historian is himself no more than another director, his narrative another product, his work another narration.
>
> (Lyotard in Bennigton 1988: 10)

Thus, by analogy we can think of a Lepagian spectator as a historian, or an analyst reflecting on the processes that construct perceptions and representations of Hamlet/*Hamlet*. But the spectator also becomes more than that. In a way the spectator becomes a co-producer, a co-director, a montageur of meaning that can be constructed from the fragmented décalage presented on stage.

In this chapter instead of perceiving décalage as a failure of craftsmanship or a superficial exhibition of technical fireworks, we can interpret and explore these deconstructive effects as post-cinematic aesthetics which reflect upon the role and influence of cinematic culture on our modes of perception and, in particular, on the way we choose to perceive theatrical representations.

3
Acinematic Montage in *Roadmetal Sweetbread* and *A Mare's Nest*

So far we have looked at the deconstruction of classical realist montage from the perspective of cinematic movement. This has enabled us to explore wider philosophical concepts concerning the perception of cinematic movement and the ways in which Lepage's post-cinematic work engages with them. In this chapter we will focus on another property of classical montage, the design of a pleasure-laden aesthetic experience – a libidinal journey. Post-theory such as that of Baudry and Lyotard has criticised classical realist montage for the way in which it can create pleasurable aesthetic experiences and lure the audience into a passive mode of spectatorship, inviting them to agree to ideological constructs and political agendas inscribed within them. These pleasures are often associated with aesthetic structures and harmonies through which realist representations are constructed. There is also a cultural expectation at play here, which is the effect of a long tradition of realist filmmaking. Going to a cinema involves suspension of disbelief and indulging the pleasures of yielding to the illusions and aesthetic structures that constitute realist montage.

In this chapter we will explore the 'politics of perception' from the perspective of the pleasure factor of realist cinematic montage. Jean-François Lyotard's post-structural critique of classical realist film montage from his essay 'Acinema' will be used as a theoretical approach in order to explore how Station House Opera's post-cinematic pieces deconstruct the realist experience of pleasure. Lyotard argues that realist cinema creates aesthetic pleasures in order to promote ideological constructs and capitalist agendas. In SHO's pieces, the deconstruction of pleasure-laden cinematic experiences can foreground the 'politics of perception' by emancipating the audience, broadening their perceptual spectrum and breaking the passive mode of spectatorship often inspired by classical realist films.

Lyotard (following Lacan) advocates a different type of pleasure, or should one say enjoyment, distinct from the pleasure of aesthetic harmonies, which he names *jouissance*. In 'Acinema', Lyotard describes *jouissance* as a boundless enjoyment, one that is always in excess of form. He associates the sense of pleasure with classical cinema, as it is historically strongly rooted in its traditions, whilst he claims that *jouissance* lies beyond the realms of the cinematic, both aesthetically and politically. He seems to locate the experience of *jouissance* in a realm which is beyond realist aesthetic frameworks of classical cinema and one which requires a certain re-framing of cinematic experience. Lyotard essentially sees the spectator trapped within a realist aesthetic framework that he defines as 'libidinal normalization' (Lyotard 1989: 175), which creates and normalises pleasures during the experience of a film and is ultimately designed to generate specific ideological representations. 'Acinema' becomes thus a manifesto advocating that film has to convey an experience of enjoyment beyond these realist aesthetic frameworks but also beyond their set ideological and political precepts.

In Station House Opera's, *Roadmetal Sweetbread* (1998) and *A Mare's Nest* (2001) an interinvolvement of theatre and film/cinema enables these pieces to engage the audience with the fleeting effect of what Lyotard calls *jouissance*. By creating a space beyond the structural confines of classical pleasure, they potentially stimulate the audience to reflect upon the ways in which normalised and structured aesthetic pleasures are instrumental in constructing representations with a particular political and ideological context.

Thematically both pieces deal with representations of sexual fantasies, hence representations of what could potentially be perceived as pleasurable acts in a literal sense. Through different intermedial configurations, the boundaries of these representations are explored and the space for *jouissance* is negotiated. *Roadmetal Sweetbread* in essence concerns a couple and their multi-faceted relationship conveyed through the juxtapositions of live and mediated spaces and their various disjunctions. The stage has a screen at the back which often doubles the action taking place on the physical stage, becoming its virtual augmentation. Quite often the space of the virtual becomes the space of the characters' fantasies, their perceptions of themselves and their relationship. The live dimension depicts their 'reality' with all their attempts to find fulfilment and realisation of their inner cravings. The contrast between the two is often used for comical effect and to highlight the often embarrassing discrepancies between fantasy and reality. *A Mare's Nest* presents a surreal world of two couples. The piece is full of uncanny scenarios, virtual characters, imaginary and real encounters, with doubling acts. There is also a multiplicity of storylines and a series of mismatches between what is happening on the screen and in the stage space. The set-up, however, is quite different to that of *Roadmetal Sweetbread*. Here, there is a wall raised in the middle of the stage with screens on either side. Around this wall four actors perform a series of disconnected episodes whose spatial and temporal dimensions are augmented by the virtual rooms projected onto the screens. The confusing interplay between live and film performances is further emphasised by the fact that the audience can move freely around the entire set and hence montage their own experience of it in real time. None of the represented relationships, through live action or film, ever attain a sense of formal completeness or closure since the audience's perception is always in a state of flux. The pleasure associated with an 'idealised perspective', if we were to go by Baudry's terms, is compromised and often denied. Both pieces seem to be reminiscent of George Coates's works, such as *Invisible Site: A Virtual Sho.* (1991). Coates's works employed an intermedial aesthetic, which as with Station House Opera was designed to jar and blur the distinctions and boundaries between the physical stage action and the virtual material on screen. Also like Coates's pieces there are affinities with installation art of the 1960s and with traits such as the 'stepped-screen staging spectacles of the Laterna Magika in the late 1950s' (Dixon 2007: 341). However Coates's aesthetic is more focused on the use of computer technologies, whereas what is particularly interesting about Station House Opera is their use of cinematic and televisual codes of representation and a performative deconstruction of film space and montage.

'Acinema'

Before analysing *Roadmetal Sweetbread* and *A Mare's Nest*, it is important to elaborate on the theoretical lens which will be applied, namely Lyotard's critique of classical realism in 'Acinema'. Lyotard sets out a project to define the possibility of a cinematic experience that lies beyond the frameworks and conventional aesthetics of classical realism which he sees as dominating mainstream cinema culture. In essence this manifesto follows his long-standing pursuit of criticising realism in art and the ideological implications thereof, which he identifies as capitalist. Consequently it can be located within the post-theory arguments of the 1980s put forward by critics such as Metz, MacCabe and Heath. These arguments also sought to redefine cinema and explore the margins of cinematic representation by criticising the realist 'cinematic apparatus', indeed defining it for the most part as being inextricably linked with the dominant consumer society. What is specific to Lyotard's take is the notion that the spectator's emotional response can be regulated through aesthetic structures. To briefly introduce the gist of his argument, one of the key functions of montage in realist film is to structure the film in such a way that it will provide pleasure through its harmonious form. This notion of pleasure is understood by Lyotard as arising from the formal harmony and order of montage, imposed as an 'artificial' system upon filmed movement. Instead of this type of cinema Lyotard craves a different sensibility and sensorial organisation altogether, a cinema that recuperates excess movements that are lost during the filming and editing process, a cinema of abject[1] movements, a cinema of movements that are 'normally' effaced in the aesthetics of realism. Thus he wishes the spectator to experience *jouissance* – a different type of enjoyment. He defines this experience as a perpetual diversion, a free dissipation of joy as a result of experiencing film material, a pure sensation that is not necessarily normalised by a specific aesthetic framework. He likens it to the experience of a child lighting a match and enjoying the diversion and dissipation of energy for its own sake. The 'simulacrum' created does not have to refer to an external representation. It does not have to be linked to other objects (such as cooking utensils in the example of the match lit in vain, where the act of lighting the match has no justification in terms of a productive purpose). Thus the simulacrum:

> is not composed with these other objects, compensated for by them, enclosed in a whole ordered by constitutive laws [...] On the contrary it is essential that the entire erotic force invested in the simulacrum be promoted, raised, displayed and burned in vain.
>
> (Lyotard 1989: 171)

For Lyotard it is like experiencing the multitude of colours produced by fireworks – an experience that Theodor Adorno once saw as an exemplification of purity in art. It is a 'sterile' form of enjoyment in that it is not linked with the production of something else or reflective of an external idea or representation. It is an experience of motion that goes beyond the point of no return, beyond meaning and productivity, exhausting itself in vain. All in all he seems to express a desire for an almost impossible experience, an impossible recuperation of the 'real' that is forever lost in the process of signification. This is especially hard for cinema to achieve, since it rests so firmly in its classical representational firma-ment. Hence it will be interesting to see how, through intermedial prac-tice, the post-cinematic pieces discussed below deconstruct and re-frame this firmament and the experiences and expectations stemming from it.

Lyotard's critique in 'Acinema'

Lyotard's critique can be viewed as concerning what is lost and made inaccessible in the process of montage that is designed to elicit an imagi-nary unity. Lyotard could be seen as proposing a more 'cubist' approach to film-making or – further – an approach to editing film in such a way that it will not be compromised by the need to form an organic whole, where the main aim is to provide a perspectivist experience so that the spectator can 'embody' the filmic reality on imaginary terms.

Lyotard begins by focusing on the elements of a filmed reality that are essentially lost during the selection process required of montage. His understanding of realist montage is focused upon discrimination of movements, which occurs during the translation of movement from the studio environment onto celluloid. It is the discrimination involved in crafting cinematic metaphors of which Eisenstein speaks. Thus Lyotard sees realist filmmaking as a process of organising inscriptions of all kinds of movements:

> for example, in the film shot, those of actors and other moving objects, those of lights, colours, frame and lens; in the film sequence, all of these again plus the cuts and splices of editing; for the film as a whole, those of the final script and the spatio-temporal synthesis of narration.
> (Lyotard 1989: 169)

What Lyotard is referring to here are essentially three dimensions of montage: the internal montage of the shot and its constituent compo-nents, the relative (lateral) montage of the different shots in a sequence and the absolute (vertical) montage of all the film's dimensions, which refer to and collapse back onto the whole body of the film which unfolds throughout the spectator's experience. The first dimension concerns shot composition, it is the so-called *mise-en-cadre* of a shot – the set of ele-ments which the filmmakers choose to incorporate in the frame. The second dimension, relative or lateral montage, is the arrangement of different shots into a sequence that make up a scene, cross-cutting dur-ing a conversation between characters for example. The final dimension is the arrangement of all the scenes within the entirety of the film. Lyotard claims that the main role of a mainstream film director is to

cut out or efface from the recorded material any 'undesirable' movement. Thus 'learning the techniques of film-making involves knowing
how to eliminate a large number of these possible movements' (Lyotard
1989: 169). Despite tensions, conflicts and instabilities within the work
of art, he argues that the art of making movies is based on a notion of
return and repetition. Accordingly, for Lyotard the 'impression of reality
is a real oppression of orders' (ibid.: 170), which is designed to create a
return to values. In other words, every image has to refer to a concept
or another image in order to make sense and have value. Movements
thus have to be exchangeable for signs, signifiers pointing to specific
signifieds that will form part of the 'whole'. Lyotard links the aesthetics of realist mainstream cinema with capitalism and productivity. All
images of movement have to return something external to themselves
like a narrative framework, a harmonised composition, or an ideology.
A film like that could be deemed valuable in the capitalist sense
'because it returns to something else, because it is thus potential return
and profit' (Lyotard 1989: 170). By contrast, movement that is not
exchangeable 'against other objects and in terms of equal quantities of
a definable unity' (ibid.) has no value.

So what specifically does this 'return' consist of for Lyotard? The
return can occur at a macro level, the level of narrative where there is
a resolution of all the themes and plots, or on an ideological level as
a recapitulation of a moral or ideological order. On a micro level there
is a constant reinforcement of compositional rules of the image, editing, music, montage and so on. In short, making a mainstream film for
Lyotard is a process of return to a wide range of predefined rules and
schemata. This return through repetition becomes a way of producing
the notion of totality. It becomes a way of conveying a whole through
the fragmented but composed material of a film. Furthermore it
becomes a way of establishing order by eliminating mistakes or 'incon-
gruities'. A film director thus 'eliminates all impulsional movement,
real or unreal, which will not lend itself to reduplication, all movement
which would escape identification, recognition and the mnesic [*sic*]
fixation' (ibid.: 175). Any abstract movement that makes no clear sense
and carries little more than an *intensity* of immediate experience must
be eradicated. Lyotard wishes to focus on this intensity that is lost and
calls for a shift in filmmaking that could recuperate these intensities. He
links them with the notion of *jouissance* or a Freudian notion of libidinal drives and hence he criticises realist film directing for being 'a factor
of libidinal normalization' (ibid.) whose goal is the 'subordination of
all partial drives, all sterile and divergent movements to the unity of an

organic body' (ibid.: 176). The organic body can be understood here as an image of the body of film created by the montaged material. It can also refer to the organic unity of the body of the actor created through montage and the spectator's subordinate identification with it.

Lyotard's problematisation of mainstream realist cinema thus becomes a speculation on how to break up the 'normalization of libidinal drives' and the organic constituency of the cinematic image instituted by the realist aesthetic and directorial habits that craft it. Lyotard claims that two directions are open for cinema and they correspond to two poles, namely 'immobility and excessive movement' (ibid.: 172). Both relate to the speed of the image (slow or fast motion), which breaks up the 24-frames-per-second realism. He quotes two murder scenes from a film about a hippie community, *Joe*. In the first scene a father 'beats to death a hippie that lives with his daughter'; in the second, when '"mopping up" a hippie commune he unwittingly guns down his own daughter' (ibid.: 174). The latter scene closes with a freeze-frame of the daughter, struck down in full movement, whilst the former is characterised by the rhythmic alternation of shots between fists falling and a defenceless hippie who quickly loses consciousness. Lyotard sees these two scenes, one of immobilisation and the other of extreme mobility as arrhythmic in terms of the representational stance of the film. But he quickly concludes that the 'strong affective charge' (ibid.) that accompanies the scenes ultimately corresponds to the 'organic rhythm of the intense emotions evoked' (ibid.) and thus ultimately benefits the totality of the narrative. We can also see this in David Lynch's films where the intensities released break up the frame of reality previously established. For example, in an early scene in *Blue Velvet* the father is having a stroke whilst watering the garden. Instead of showing the reaction of the family and the effect this has on a previously established reality frame, the camera randomly homes in on the microcosm of the lawn. We see beautifully filmed droplets of water from the hosepipe draining into the lawn in slow motion and excessively fast images of moving dung beetles. According to Lyotard, by occupying these poles of excessively slow or fast motion, cinema would cease to be an ordering force and produce 'true, that is, vain, simulacra, blissful intensities, instead of productive/consumable objects' (ibid.: 172). The initial assumption here is that by altering the duration of events the spectator can become somehow liberated from an objective perception of the material; thought is a process in time and data require not only a certain amount of time but also rhythm in order to be digested. In the example from *Blue Velvet*, Lynch's surrealism can be easily read as a profound psychoanalytic exploration of human family relations (Lynch himself strongly encourages those readings when he talks about his work).

But Lyotard insists and persistently attempts to envision and speculate upon a film that would have to form what he calls a 'composite of decompositions' (ibid.: 171) – an abstraction. What this means is that it would be a non-functional whole, one that no longer has representational or dramatic function. The movements would not be organised into gestures that would perform a dramatic or representational function returning an image of a reality but would comprise a composition in the process of deconstruction. Lyotard's next suggestion is that the compositional rules that render the cinematographic object as transparent, whilst remaining unconsciously perceived by the spectator, would have to be brought to one's attention.

Lyotard attributes cinema's compelling power to create a libidinal cathexis to the unconscious (with recourse to Klossowski). He explains that: 'the support itself must not submit to any noticeable perversion in order that the perversion attack only what is supported, the representation of the victim: the support is held in insensibility or unconsciousness' (ibid.: 178). Perversion of the support in this case refers to opacity of technique. This means making cinematic conventions and filmic techniques perceptible and making them the subject of the piece. In art one could think of Jackson Pollock's canvases that abandon figuration in favour of exposing and aestheticising the materiality of paint and the gesture of the painter. Pollock pays close attention to the physical properties of paint which condition its flow and reaction with other pigments and paint consistencies upon a canvas. Now for Lyotard, *acinema* is achieved when intense emotions are always displaced. This is where Lyotard postulates that the support that renders a representation (a medium and/or an aesthetic in this case) has to be perverted. Lyotard claims that one way in which cinema can escape libidinal organisation is to get rid of the libidinal fragmented object (montaged character), which evokes the 'loss of the unified body' (ibid.: 179) and therefore stimulates its reconstitution in the spectator's mind. When the object is removed, however, we arrive at abstract cinema:

> the represented ceases to be the libidinal object while the screen itself, in all its most formal aspects, takes its place. The film strip is no longer abolished (made transparent) for the benefit of this or that flesh [he means representation here], for it offers itself as flesh posing itself.

> (Ibid.)

This would reverse the 'client-victim' relationship and once the 'victim' or the object of representation is abolished, the spectator/'client' becomes the victim. Yet, this is also the point at which Lyotard encounters a limitation as far as cinema is concerned. He quickly concludes with a rhetorical question: 'If the victim is the client, if in the scene is only film screen, canvas, the support, do we lose to this arrangement all the intensity of the sterile discharge?' (ibid.). Thus what Lyotard seems to imply is that a constant oscillation between representation and abstraction of its 'support' is necessary. The experience of *jouissance* lies somewhere in this dynamic shift between an object's representation and the presentational aspects of its 'support'. To relate it to his terms: between the immobility of the victim (representation with a transparent support, form) and the mobilisation of the support (opaque support, form as the subject of art). What is also interesting is the transition he makes from the concept of a phantasmagorical body,[2] the representation of 'flesh', to a more corporeal notion of cinema, screen and film as 'flesh itself'.

Lyotard supports his argument with reference to Pollock's and Rothko's paintings and the almost imperceptible movements of Nō Theatre that bring out the support, the flesh of the artwork itself. Lyotard states that:

> abstract cinema, like abstract painting, in rendering the support opaque reverses the arrangement, making the client victim. It is the same again though differently in the almost imperceptible movements of the Nō Theatre.
>
> (Ibid.: 179)

It is at this point that Lyotard tries to 'theatricalise' the encounter with the cinematic image. The experience of film is to become an experience of an opaque medium not a transparent screen, a mere carrier of meaning. The post-cinematic pieces that will be looked at in this chapter deliberately theatricalise film and make the relationship between 'victim' and 'support' aesthetically unstable.

Another feature of post-cinematic performance which will be exemplified through the case studies is what Peter Boenisch called the '*ais*thetic' experience of staging film in theatre. Peter Boenisch has argued that films can remediate other media, but theatre can remediate remediation, by confronting 'its spectators with the ever changing workings of perception' (Boenisch 2006: 113). However film can only offer an aestheticisation of other media, unlike theatre, which has the potential of *ai*sthetic effects. This is what Boenisch argues is the difference between aesthetics and aisthetics:

> We must go beyond theatre's alleged aesthetic originalities (the beautiful and the sublime) to scent that microscopic, yet ever so obvious effect. It is no technical, no mechanical, nor a digital effect – but an aisthetic one, which does not transform nor physically affect the actor, photo, or video-tape, as their mediation by means of a camera, scanner, or TV screen did. This trace of theatrical mediation is produced in the observers' perception alone: the actor on stage is no longer the actor, but the actor exposed on stage. That photo becomes a photo placed on stage and strangely different from the very same photo hanging stored back-stage before the show...
>
> (Ibid.: 114)

Films remediate other media including theatre itself but theatre is of a different order.[3]

Post-cinematic theatre has an *ai*sthetic mode because it is essentially intermedial. This intermediality, in this case the interinvolvement of film and theatre, allows for two different modes of perception that are being shown to the spectator. If any attempt at deconstruction is ultimately met with an attempt to piece things together and create a coherent reading then the only effective way to disorient the spectator is to create at least two modes of readability (perception) simultaneously.

Lyotard concludes his essay with a pessimistic stance, reflecting on the culturally dominant status of realist cinematic tropes. This reflection is encapsulated in the following rhetorical questions:

> [M]ust we then renounce the hope of finishing with the illusion, not only the cinematographic illusion but also the social and political illusions? [...] Must the return of extreme intensities be founded on at least this empty permanence, on the phantom of the organic body or subject which is the proper noun, and at the same time that they cannot really accomplish this unity?
>
> (Lyotard 1989: 180)

His argument consolidates the fact that the social body represented in realist films becomes a 'region of de-responsibility at the whole which *ideo facto* is posed as responsible' (ibid.: 175). An affinity could be found here with the arguments of Lehmann who claims that our experience of the world through media such as televisual newsreel or fictional representations such as we find in cinema makes us insensitive and 'de-responsible' in relation to people and realities represented. Lehmann's argument is that we are physically separated from the site of production of the images both in space and time when we experience mediated images, thus we do not have an immediate capacity of response, 'there is no experience of a relation between address and answer' (Lehmann 2006: 185). This is where locating post-cinematic theatre as exploring this reversed transition from *mise-en-scène* to *mise-en-cadre* becomes interesting because it brings together the mediated image and the physical stage space that is often also the site of production of live feeds for the show.

Following Lyotard's critique it can thus be concluded that realist cinema creates aesthetic pleasures in order to induce ideological constructs and capitalist agendas. Hence this chapter will look at how post-cinematic pieces deconstruct the realist experience of pleasure through the evocation of *jouissance* and by doing so carry the potential of a cultural and political resistance to dominant cinematic conventions. *Jouissance* will be seen as having the potential to disrupt the chain of pleasure, representation and ideology and thus allow a certain perceptual freedom. Consequently this freedom will allow for a foregrounding of the 'politics of perception' – a mode of reflexivity on the relationship between the spectator's potential perceptual choices and the political and ideological agendas implicit in them.

Roadmetal Sweetbread and the 'post-cinematic apparatus'

Station House Opera's *Roadmetal Sweetbread* was first performed in 1998 and toured for many years around Europe with a changing cast. The performance referenced here is the 2005 performance in Nevers, France, with Julian Maynard Smith and Susannah Hart. Maynard Smith's comments on the title of the show suggest that what is at stake is the juxtaposition of actual and virtual, real actions and imagined relationships, framed through the interinvolvement of theatre and film. He claims that both words in the title 'sound like something they are not. Sweetbread isn't sweet and it isn't bread, it's brains or organs of animals and road metal is Tarmac, it isn't metal at all' (Jones 2001). *Roadmetal Sweetbread* is a theatre piece about a couple, a man and a woman, and their complex relationship portrayed through a series of games they play with each other. This spectacle is construed through juxtaposed dimensions of stage and filmed action which often double one another. The two worlds – that of the virtual film and the stage reality – often show different actions that are reflective of the differences between the fantasies and the reality of the couple's relationship. The games that the characters play with each other often involve sexual fantasies, playful deceptions, hide and seek, role-plays and pranks relating to fairly mundane actions such as drinking tea or trying to take a nap. As suggested by Greg Giesekam, apart from functioning as simple pieces of 'theatrical' magic, they 'resemble some Freudian game of fort/da' (Giesekam 2007: 207), a symbolic exploration of the loss and recovery of the loved one through a transgression of boundaries between the real and the imaginary. The space of the virtual film becomes representative of the characters' fantasies, their perceptions of themselves, their inner thoughts and the psychological dimension of their relationship. By contrast the stage space seems to depict their 'reality' with all the limitations and boundaries which the 'real' world entails. The contrast between the two, conveyed through the discrepancies between the virtual and the actual is what establishes dramatic tension and drives the piece forward. Following this interpretation, one could argue that *Roadmetal Sweetbread* challenges the ideological representation of a heterosexual married couple or heterosexual normality that is often expressed in mainstream cinema. This is because it explores sexual fantasies that lie below the surface of mundane life and are potentially disruptive of it. Thus I will look at how the intermedial strategies in *Roadmetal Sweetbread* disrupt cinematic conventions that would underlie such normative constructs by enabling an experience of *jouissance*.

Let us first consider instances in *Roadmetal Sweetbread* where *jouissance* can arise out of the interinvolvement of theatre and film, which can be seen as disruptive of the realist aesthetics of pleasure that are instrumental in the ideological constructions of the mainstream. The first convention to consider is the relationship between the performance and the audience. As mentioned previously, one of the features of the realist cinematic experience is the separation of the audience from the site of the production of images, which induces a sense of de-responsibility. One of the key post-cinematic features of *Roadmetal Sweetbread* and many other works of Station House Opera is the implication of the audience within the production of film images. This is a post-cinematic feature that effectuates a relationship with the audience that is starkly different to that of an arguably passive spectator of Baudry's 'cinematic apparatus' around which post-theories such as that of Lyotard are based. This is achieved through an interinvolvement of virtual film action and live performance – a montage – which challenges the potentially perspectivist, passive perception associated with the more traditional cinematic apparatus. At the beginning of *Roadmetal Sweetbread* a film sequence of the male protagonist is displayed on a screen on stage. The film shows the man walking in the vicinity of the theatre where the piece is being performed.[4] He enters the building, walks along the corridors, passing the ushers, and enters the audience space. At that moment the live performer enters the theatre through the same door as his virtual image on screen.

This device is used in many Station House Opera pieces and immediately establishes a link between the filmed representation and the live space. As I watched the scene my imagination drifted into the filmic reality, but at the same time I was made aware of my own material presence within the space of the auditorium and then of the live presence of the performer who materialised from the film into the physical space before me. In that sense the relationship between the film representation and the real space from which it was being derived (the *mise-en-cadre* and *mise-en-scène*) was recuperated. As a result of this, the potentially alluring yet illusory imagery of film and the one-sided relationship of a cinema audience to film were disrupted and a new mode of perception was negotiated. Lyotard talked about the shift in perception, when the client (spectator) becomes the victim, making them self-aware and part of the spectacle. This scene can be understood to effectuate a similar change in perception; merging the filmic world with the reality of the spectators. The voyeuristic cinematic spectator who traditionally can be perceived as immune and safe within their alienated position is all of a sudden construed as a witness and implicated within the social milieu of the performance. As a result of this theatricalisation of the film process and the blurring of boundaries between the live action on stage and the filmed material, the re-positioning of the spectator brings forth the notion of an aesthetics of 'response-ability' that Lehmann talks about.

At this moment, as a spectator, I felt somewhat disoriented, but also empowered to frame the spectacle in my own way. Even though in itself this scene did not carry overtly 'political' connotations, the fact that I felt emancipated encouraged in me a mode of reflexive perception, which later on in the show became significant in perceiving the politics of heteronormative couples. Unlike in the case of what Baudry described as the 'cinematic apparatus', as a spectator I felt I had the freedom to make perceptual choices that were no longer singularly conditioned by the aesthetics of film alone. Instead of offering just a transparent illusionary construct, designed to create a specific journey of immersive pleasurable moments, the piece framed itself as a hybrid form – a form containing illusionary aesthetics underscored by the opaqueness of support which produced it. This in turn inspired a wondering mode of perception, a particular enjoyment of perceptual freedom that is akin to *jouissance*.

In the scene described above, the actions that the man performs on stage and on the video screen are closely coordinated and synchronised, giving the impression that the action on stage is being filmed live. It is as if the film world was a mirror double of reality. Then a woman (Susannah Hart) runs into the theatre. She circles around the man and then goes offstage. She does not appear on the film though the male character's reactions to her appear on both stage and film. Then the inverse of this dynamic occurs. Hart runs into the space on film but she is absent from the stage; onstage, the man seems to react to her running around him, following her with his gaze. This routine is repeated, with the female character alternately appearing on the stage space and on the virtual image. The man's searching gaze and the camerawork – panning as if it was framing a running figure – prompt the spectator to imagine the absent woman. Not only the space is being doubled in this scene, but so is the time. Whenever the woman runs offstage she goes out of field but then appears immediately on film running around the stage as the performer is going around the back to make it back on time for the live performance. The film material in this scene functions as an augmentation of reality both in spatial and temporal terms (Figure 3.1 shows a part of this scene).

If we were to apply Lyotard's critique of realist montage here then the spatial and temporal excess of performance in this scene could be deemed as inorganic, since its multiplicity of action and space does not amount to a unified image of a dramatic event – a unified dramatic event being a traditionally perceived event with unity of space, time and action. It is also inorganic and non-figurative (in a narrative sense) if we were to go by the notion of vertical montage, which in classical cinema reconstitutes all smaller elements of montage into a cohesive narrative whole. Even though one could make a reading that the two characters are playing games with each other, this potential representa-tion comes into tension with the exhaustive, futile repetition of this sequence, which potentially renders the scene abstract by foreground-ing its formalities. Much as in Beckett's later theatre works, such as *Quad*, the abstract logic of the scene's structure replaces the organic logic that would tie it into the category of realist representation. Thus it becomes a diversion from representation in Klossowski's sense, or as Lyotard elaborates in his essay, a 'kinetic problematic [...] a composite of decompositions' (Lyotard 1989: 171). In Lyotard's terms the scene does not necessarily return to a specific dramatic form or concept, and

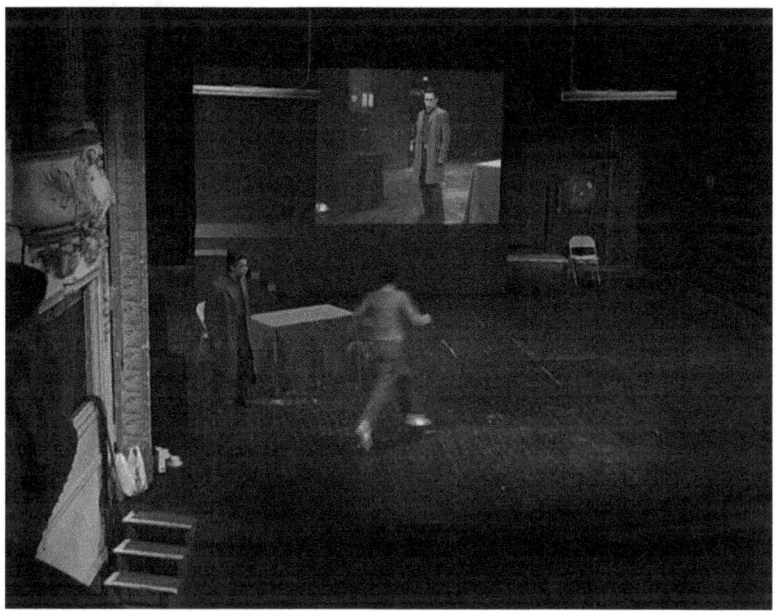

Figure 3.1 'The running game', *Roadmetal Sweetbread.* Photo © Station House Opera, 2005

despite there being a possible representation at play there seems to be an oscillation between the scene's representational aspects and the presentational ones – those that foreground the 'support' as Lyotard calls it.

As a result, reading the scene with Lyotard's critique in mind, we can say that the *pleasure* of spotting congruence between the material presented in performance and a realist sense-making frame is being disrupted. There is, however, *jouissance* in this non-productive excess that Lyotard would call spillage, as the action on stage is always potentially more and in excess of its pre-recorded double. One of the aspects of mainstream filmmaking to which Lyotard attributes the loss of *jouissance* is the transition between the *mise-en-scène* and the *mise-en-cadre*. Lyotard criticises this process of creating a cinematic illusion as a process that consists of a reduction and elimination of the undesirable, unproductive movements. Arguably the intermedial set-up in the above scene shows the potential of reversing this dynamic, as it exposes live some of the incidental movements that would normally be cut out or removed. Through an interplay of film and live action, the virtual characters from film materialise on stage and become part of the *mise-en-scène* action. Through this intermedial playfulness and by re-enacting the transition between *mise-en-scène* and the *mise-en-cadre* in a back and forth mechanical manner, the scene negotiates a space for *jouissance* of spectating movements lost in the process of setting them to a filmic frame. These movements do not necessarily conform to an aesthetic framework, but potentially disrupt it. As Lyotard writes: 'the motion which is going beyond the point of no return spills the libidinal forces outside the whole, at the expense of the whole (at the price of the ruin and disintegration of the whole)' (ibid.). The point of no return is a place beyond an aesthetic framework that would emotionally justify an action within a framework of meaning. It is a place where the enjoyment of classical pleasure fulfilment is substituted by a *pleasure/pain* enjoyment which is akin to the concept of *jouissance*. It is a place that carries a potential for a perceptual freedom, free from the need of returning a narrative structure.

What further heightens the *jouissance* of this scene is that it plays with the notion of chance by juxtaposing the temporality of film and theatrical action. Every time the woman makes it around, the male character attempts to trip her. An audience could be certain that the recorded material was staged and happened in the past, whereas the live stage action always suggests a possibility of the woman actually tripping. The almost perfect staging makes this uncertainty even more pronounced. This is because the formal rules are clear but at any moment they can be broken as a result of a potential accident. The temporality of events in classical realist film montage usually serves specific patterns and intensities of events which, as elements of an aesthetic structure, are designed to generate pleasure and are subordinate to a 'libidinal normalisation'. An example of this in cinema would be the structural montage technique of 'recoil'.[5] Of course not all films follow this technique and even in classical film montage there are moments of *jouissance*. However these moments eventually collapse onto a sense-making frame which normalises them into a more pleasure oriented experience. What Lyotard envisaged was a more perpetual experience of *jouissance*, a more mechanical deconstruction of aesthetic pleasure. In the running scene, the constant repetitions create a degree of potentiality, almost like a rehearsal for something to happen, something beyond the established formal and aesthetic confines of the scene. It becomes more of an experience of a *process* than a *product*. The enjoyment of the scene is no longer confined to a fulfilment of a structural pleasure within a set aesthetic structure, but becomes an oscillation between the *pleasure/pain* of dissipating away from that structure in a more ambiguous, *ai*sthetic setting.

In *Roadmetal Sweetbread, jouissance* is disruptive of realist cinematic conventions, particularly when we look at it in relation to cinematic 'suture'. Cinematic suture is a concept which explains the pleasures which underlie the identification process of the spectator with a character in realist cinema. Assuming the perspective of a character can often imply assuming an associated potential ideological or political discourse. Hence disrupting this effect allows for a certain degree of emancipation of the spectator and a foregrounding of the 'politics of perception'. In *Roadmetal Sweetbread* this is exemplified in the sexual fantasy scene. Giesekam suggests that this is reminiscent of 'Pinter's 1963 play *The Lover*, in which a married couple spice up their relationship through playing at being each other's fantasy lover' (Giesekam 2007: 207). It is in this scene that disruptive sexual fantasy challenges heterosexual normality and the mundane. The man is on stage, standing at the side of the table. He seems to be surprised and amazed as the woman is dragged below the table by an invisible hand. As the action progresses she becomes more and more ecstatic and sexually excited. The situation is absurd and she may appear as delusional. On the film, however, it is the man dragging her beneath the table, kissing and licking her feet and engaging in what would appear as foreplay. On stage we see the woman fantasising about a sexual act with the man as a voyeur, apparently puzzled by her unexplained excesses. The action onscreen could be read as portraying the woman's unfulfilled fantasies. The lack in the staged reality prompts an imaginary fulfilment on the screen. But the stage reality that is *lacking* can also be seen as a fissure within composition. This occurs when the binary model in which the stage reality is interpreted as an objective representation of their relationship and the film reality as a subjective representation of sexual fantasies is further complicated and the man appears on top of the table in the film, thus becoming the third multiple (doppelganger) of that character, and starts to watch the act taking place between himself and the woman, apparently unaffected and bored by what he sees. This chimerical structure not only causes confusion as to what the different spaces represent but could also be seen as a deconstruction of cinematic suture, as it is no longer clear where the boundaries of subjective experience lie. The space of subjective fantasies, the film, has been invaded by yet another version of the voyeur (Figure 3.2).

It is worth looking at this scene through the concept of suture because the linkage it provides can be associated with the construction of

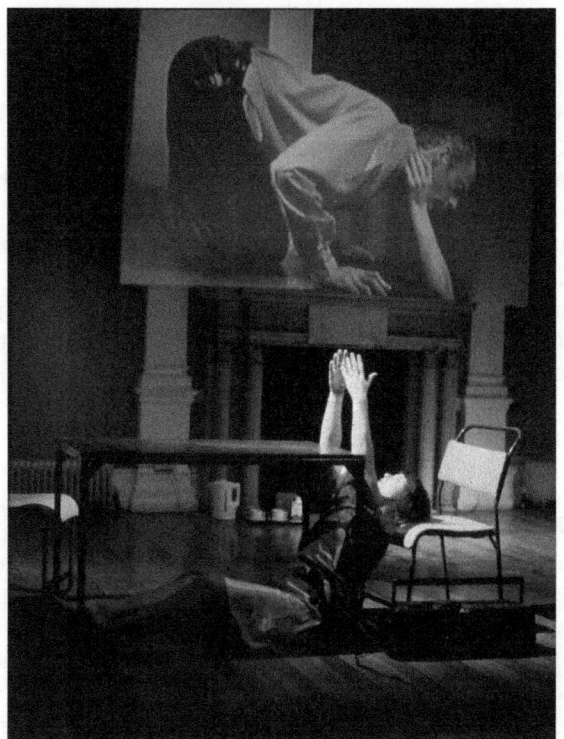

Figure 3.2 Fantasy scene from *Roadmetal Sweetbread*. Photo © Jan Poloczek

pleasure in cinema. Conversely, its deconstruction may be revealing of *jouissance*. Suture is a Lacanian concept that was transported into film studies from linguistics by Jean-Pierre Oudart. Since then many critics have applied it to the study of film syntax in varied ways. Despite suture being achieved in a number of ways (shot composition, camera movement, lighting and so on), the most often analysed component of the cinematic discourse in relation to this disclosure is the shot transition. Kaja Silverman defines cinematic suture as follows:

> [T]he shot/reverse shot formation derives its real importance and interest for many of the theoreticians of suture because it demonstrates so lucidly the way in which cinema operates to reduplicate the history of the subject. The viewer of the cinematic spectacle experiences shot 1 as an imaginary plenitude, unbounded by any

gaze, and unmarked by difference. Shot I is thus the site of a jouissance akin to that of the mirror stage prior to the child's discovery of its separation from the ideal image which it has discovered in the reflecting glass.

(Silverman 1983: 221)

What she argues later is that this moment of *jouissance* is interrupted by recognition that this view is essentially disclosed; it is a negation of the out-of-field of everything that the camera does not show. The conclusion is that there is an 'other', who has authority of the image, hence the initial plenitude and *jouissance* of the cinematic experience is lost. It is this awareness of negation and the existence of a complementary set (the set of elements that are not disclosed by the shot) which produces a lack that causes a discomfort of not knowing who the image belongs to and thus stimulates a need for closure. Silverman argues that classical cinema requires a fictional gaze of a character to justify who the viewer is and to stand in for the absent other. The character thus becomes a signifier for the signified to come, for the reality that has not yet been disclosed and is still to appear; hence it is not yet a signifier but a signified wavering in the spectator's imagination. Putting it in simple terms, shot 1: we see a beautiful coastal landscape, then in shot 2: we see a fisherman, and the discourse is established.

Films can disrupt this mechanism aesthetically. Silverman quotes the famous shower scene in *Psycho* at the end of which the only character with whose gaze we could have identified, namely the victim Marion,[6] dies leaving the spectator in an uncomfortable position. At that 'point we find ourselves in the equally appalling position of the gaze which has negotiated Marion's murder, [...] we acknowledge our own voyeuristic implication' (ibid.: 227). After that disruption the narrative is resumed with the money theme. Moments of *jouissance* exist in classical montage but are only temporary and form part of an elaborate narrative strategy, as in the case of *Psycho*, where what is at stake is the creation of a sense of psychosis, of being watched. However these momentary glimpses are not what Lyotard seeks to articulate. He seems to be more interested in a perpetual, almost mechanical or even Artaudian (to risk the comparison) sense of disruption.

Thus in the sexual fantasy scene in *Roadmetal Sweetbread* the cinematic suture is disrupted by two simultaneous forms of montage: the filmic montage but also the montage constructed by the audience as they experience the whole spectacle. In theatre, even though the action on stage is not framed and does not have a discretely defined out-of-field in the way that film would, the spectator's attention is directed through gestures and performance moments that are made more significant than others. If this were not the case an act would become unclear and its perception fortuitous. The simultaneous exposure of the film and stage action also means, however, that it is almost impossible to capture the event through one frame or perspective; instead the perception of the act is more fragmentary than unifying. If *jouissance* is enjoyment unbound by form, then unlike pleasure it offers the freedom of perception from endless perspectives. By evoking this freedom one may enjoy instances of identification with the characters in a more 'focalised' way without their enjoyment having to be necessarily informed by the perspective from which the representation is constructed.

Maaike Bleeker devised the concept of 'focalisation' through which she articulates a process of identification with a representation or a potential character, as in the case discussed here, that is not unaware of different possibilities of perceiving the representation. She explains that:

> 'Identification' here does not mean the kind of non-critical, passive reception whereby the spectator imagines him- or herself to be a character represented on stage. The concept of focalization involves a type of identification that does not aim at erasing difference between seer and seen.
>
> (Bleeker 2008: 28)

The re-articulation of the difference between 'seer' and the 'seen' or, in Lyotard's terms, the 'client' and the 'victim', is effective in *Roadmetal Sweetbread*. Classical cinema and theatre often work towards erasing this difference and achieving suture, through aesthetic operations that work towards harmonious sensibilities and a sense of pleasure in matching up perspectives and discursive points of view. By deconstructing the aesthetic structures that yield pleasure and by evoking *jouissance*, a freer and more reflexive, self-aware perception can be achieved. Thus the concept of *jouissance*, the dissipatory 'sterile' enjoyment, can be inextricably linked with a dissipatory, reflexive perceptual mode.

For Lyotard the break with realist aesthetic structures opens up the possibility of resistance to the permanence of the capitalist ideology and political agendas that are usually reinforced and returned. In what sense can the *jouissance* of *Roadmetal Sweetbread* be seen as opening up possibilities of resistance to hegemonic ideological constructs? How does this effect challenge the political context of this piece? As will be explained shortly the piece engages with notions of heteronormative politics and it complicates its perceptions precisely through its intermedial aesthetic.

Consequently it can be argued that this free wandering of perception leads to a heightened sense of 'politics of perception' as the audience are made aware of what constitutes their perceptual choices. These choices may, for example, lead to an awareness of the heteronormative implications of the representations portrayed in the sexual fantasy scene. As mentioned before, in that scene the spectator's gaze and the cinematic suture is not realised in such a way as to direct the audience's identifications with the characters in order to establish a singular idealised perspective on their relationship. Instead the perspective is made ambiguous. As a spectator I felt I could either choose to identify with the unfulfilled woman and construct my own montage of the scene out of the theatrical and filmic actions accordingly or opt for a linkage that favoured the man's perspective. There was also the possibility of switching back and forth or succumbing to confusion and getting lost in the attempt to grasp the whole multiplicity of interpretative options. What foregrounded these choices, however, was the continuous interinvolvement of theatre and film, which constantly disrupted the possibility of pleasure gained from piecing the spectacle together into one privileged perspective. If classical realist montage works towards a constant effacement through suture of moments of *jouissance* in favour of an experience of aesthetic *pleasure* in a singular perspective, then the 'post-cinematic montage' of *Roadmetal Sweetbread* could be said to reverse this dynamic. In other words it seems to attempt to efface the instances of aesthetic, structural *pleasures* through a perpetual evocation of *jouissance*.

So far I have looked at how intermedial strategies in *Roadmetal Sweetbread* deconstruct and challenge realist cinema montage conventions and the aesthetics of pleasure and potential spectator expectations associated with them. I have argued for a perceptual freedom which foregrounds the 'politics of perception' in the act of spectating and which could be seen as a resistance against the more passive, mono-perspectivist approach to cinema. Whereas *Roadmetal Sweetbread* challenged deconstructed cinematic montage by re-establishing the relationship between the *mise-en-scène* and the *mise-en-cadre*, *A Mare's Nest* introduces the concept of a moving spectator.

A Mare's Nest

Traditionally a spectator who is fixed in an end-on position is associated with perspectivism and dramatic narrative forms both in cinema and theatre. Colin MacCabe has famously criticised realist cinema for imposing a privileged discursive position on the spectator and its resultant ideologically singular implications. This notion of a privileged discourse, a privileged total perspective which encompasses all significant representations and gives the spectator the optimal experience is a prominent cinematic convention which not only affects the way in which we perceive cinema but also might affect our expectations of the way theatre and other forms of art should be perceived. What is also interesting here from the perspective of Lyotard's critique is that from a classical standpoint there is a lot of aesthetic *pleasure* to be derived from following and reading these perspectives and forms – as was argued above with the notion of cinematic suture. In that sense there is a potential for *jouissance* if the spectator's position is destabilised and mobilised, made flexible and flux-like in relation to the presented film and stage material. Station House Opera's *A Mare's Nest* offers such mobility and deconstructs the convention of perspectivism.

In this piece two screens are set back to back on either side of a wall placed in the middle of a raised stage. The screens are connected by a door. The raised stage with the screens is placed in the centre of a large space and the audience may move around this set (see Figure 3.3). Four performers act out unrelated scenes whose spatial and temporal dimensions are augmented by the spaces projected on film. Unlike in *Roadmetal Sweetbread* the audience is not seated in front of the action but is expected to move freely around and hence montage in real-time what is happening in performance. The arguably post-cinematic experience of this montage is very different to that of film editing or even choosing from an array of angles on an interactive DVD because it is unrepeatable and corporeal. It is unrepeatable because it concerns the individual framing of live performance, both of the performers and the audience. The experience is subject to the continuous space and time of theatre and not the discontinuities of realist film. The corporeal aspect of it comes from the fact that each spectator physically becomes their own 'editing suite'. Arguably the body of the spectator and the spectator's perceptual apparatus become the technology through which the spectacle is montaged.

In this section I will look at how *A Mare's Nest* foregrounds the 'politics of perception' by emancipating the agency of the spectator and evoking *jouissance* through a denial of pleasure attributed to realist cinema spectatorship conventions. This is achieved by offering a multiplicity of perceptions and by challenging pleasurable viewing habits and aesthetics that culturally serve as lenses through which reality can be

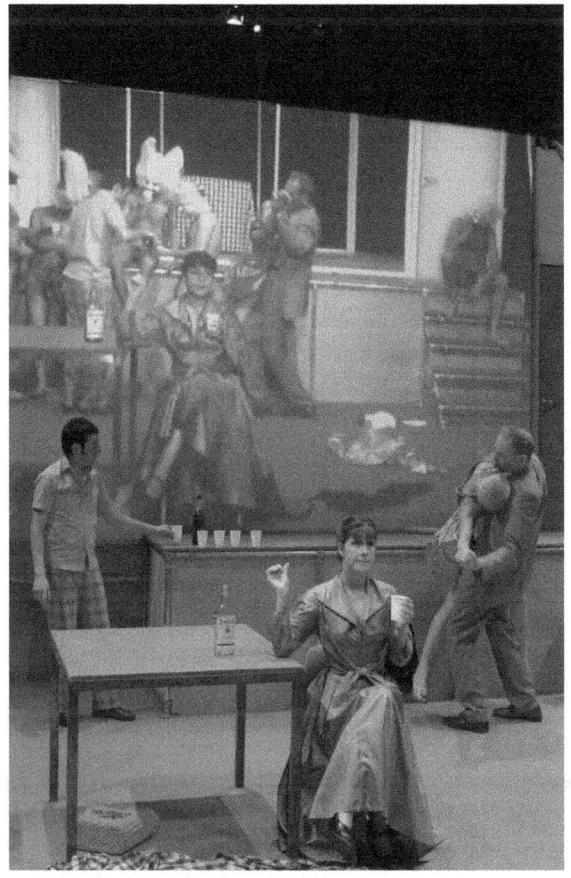

Figure 3.3   *A Mare's Nest*, Station House Opera. Photo © Christian Enger, 2001

represented and consequently potentially perceived. By moving beyond the confines of pleasure-generating forms and potentially amplifying an experience of *jouissance*, *A Mare's Nest* explores the uncanny landscape that lies between our immediate experience of the real and the virtual fantasies to which we are exposed and which we inhabit on a daily basis. Lyotard's critique applies here in an interesting way since the piece takes on the form of an installation, emancipating the audience and implicating them within the process of production of images but also making them more vulnerable through their involvement as a part of the physical reality of the show. By bringing the mechanics of film and theatre to the forefront of the spectator's attention – or in Lyotard's words by 'rendering the support opaque' (Lyotard 1989: 179) – *A Mare's Nest*, like *Roadmetal Sweetbread*, also reverses the 'client-victim' relationship that Lyotard argues is so solidly ingrained within classical film realism. By reversing this relationship it also dismantles the unity of an organic cinematic body and denies the pleasure of a gestalt perception.

The experience offered by *A Mare's Nest* is not merely a question of extending theatrical space by means of using film, as we have seen in *Roadmetal Sweetbread*, it is also a question of extending film by making it part of a theatrical space. Often during the piece, performers move between the two sides of the screen. Sometimes they run around the screen and sometimes they go through the door in it. By 'entering' the screen, they virtually appear in the film and continue their action whilst physically they are on the other side where a slightly different physical space and film space are to be seen. These games can cause much confusion. According to Giesekam the screen becomes:

> both form and image, a liminal place of transition between both physical playing spaces and virtual playing spaces, with the performers functioning simultaneously as material and immaterial beings, an interweaving that confounds attempts to distinguish between real and unreal.
>
> (Giesekam 2007: 211)

If we look at the piece from the perspective of deconstructing the cinematic apparatus, by allowing the audience members to walk around the screen and, as it were, to take on the role of film editors, the relationship between the spectator and the film screen is undermined. There is no conventional narrative or storyline as such, although one could infer that the thematic is one of a surreal party with four characters who leap in and out of a world of erotic fantasies. There is very little dialogue and a lot of the action is very mechanical, in part to establish the relationship between the virtual and the onstage action. For example in one instance Mem Morrison runs around the screen placed on the stage platform. (The cast in the performance discussed here was that in the première of the piece at La Batie Festival, Geneva, in 2001.) He randomly takes different objects and elements from the set – glasses, cups, bottles, boxes – and carries them over to the other side of the screen, placing them in new configurations. Again an affinity is to be found here with Beckett's drama since these tiresome routines are reminiscent of the futile exercises Beckett makes his characters go through. Clov's tedious searching for the 'centre' in *Endgame* springs to mind. In *A Mare's Nest* there are scenes in which the stage action is perfectly synchronised with the projected film action, offering an extremely exciting spectacle of precision and synchronisation. Other scenes are deliberately out of synch and exemplify divergences between the virtual and the live action. For example, on stage, Julian Maynard Smith offers an ashtray for Susanna Hart to tap her cigarette into. This action is doubled on the screen but instead of the ashtray Maynard Smith places his face below the cigarette so that Hart drops ash into his mouth. This bizarre ritual is somewhat reminiscent of the uncanny games and routines the characters from *Roadmetal Sweetbread* engage in. In that sense, this scene can be interpreted as destabilising the perception of mundane, quotidian life where the boundaries between repressed fantasies and reality, the imaginary and the actual become blurred. This blurring of boundaries between the real and virtual and the simultaneities of exposing them through different media, have an effect of destabilising perspectivist perceptions of events and complicating the possibility of narrative structures.

But the deconstruction of imaginary film space through the juxtaposition of material action is not the only way in which cinematic conventions are being deconstructed here. Lyotard's 'immobilised' spectator is mobilised by the set-up of the piece. Faced with a set like an art installation, the audience in *A Mare's Nest* is physically emancipated and liberated from the conventional fixed theatrical/cinematic positioning in an auditorium. The auditorium is an element of a perceptual apparatus both in theatre and in cinema which traditionally has a perspectivist implication and is usually associated with a liberal humanist discourse. It can be seen as part of an apparatus that is designed to produce and reinforce specific ideological and political perspectives, and historically this has been the case. This is in the sense that the optimal perspective which it was designed to uphold has often represented the culturally dominant discourse.

Thus the 'politics of perception' become foregrounded in *A Mare's Nest* by the fact that the audience can never get the full picture of the show. The set-up is such that no spectator can ever see all the action. Seeing the action on one side of the stage means not being able to see the action on the other. Thus any potential narrative thread will always be the outcome of how a particular spectator positions him or herself around the stage. At the same time, any identification with the characters is made difficult since they confusingly mingle with their virtual counterparts and displace themselves in different dramatic situations occurring on stage. One could argue that the pleasure of experiencing movements that fall into discrete temporal and spatial structures is thwarted. The syntax of the piece becomes heavily dependent on the spectator's' choices. It is impossible to get any ideal perspective of the show. There is a dissatisfaction linked with this but also an enjoyment in being able to choose or ignore certain aspects of what is happening. One could of course not move at all and simply see one version of the show but the potential of diversion is tempting. This temptation to divert links with Lyotard's notion of *jouissance*, which is a non-productive experience of enjoyment, in this case an enjoyment that is not geared towards a production of a cohesive narrative and sense-making frame. There is a potential for anxiety in that the audience may not experience the ideal montage and no intended narrative structure will be returned. The spectator cannot rewind the show, not only because it is a theatre piece but because they would have to rewind themselves too. Once a choice is made there is no going back. By moving around, spectators become aware of their choices and the fact that they may not be able to grasp an optimal version of the spectacle. The pleasure of piecing the material together into an organic whole, an undertaking that is fundamental to classical montage, is constantly denied because moving around and switching viewpoints breaks up a possible frame. Through this structure *A Mare's Nest* also articulates the demand for the pleasure of imaginary organic unity. *Jouissance* becomes thus a perversion, a form of torture for the spectator who is constantly denied the holistic perspective but also a resistance to the dominance of perspectivism in our contemporary cinematic culture.

Because the experience of a classical film is usually set against the knowledge that all material – no matter how uncanny and exhilarating – has been filmed and is unchangeable, the perceptual process is conditioned by referring the experience to a constant. This constant in the case of film is the structure and organisation of images within the discrete timeframes of the cinematograph or other technology projecting the film and its fixed screen. In *A Mare's Nest* this perceptual constant, a referring back or a return to an aesthetic structuring, is set in motion and thus becomes a variable. Where film can achieve different duration effects by altering the velocity at which images are displayed, *A Mare's Nest* achieves an acceleration of perception, a double relativity so to speak, as a result of allowing the audience to move and actively assemble the spectacle themselves.

But an experience of re-editing in real time is not the only effect of the interstice of the live action and video images. During the spectacle there are a few instances where objects such as metal chains are dropped from the ceiling into the audience space. The menace of a potential physical danger breaks the illusion of filmic realities within the piece, reminding the spectator of the materiality and physicality of theatre in a somewhat shocking and violent manner. This is a postdramatic aspect that Lehmann defines as the 'irruption of the real', a breaking up of a theatrical frame, where the traditionally 'unwanted' elements become a 'co-player' (Lehmann 2006: 100). This has much affinity with Lyotard's call for the recuperation of 'unwanted' movements that are usually cut out of the final montage version of a movie. Thus all these elements break the framed notion of a *mise-en-cadre* by introducing the unpredictability and potentiality of the *mise-en-scène* action. There is also a materialisation of the experience of the virtual image itself. The film screen becomes a canvas as well as a skin of a virtual reality, it is made flesh. For example, a door within the screen through which characters can pass onto the other physical side but that also appears in the virtual realm on screen. This is where Lyotard's wish for a film to be more like a painting on a wall becomes more fully realised. Films aren't usually perceived as paintings on a wall unless they are part of an installation thus reframed. In *A Mare's Nest* the projected films are no longer only invisible transparent portals into a different dimension but physicalised spaces in theatrical terms on stage. More importantly this also changes the ontological status of a spectator in relation to film material. Spectators are no longer absent receivers but corporeal witnesses to the event taking place in front of them. Going back to Lehmann's distinction, they also play a more active part of the performance text of the piece.

This *aisthetic* displacement of the audience's relation with the virtual and live is further emphasised on a more fundamental level of visual perception. In cinema it is important for the audience to be drawn into the virtual world, carried through the portal of the silver screen into a different dimension. All lights are dimmed in the movie theatre, the sounds of the external world are blocked out and comfortable chairs make the spectators almost forget they physically exist. Here again Lyotard's notion of the effacement of support can be applied. The support is not only the aesthetic rules and conventions, the inner workings of the cinematic apparatus that convey a filmic reality, but also the whole of the spectator's body that reacts and processes information, most importantly for film the eye-cortex apparatus.

A Mare's Nest physicalises the act of visual perception of film as can be seen at a rudimentary anatomical level. In order to understand better what is at stake in the visual perception of film let us turn to cognitive theory. Cognitive theory distinguishes two main types of visual

perception: mental and physical. Mental phenomena are a set of properties of the image through which we can judge its composition. Let us
consider judgement of depth, which is crucial for comprehension and
orientation in space. Amongst the most common mental visual cues are
perspective cues that organise objects in space, the relative scaling of
objects, texture gradation, interposition of objects, shading and motion
parallax. All of these features can be implemented through cinematography to give an impression of depth but a real life visual experience is
more than just deducing these phenomena. There is also the physical
optical dimension, which consists of accommodation, convergence and
retinal disparity. Accommodation is the movement of ciliary muscles
that contract or stretch the eyeball lens in order to focus the image on
the retina, stretching for objects further away and contracting for closer
objects. Convergence is the angular orientation of the eyeballs relative to
each other around their vertical axis. For distant objects they will look
more ahead whilst for closer they will, in turn, move towards each other.
Retinal disparity is the difference in the object's position within the visual field that the two eyes see. The difference should increase, the closer
the object is to the eyes. All these physical phenomena send signals to the
brain about the space that surrounds it. So to an extent our mind physically *feels* the space around it even though we are not very conscious of
it. We can become conscious of this after a long dull film where our visual
apparatus has been focused on a static object for three hours (the screen
doesn't physically move), when we leave the cinema and possibly get a
headache. This difference relates to ontology, aesthetically movies can
simulate most mental cues of depth through cinematographic technique
but the physical cues are abandoned. The vigorously lit top of Mordor in
the background is still at the same physical distance from the spectator
as a backlit Frodo in the foreground. The eyeballs do not react physically
to that spatial difference. This is intensified by the darkness in movie
theatres. In this sense movies are designed not only to make the audience
forget about their bodies but also about the fact they have eyes.

In *A Mare's Nest* the physicalisation of the film screen and the fact
that it is interinvolved with the theatrical space and action juxtapose
the two modes of visual perception by adding a biological embodied
perspective. The perception of live, three-dimensional objects, whose
qualities can be perceived by the spectator by physically moving around
them, is juxtaposed with their virtual representations. The constant
oscillation between these perceptions potentially makes the audience
aware of the inner workings of their visual perception. Even though the
'hypersurface' has the potential to 'blend' the two realities, there is a

mesmerising quality to this experience. There is a subtle disjunction of the real and the virtual that is not only to be cognised visually but also physically 'felt' by the spectator's visual apparatus.

Despite the ontological mayhem of *A Mare's Nest*, which is also suggested by its title, the piece maintains a promise of narrative and a degree of intertextuality with cinema culture. For example, the costumes and the hair-styling echo a Hitchcockian stylistic, and the appearance of naked men within the virtual film component of the piece, wearing carnival masks and feathery tiaras on their heads is a surrealist convention that could have come from Lynch. Without these exotic touches and the promise of dramatic scenes such as fights, arguments and chases between the characters – even though there is hardly any dialogue to ground interpretation – the piece would risk being both boring and uninteresting. In many ways the inclusion of film into theatre space brings about a promise of narrative and interinvolves the theatrical with potential film intertexts. It potentially conveys an experience of oscillation between the knowable cinematic conventions, the promises of imaginary unity and a more open disorienting experience of *jouissance.* Jean Mitry once suggested, when referring to realism in cinema as a highly conventionalised aesthetic, that 'the real is nothing other than a form of the fantastic to which we have become accustomed' (Mitry in Ezra and Harris 2000: 151). Thus *A Mare's Nest* explores the 'politics of perception' by emancipating the agency of the spectator and denying a relationship of pleasure that is attributed to perspectivist cinema spectatorship conventions. Station House Opera achieves this by offering a multiplicity of perceptions and challenging pleasurable viewing habits and aesthetics that culturally serve as lenses through which reality can be represented and consequently potentially perceived. By moving beyond the confines of pleasure-generating forms and potentially amplifying an experience of *jouissance, A Mare's Nest* explores the uncanny landscape that lies between our immediate experience of the real and the virtual fantasies which we inhabit in our daily lives. This attempt to explore what is in between is nicely encapsulated by a remark made by John Maynard-Smith: 'Existence carries on [...] There are no resolutions, there's no catharsis. The problems always return, the misery seeps back in. What else is life, but nice sunsets and bits in between?' (Maynard Smith cited by Kent 1998: 134).

Conclusion

This chapter has looked at the way in which the pleasure factor of realist cinematic montage affected perceptions and their potential ideological and political underpinning. Consequently it shed light on how intermedial strategies in *Roadmetal Sweetbread* and *A Mare's Nest* deconstruct and challenge realist cinema montage conventions and the aesthetics of pleasure and potential spectator expectations associated with them. In the case of *Roadmetal Sweetbread* it was the interplay between the *mise-en-scène* and the *mise-en-cadre* which played the key role in the deconstruction but also the way in which some of the scenes disassemble the potential for cinematic suture. With *A Mare's Nest* it was the deconstruction of a perspectivist mode of spectatorship and the pleasures and expectations associated with a privileged discourse. Following Lyotard's critique, I have argued for a potential of post-cinematic theatre to articulate a space for the experience of *jouissance*, an intermedial, in between space beyond the aesthetic and structural realms of pleasure. Whereas classical realist montage works towards a constant effacement of moments of *jouissance* through suture in favour of an experience of aesthetic *pleasure* in a singular perspective, post-cinematic montage (*acinematic* montage) reverses this dynamic. It essentially attempts to efface the instances of aesthetic, structural pleasures through a perpetual evocation of *jouissance*. The experience of pleasure and *jouissance* is thus a polarity, not a binary opposition that has a different dynamic depending on each specific work of art. I have argued that this *jouissance* has an emancipatory character affecting the perceptual choices made by the audience because it opens up the perceptual spectrum, allowing more possibilities for interpretation as the representations are not bound by a rigid aesthetic frame. Hence Lyotard's search for *jouissance* in avant-garde art is really a search for an individual freedom of response beyond the imposed external order of representation. Thus in trying to recuperate *jouissance*, Lyotard is trying to recuperate 'ownership' of emotive experience for the individual spectator. This perceptual freedom in turn foregrounds the 'politics of perception' in the act of spectating, which can be seen as a resistance against the more passive, mono-perspectival aesthetic cultural tropes of realist movies and their political implications.

4
Guilty Pleasures and Intermedial Archaeologies in the Wooster Group's *House/Lights* and *Hamlet*

This chapter will follow and extend the theoretical context outlined in Lyotard's 'Acinema' which was discussed in the previous chapter. It will discuss the concept of *pleasure* in mainstream cinema and the possibility of post-cinematic performance to move beyond this aesthetic framework and recuperate the experience of *jouissance* (divergent libidinal pleasure). The theories will be explored by looking at two post-cinematic pieces by the Wooster Group, each of which explores libidinal pleasures albeit in contrasting ways. These are *House/Lights* (1998) and their more recent production of *Hamlet* (2009). I will argue that the interinvolvement between theatre and film in these pieces deconstructs the aesthetics of pleasure and evokes *jouissance*. Consequently, I will argue that this negotiates the 'politics of perception' concerning the representations of pleasures in the two productions.

The Wooster Group is an American experimental theatre collective led by director Elizabeth LeCompte. It was set up in 1975 by Spalding Gray, Jim Clayburgh, Ron Vawter, Willem Dafoe, Kate Valk and Peyton Smith as the original founding members. Among their past works are *Rumstick Road* (1977), *Route 1 & 9* (1981), *L.S.D. (...Just the highpoints...)* (1984), *BRACE UP!* (1991) and *La Didone* (2009). Their work is heavily influenced by mass media, in particular cinema, as a result of which they often incorporate films as part of their *mise-en-scène*, but they also base a lot of their material and devising processes on film aesthetics.

House/Lights deals with the embodiment and staging of cinematic conventions. The theme is sexual perversion and its structural basis is an interweaving of the horror film *Olga's House of Shame* (1964) and Gertrude Stein's *Doctor Faustus Lights the Lights* (1938). Film material other than *Olga's House of Shame* includes *Young Frankenstein* (1974), *I Love Lucy* (1951) and a live feed from a camera placed centre stage.

The actors on stage seem to channel and react to film material being fed through two TV sets, where their choreography takes on the structural language of film. In doing this they explore the tension between the specific film aesthetics they quote and their presentational theatrical style. This tension becomes a way of negotiating what is at stake in the filmic representations of sexual desire they set out to explore. In contradistinction to Station House Opera, the Wooster Group do not use immersive strategies to explore intermediality. Instead they develop a more dialectical, presentational, almost post-Brechtian approach that can also be found in the stylistics of The Builders Association, in pieces such as *Jump Cut (Faust)* (1997). Not only the topic is similar but so is the deconstructive approach that interrogates illusionistic narrative forms. The dialectic they establish gives an interesting insight into that between the notions of *pleasure* and *jouissance*.

Hamlet is altogether different. In many ways it is a substantial recon-struction of Richard Burton's 1964 Broadway production of *Hamlet* directed by John Gielgud. This was an unusual production mainly because of the intermedial experiment that was being made in regards to its distribution. Katia Arfara recounts:

> Seventeen cameras were used to film this performance so that it could be broadcast live during two days in 2,000 movie theatres all over the United States. The idea was to provide thousands of viewers with a theatrical experience that would take place simultaneously in different cities. This new form of performance became possible due to Electronovision and it was named 'Theatrofilm'.
>
> (Arfara 2008: 134).

Thus the mode of distribution located the production firmly within film and cinematic culture, but the way in which the production was staged and cast was also indicative of the influence of cinema on American theatre. Richard Burton was a famous film actor at the time, having just completed *Anthony and Cleopatra*. Director John Gielgud also had a track record of film performance. Wooster Group director Elizabeth LeCompte has stated in an interview that one of her main interests in that specific production was that it signified a change in American theatre, 'a change into a kind of performance [style] that comes out of film rather than theatre' (Shevtsova 2013: 122). The Wooster Group production of *Hamlet* also used other films as sources, mainly Kenneth Branagh's film version of *Hamlet* from 1997. As Johan Callens pointed out, the production 'emphasizes the company's "archaeological" excursion into America's cultural past, [their] reconstructing a hypothetical theatre piece from the fragmentary evidence of the edited film, like an archaeologist inferring an improbable temple from a collection of ruins' (Callens 2009: 545).

A striking feature of the production is the way in which the actors attempt meticulously to recreate most of the movements, actions and vocal performances in Burton's *Hamlet* in a manner that could be described as resembling 'a very sophisticated form of karaoke' (Worthen 2008: 315). With the original as a digitally manipulated backdrop projection, the live performance adopts a deconstructive approach that interrogates illusionistic narrative forms. This technique is reminiscent of the techniques used in *House/Lights*. However, where *House/Lights* focused on the embodiment of cinematic conventions, *Hamlet* is more focused on the embodiment of the end product and on the exploration and foregrounding of the libidinal intensities and viewing pleasures of Burton's *Hamlet*. In that sense the production can be seen as an attempt to embody the pleasures and the emotional journey of viewing Burton's piece or as a representation of what Marvin Carlson calls 'ghosting' – 'trying to represent what happens in the mind of a spectator when they watch this new representation of something that they have seen several times' (Carlson in Shevtsova 2013: 130). This removal from immediate representation into a representation of the experience of representation, a 'post-representation', is interesting in terms of Lyotard's theories; the experience of *jouissance* requires a degree of removal from the representational frame.

House/Lights

House/Lights, as noted above, is based on an interweaving of horror film *Olga's House of Shame* (1964) and Gertrude Stein's *Doctor Faustus Lights the Lights* (1938). Stein's autobiography (Toklas 1933) is also used as a supportive intertext. The two main intertexts deal with the theme of forbidden pleasures that could be considered abject from a mainstream ideological point of view. *Olga's House of Shame* is about a woman who runs a crime syndicate in a deserted mine in upstate New York, dealing with prostitution, narcotics and jewel smuggling. The substance of the film is how she brutally tortures and molests young girls in her den, taking perverse pleasure in the torments she inflicts. Gertrude Stein's *Doctor Faustus Lights the Lights* is a rewrite of the Faustian myth and is essentially about temptation. Affinities can be drawn between *Olga's House of Shame* and Stein's text but also with Stein's autobiography. At the heart of the film there is a power struggle between Olga and her protector

Elaine which could be seen as reflective of the struggle between the Devil and Faustus in Stein's text. A further parallel could be drawn to Stein's lesbian relationship with Alice B. Toklas. However, the performance does not adopt a narrative structure through which to explore the thematics of perversion that comprise the content of these intertexts; instead it picks moments and elements from the two intertexts and organises them into a complex, multi-layered assemblage. Unlike its filmic intertext, *House/Lights* does not convey the content of perversion through traditionally dramatic means, that is by adhering to a coherent narrative and characterisations. The performance rather emphasises what could be termed as a process of deconstruction. As Andrew Quick relates,

> the wing space and proscenium arch, so crucial to the production of the forms of realism that have dominated the theatre since the late nineteenth century, are pared down to see-through metal structures, which open out all the technologies of reproduction and manipulation to the gaze of the spectator.
>
> (Quick 2009: 33)

The emphasis on the interweaving and juxtaposition of multiple texts, video, live performance and the bare grid-like structures of a theatrical set, potentially shifts the audience's attention from the signifieds to the signifiers. The signifying structures of theatre are no longer an invisible form, a 'support' that would make 'meaning' potentially transparent and clearly readable. Instead the support itself becomes 'perverted' not only on an aesthetic level and a level of representation and meaning, but also on an *aisthetic* level, as the hierarchy of organisation of the different theatrical elements in the piece is set into motion.

In his book *Staging the Screen*, Greg Giesekam claims that Stein's text was more than just a thematic inspiration or 'quotable' text for performance but also an inspiration for the philosophy of structuring the performance. According to Giesekam:

> [t]he resulting focus on the signifier rather than the signified echoes the spirit of Stein, a writer more concerned with the process of representation than the object of representation, and for whom the shape and rhythm of a sentence was always paramount.
>
> (Giesekam 2007: 106)

The focus on the 'process of representation' or in other words the process of the production of meaning can also be seen as one of the key

post-cinematic features of *House/Lights* and an important strategy
through which the piece deconstructs cinematic conventions. Thus
before moving on with the analysis of the piece, it would be worth
taking a look at some of Stein's artistic principles and agendas as they
inspired many of the intermedial and deconstructive strategies in *House/
Lights*. Because *House/Lights* deconstructs cinematic montage conventions that are designed to impose a more perspectivist experience on the
spectator, Stein's approach – which essentially challenged perspectivism –
will be insightful here. Stein was greatly influenced and inspired by the
cubist movement in visual arts, especially by her friend Pablo Picasso.
Even though her work consisted of writing for theatre, she tried to
adopt the cubist 'spirit' of aesthetic innovation especially concerning
her use of syntax to structure her material. As indicated in the discussion on Eisenstein's theories in Chapter 2 above, one way of describing
the aesthetic shift which cubism was implementing would be as a shift
away from a notion of organicity. It could be seen as an attempt to
liberate perception from a single perspective that would organise and
arrange the viewer's experience of vision-scape or landscape. The classical landscape paintings against which cubism as an artistic movement
might have been reacting, such as the impressive nineteenth-century
landscapes of Constable and the near-expressionism of Turner, the
Impressionist and later mesmerising post-Impressionist landscapes of
Van Gogh, were to various degrees reconstructed and re-imagined by
these artists. However, it would be wrong to say, and one must be careful here, that all of these landscapes are purely imaginary, made up in
a state of delirium or other stance of inspiration. Most of them were
derived from meticulous observation and encounters with the 'real'
landscape accompanied by dozens of sketches and drafts. It is true that
they were submitted to an abstracted syntax, for example, geometric
rules of composition, colour balancing rules, linear perspective scaling and organisation in relation to a vanishing point/points and so
on. Each work, however, constitutes the montaged end product of a
long process taken by the artists to formulate and articulate through
specific syntax the experience they had in the encounter with the 'real'
landscape. Note that the classical landscape was by no means a true
'snapshot', it was made up of discontinuities and temporarily disjointed
instances of perception but they were bound by form which gave them
organicity and hence implied the viewing subject within it, putting the
chaos of experience into 'perspective'. Conversely cubism would offer
multiple instances of perception and multiple perspectives all in one
painting with no adherence to an organic form.

Thus the main preoccupation for Stein when transposing cubist aesthetic into dramatic form would obviously have to be the implication of the subject. As Jane Palatini Bowers argued, Stein had to find a way to create a 'lang-scape' (Palatini Bowers 2002: 132) that would appropriate the syntax of cubist painting for theatre. In many ways what creates perspective and a subject's cohesion in dramatic theatre is narrative. Theatre has a special potential here since speech and action in theatre move along a temporal continuum. Arguably, the greatest source of continuity in dramatic theatre is the actor who is always in *propria persona*, always present. Finding ways to dismantle the potential for this temporal horizontality of perception in dramatic theatre, would become one of the main aesthetic directions that Stein's work in theatre took. Palatini Bowers argues that:

> Stein's verbal compositions for the theatre resist the temporal thrust of speech and linear sequence of thought and narration. Each utterance in a Stein play is meant to be responded to as we respond to space – as a totality, present in each instant but not connected to subsequent instances except by juxtaposition or echoing. A Stein play comes into being as a series of perspectives. Its whole is not experienced as a unit but as an accumulation of multiple engagements of the listening self with the spoken and sung words. For the American Stein as for the Spaniard Picasso, juxtaposition, simultaneity, and multiple perspective are the relational principles expressed by the land/lang-scape.
>
> (Palatini Bowers 2002: 132)

Stein tried to achieve what could be called a 'disorienting landscape',[1] a landscape that resists the imposition of a framework and allows for a simultaneous experience of multiple perspectives. She likened her plays to 'landscapes': 'A landscape does not move, nothing really moves in a landscape, but things are there, and I put into the play the things that were there' (Stein in Meyerowitz 1971: 81). These aesthetic principles underlying Stein's approach to language and theatre were a starting point for the post-cinematic strategy for *House/Lights*. In many ways the strategy behind *House/Lights* was to dismantle and unsettle pleasures associated with perspectivism, classical film narration and montage aesthetics. In that sense they can also be said to follow Lyotard's project in 'Acinema', in which he advocated a more 'cubist' approach to filmmaking, one not bound by aesthetic forms that elicit perspectivist forms of identification and subject implication.

Now let us look at how the intermediality of *House/Lights* disman-tles cinematic representations of pleasure and evokes *jouissance*. Once again Lyotard's critique acts as a point of reference for the analysis, which will begin with the filmic intertext and its relationship to the thematic of perverse pleasure. *Olga's House of Shame* is a horror movie, an unspeakable 'nightmare of eroticism' stripped of all political correctness.

> Olga, the ultimate sadist, moves her headquarters from Chinatown to a deserted ore mine in upstate New York. There, with the help of her malignant brother Nick and numerous semi-clad gals in push-up bras, she controls a crime syndicate involving narcotics, prostitution, and jewel smuggling. But what the film is really about of course, is scene after scene of gals being tortured, whipped and beaten.
>
> (Henenlotter in Quick 2007: 167)

Despite its aesthetic strangeness and independent cinema feel, charac-terised by 'odd angles, strange edits, jump cuts' (LeCompte in Quick 2007: 214) the intertext film itself only offers an aestheticisation of perversion. Its syntax and language still remain transparent and 'hid-den' so that the viewer may focus on the acts depicted within the cinematic image. For Lyotard the syntax of mainstream film but also of any simulacrum must normally be seen as held in 'insensibility or unconsciousness' (Lyotard 1989: 178) in order to achieve transparency. This syntax allegedly 'vanishes' as the studio space is transposed onto the screen. What is interesting about this Wooster Group piece is that its somewhat hectic choreography takes on the structural language of film, potentially reversing this presupposition. As noted above, the actors on stage seem to respond to material being fed through two TV sets, located left and right of the stage. The director of the piece, Elizabeth LeCompte, used close-ups, camera moves and different types of shots as a means of generating movement on stage. She gave her performers the freedom to decide which aspects of the film stylistic to mark in performance, since video material provides such a rich set of stimuli for the devising process:

> there are so many impulses that can be generated by a visual picture. One day you might respond to the way the camera moves and the next day you might respond to the fact that the person on the film looks in a certain direction.
>
> (LeCompte in Quick 2007: 217)

Thus a close-up on one of the TV sets may force the performer to move front stage whilst a long shot will make them move backstage. By doing so they embody the cinematic apparatus, abstracting what Lyotard calls the 'support' and bringing it to the spectator's attention as significant. Thus, that which is normally hidden and comprises of cinematic tricks is made into a material for performance. As in the case of *Roadmetal Sweetbread*, through this embodiment (not of character but of the cinematic apparatus) the performers seem to reverse the transition from *mise-en-scène* to *mise-en-cadre*. One of the scenes where this is particularly noticeable is when Kate Valk's character is running through a forest. The film action is displayed on the central television whilst four performers, each embodying different cuts of shots, keep running in between the front and backstage depending on the positioning and spatial framing of her body. For example, if the video cuts to her feet, a performer runs front stage and mimics the movement of her feet. By attempting to embody the filmic spatiality the organic action of film is made corporeal. All moments and gestures that could yield significance within a narrative frame are displaced and dispersed and thus a disassemblage of the cinematic apparatus occurs. A strange power struggle takes place between the performers and the mediated material.

This seemingly playful set-up, which evokes a studio, allows the performers to de-contextualise, repeat, confuse and distort the mediated moments that comprise the body of film. However, if we take a closer look at the interinvolvement of the two ontologies the piece becomes a more profound exploration of cinematic syntax and language. One of the properties of realist film is its ability to assemble discontinuous depictions of movement. This does not only occur at the micro level of a frame (the fundamental level), but between different shots and, consequently, scenes. A montage of different shots depicting an event stimulates a perception of that event. The movement of the whole no longer is a depiction (like a single long shot of a scene) but an image of movement. The discontinuities of the filmic space and time become fragmentations in a continuous stage presence. If we were to take Eisenstein's analogy of the Laocoön, what the performers in *House/Lights* do is an attempt to embody an impossible filmic action, in the same way that the pose of the Laocoön embodies what would be anatomically impossible for a corporeal performer. The failure to achieve this 'impossible' unity is what de-composes the illusion of cinematic montage. Time in a live theatre show is continuous at its most fundamental level, even if the action has been slowed or distorted as in a Robert Wilson performance. Even though there can be montage in the theatre – where certain moments and events are brought into significance and thus to the audience's attention through various aesthetic means – the physical and temporal continuity of a live theatrical space, the opaqueness of the live bodies physically present to the audience makes theatre less unified than the phantasm of the cinematic.

This enunciation of the support, in this case the mechanics of film, reconfigures Lyotard's 'victim-client' relationship. In one of the scenes, the video shows Olga lifting one of the girls by her legs and biting her thighs, whilst on stage the performer's legs are supported and held by an additional two performers who do not feature on the screen (Figure 4.1). This scene is evocative of a moment in the original film that depicts perverse tortures. It is portrayed partially on the TV screen and partially on stage. The effect is almost as if her legs on stage were an extension

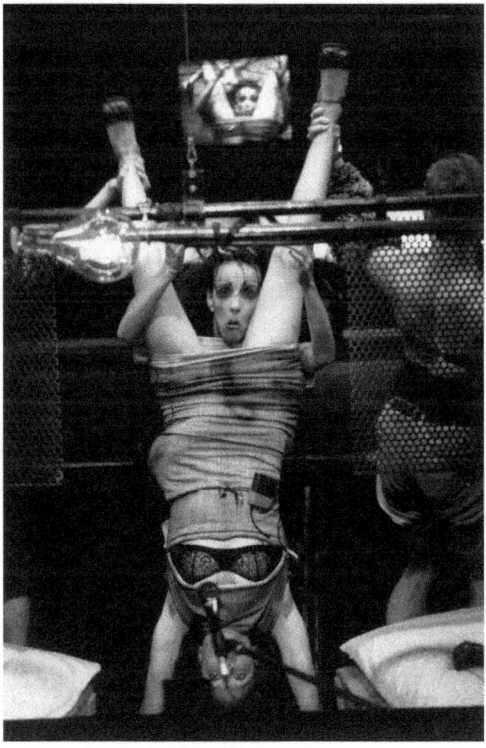

Figure 4.1   House/Lights, The Wooster Group. Pictured: Suzzy Roche, Kate Valk (upside down), Ari Fliakos. Photo © Mary Gearhart

of her body (her crotch) captured on the film. The culmination of the scene is when Olga bites the girl's thigh. This is visible both on the screen and on stage, yet the screen image seems to have an awkward unity and realism to it that the theatrical image does not, even though the former is a live feed of the latter.

In this scene the support (cinematic mechanic) is being performed and the 'victim' is being physically held on stage as character and performer and simultaneously remediated on screen, hence the possibility of experiencing an aesthetic pleasure from the filmic image is constantly undercut by the continuous excessive theatrical action. Instances of identification are juxtaposed with a performance of a *mise-en-scène* that constructs the cinematic image on screen. Apart from the image on the screen we also see the excess of performance on stage from which the virtual image arises. The fragment of the body on screen is juxtaposed with the live bodies. This complicates the possibility of 'libidinal normalisation' which relies heavily on the invisibility of the support and instance of identification with the victim. The scene thus becomes an *ai*sthetic disassemblage of cinematic illusion. The pleasure of the victim being conveyed through the support is replaced by the *jouissance* of an impossible embodiment of the support on stage – the Eisensteinian statue of Laocoön seems to shatter into a myriad of fragments and instances beyond its imaginary constituency. It is thus this intermedial shattering of the body of film, the formal, the beautiful, through live performance, which articulates *jouissance.* In many ways it is the incompleteness achieved from the intermedial chimerical hybridity which denies pleasure and fulfilment, thus creating a space for the experience of *jouissance.*

This sense of joyous incompleteness is also emphasised by a theatrical exposition of the process through which cinematic representations achieve their aesthetic forms: namely film editing (montage). Therefore an interesting way in which *jouissance* is evoked in *House/Lights* is by dismantling unity achieved through film montage by having the live action embody the film editing process. In order to achieve this some of the scenes have their choreography directly sourced from the technicalities of the film editing process. This also results in an interesting treatment of time in the piece. The stage space is divided into two parts so there are effectively two frames, one on each side. There is a lot of action being doubled, or passed from one square to another as though between two different time frames, one just before and another just after. LeCompte recounts:

> I thought of it a bit like when you're editing a Super 8 film. You see the film running through the editing machine and you watch the

two frames go by. It was like that. You see the same action in the next frame – just a fraction of a second later.

(LeCompte in Quick 2007: 215)

The movements were often improvised and LeCompte recalls wanting the performers to be responsive and open to new possibilities offered by the film material. This multiplicity and divergence of action gives the sense of a fleeting present. Theatre is always dying and being reborn whilst film always belongs to the past. Temporal discontinuities in cinematic montage can produce an indirect image of time. Not time itself but an image thereof. The physically impossible leaps in time available through the montage of film enter into tension with the physical performance that attempts to embody and disfigure them. Theatre here becomes a machine, a physical performance of the film editing process. The temporal unity of the imaginary cinematic body is disassembled. In one scene Kate Valk's character performs a monologue on stage which is also shown on screen as a close up and in which she ponders existential matters and whether Dr Faustus will cure her viper bite (Figure 4.2). The monologue has strong sexual and sadistic overtones, oscillating between notions of pleasure and pain; pain being associated in Lacanian psychoanalysis with *jouissance,* an excessive pleasure.

The notion of excess is emphasised in this scene through repetitions and the overt theatricalisation of cinematic images which constantly thwart the possibility of perceiving a 'normalised' cinematic illusion. Kate Valk's on-screen close-up often freezes, at which points she turns and talks to her frozen image. This is achieved via superimposition in the live editing of the stage feed. Instead of editing a linear monologue, multiple time frames are being overlaid. The frozen moments are displayed beyond their time frame and juxtaposed with the new live feed and live performance. A temporal confusion arises when recorded images that belong to the past are juxtaposed with the present of the performance and made apparent as present when the live performers interact with them. Again in this case it is the live performance and theatre's *ai*sthetic effects which break the temporal unity of film montage, allowing for the perception to oscillate between instances of identification and uncanny moments of witnessing the disassemblage of cinematic illusion – the exposition of representation and its presentational construction.

House/Lights is full of chaotic, confusing and anarchic moments, nonetheless they only come about as a result of a deliberate amplification through the often disorienting interinvolvement of the theatrical and filmic space. It is in these moments that a potential experience of

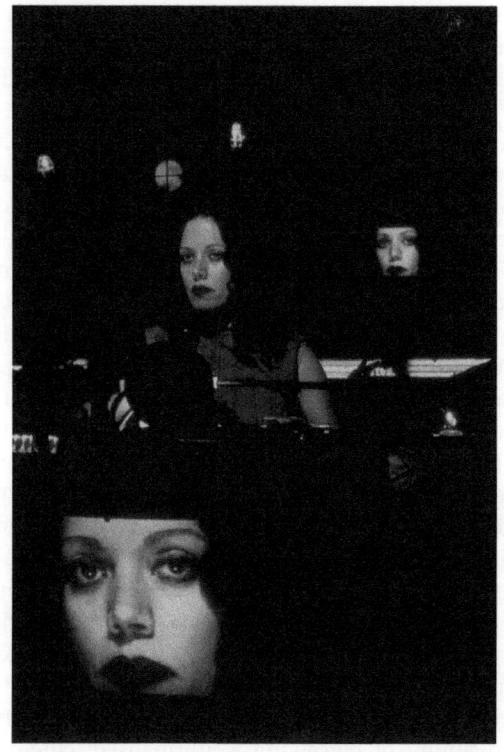

Figure 4.2   House/Lights, The Wooster Group. Pictured: Kate Valk. Photo © Paula Court

pleasure is diverted into *jouissance* making it noticeable for the spectator. Arguably it is the incomplete, in-progress and disassembled nature of this Wooster Group show which prompts the audience to connect and piece all of the disjointed elements together. 'Insofar as the work seems to be in progress, incomplete', Natalie Crohn Schmidt suggests, 'it invites our participation in the act of completing it. We become part of the process' (Crohn Schmidt 1990: 51). It is in these 'acts of completing' that a foregrounding of the 'politics of perception' occurs. This is because enjoyment is no longer aesthetically controlled by the spectacle, which is an important agent in imposing a perspective on the spectator. There is a deconstruction of cinematic montage conventions that are designed to impose a more perspectivist experience. Instead arguably the spectator gains a greater choice of how to frame what they experience and what attitude to develop towards the events presented. But what role does the free dissipatory nature of *jouissance* play in stimulating the spectator to reflect upon the pleasures that are to be derived from the spectacle and their political connotations? To return to the connotations of pleasures associated with sexual fetishism, torture and the male gaze, in the torture scene where the woman's thigh is bitten the spectator could choose either to focalise and indulge in that image of perversion or instead perceive the whole apparatus as precisely a deconstruction of that kind of pleasure to be derived from representation. Thus the perceptual choices can oscillate and there is a certain politics behind what one chooses. The very fact that this deconstruction is occurring and that the piece stimulates a freer mode of perception can also be seen as a form of political resistance to the culturally dominant cinematic tropes. One could argue therefore that the piece induces a state of awareness and reflexivity in the spectator, precisely by positioning their perceptions in the intermedial, in between spaces of *jouissance* – spaces which lie beyond representation, hence making the spectators more conscious of the forms and structures of their perceptions.

Hamlet

Hamlet's aesthetic is different to that of *House/Lights*. In *House/Lights* the focus is on the embodiment of the cinematic conventions of its intertexts, whereas, as noted above, in *Hamlet* it lies on the embodiment of the end product and on a 'visual karaoke' style exploration of Richard Burton's 1964 Broadway production. In that sense the production can be seen as an attempt to embody the pleasures and the emotional journey of viewing Burton's piece; an example of representative 'ghosting' – a 'post-representation' that lends itself to discussion in terms of Lyotard's theories. Thus the two main questions to consider in this case study are: in what way does Wooster Group's *Hamlet* stage the representation of a spectator's experience of the earlier performance? And how does this staging recuperate *jouissance*, consequently foregrounding the 'politics of perception'? In order to answer the first question let us look at the way the piece is staged and the interinvolvement of the filmic and theatrical elements in the piece.

Materialising cinematic ghosts

The Court scene, one of the earliest scenes of the performance, establishes some of the main intermedial conventions of the piece. As becomes evident, the back film projection is central to the scenographical design. This is where the edited and digitally manipulated version of

Richard Burton's *Hamlet* is screened. This film acts as the main 'source' for the performance which takes place on stage. It acts as a blueprint, a filmic script which is meticulously replicated in the live performances. The staging itself is fairly minimalistic with a few elements and props that represent the props and set used in the Burton production: a table, a few chairs, a television screen centre-stage, a live feed camera front-centre-stage and a raised platform stage-right. Most props are on wheels and are mobile. Additional elements such as a screen with frosted glass, a clothes rack for the closet scene and a chest for the grave appear whenever the scene calls for it (Figure 4.3). An initial impression of the relationship between the live action and the film performances sees the stage action as a doubling of Burton's production. The performers' positions, actions and stage impersonations come across as meticulously timed and replicated instances of the events on screen.

One way of looking at this aesthetic is as an attempt to recuperate the *mise-en-scène* from the *mise-en-cadre* in a similar fashion to that of the performances analysed so far. The doubling of performances creates an abundance of presence and allows a simultaneity of perspectives to emerge

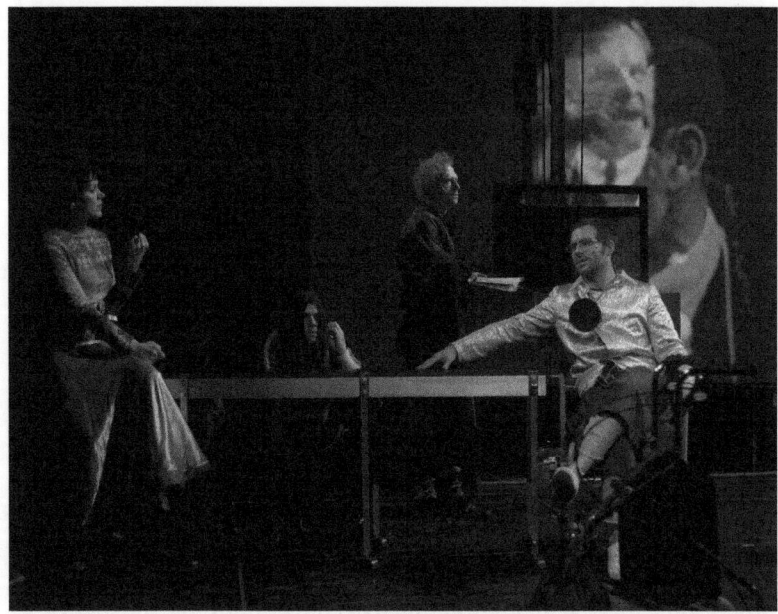

Figure 4.3   Hamlet, The Wooster Group. Pictured (l–r): Kate Valk, Casey Spooner, Scott Shepherd, Ari Fliakos. Photo © Paula Court

as far as potential audience identifications are concerned. For instance a close-up of Burton on screen has to compete for focal attention with Scott Shepherd's characterisation of Hamlet on stage. Thus, as in the other productions discussed so far, the audience is invited to engage in an act of live montage. Similarly to *House/Lights* the sense of simultaneity is further emphasised through the use of a flat screen on stage which often mediates close-ups of the live performances. However the difference here is that the staging is not an attempt to embody the impossible fantasies of cinema, but rather to explore the final visual enunciation on screen, focusing on many superficial technicalities and artefacts of cinematic imagery.

This explicit focus on the artificialities and technicalities of filmic conventions is established early in the piece and carries on throughout. For instance, a lot of attention is paid to the replication of the positioning of the set and the performers. Whenever the camera on the projected film pans slightly to the left or right the table and the chair are moved so that their positions correspond exactly with the visual perspective of the filmed image. The performers on stage reposition themselves accordingly, so as to adjust to the new angle. These instances of camera movements such as pans, tracking shots, cuts between close-up shots and establishing shots are made quite explicit during the performance. They are further accentuated by loud sound effects such as 'whooshes' which accompany the movements of chairs and tables and work as indexes of the set's mechanical movements. Quite often during these instances white noise has been digitally added to Burton's film and the exposure of the image has been intensified in order to highlight and punctuate these moments as flashes. A further emphasis has been added by picking these moments through the live-feed camera and then displaying them on the flat screen as freeze frames. Sometimes these moments of heightened intensity work to accentuate the dramatic momentum of the scene, at other times they work to undermine and obstruct the clarity of it instead. For instance Hamlet's first soliloquy was constantly upstaged by the mechanical movements of the set and distorted sound effects which distracted from the meaning and content of the speech, emphasising the artifice of the film. Arfara commented on these moments as a means of creating visual abstractions out of gestures, facial expressions and close-up details which would otherwise be embedded in a sense-making frame:

> those screens focus on pleats, hairs or the texture of the clothes. Due to coloured filters, those details become pictorial (to recall the distinction established by Daniel Arasse) since they enable us to see

the impenetrable intimacy of the creative act while remaining out of language, [...] They are 'accidents of the surface of things' that turn into 'real' abstract paintings.

(Arfara 2008: 134)

This positioning of images 'out of language', out of a realist montage sequence, emphasised the technical aesthetics of film over the actual dramatic content, creating an instability within a possible dramatic representational frame. The focus oscillated between identification with the onscreen drama and the intensified re-enactments of the filmic artefacts, 'between Brechtian distanciation and Stanislavskian interpretation' (ibid.: 135). This aesthetic creates a particular form of intermedial 'parataxis', a de-hierarchisation of conventional dramatic elements in order to shift the emphasis from dramatic content, text, meaning and representational logic, to that of the formal 'support' structures such as set movements, sound and lights. Lehmann quotes Heiner Goebbels to explain this postdramatic effect:

> I am interested in inventing a theatre where all the means that make up theatre do not just illustrate and duplicate each other but instead all maintain their own forces but act together, and where one does not just rely on the conventional hierarchy of means. That means, for example, where a light can be so strong that you suddenly only watch the light and forget the text.
>
> (Goebbels in Lehmann 2006: 86)

Lehmann then sums up the effect of parataxis: 'the spectator of postdramatic theatre is not prompted to process the perceived present instantaneously but to postpone the production of meaning (semiosis) and to store the sensory impressions with "evenly hovering attention"' (ibid.: 87). What is particular about this form of parataxis in the Wooster Group's *Hamlet* is that it accentuates the fetish of the filmic form, emphasising the sensorial impressions of film whilst postponing the content and meaning of the unfolding drama. The piece becomes a staging of a perception of the film itself. The focus of the production seems to be on staging the feeling, or the sensorial libidinal experience of watching Burton's *Hamlet*. The content and meaning of *Hamlet*'s narrative is still there but it is often postponed in favour of sensorial challenges to the filmic conventions. This movement away from the representational frame, which would instil a focus on the interpretation of the dramatic text is also embedded in the company's aesthetic strategy. Kate Valk remarks on the Wooster Group's approach to narrative and meaning in the piece: '[w]e don't talk a lot about how we are going to interpret it. It just happens in the alchemy of our physical, modern beings and we bring all of this stuff to the room, encountering the system that Liz sets up from the beginning' (Valk in Shevtsova 2013). The 'system' to which Valk is referring is the whole performative methodology of the production – the use of Burton's film as a source material for the physical performance on stage.

Another key feature of this production which contributed to the effect of parataxis and the movement away from the focus on dramatic content was the effacement of actors on the film. Throughout the whole piece the actor's images on film were being constantly effaced. At times they would appear and disappear, partially fade away or distort. At other times they would appear as partial objects with selected elements of actor's bodies being exposed. Most of these effacements and fragmentations were not planned for by the director LeCompte but were made during the editing pre-production process by the technical staff. LeCompte instructed the video editors as follows: 'I would just say, "Do what you want with this scene. Take out who you want, put in who you want, if you want to leave a leg, if you want to leave an arm, if you want to leave the whole thing and just take out the background"' (LeCompte in Shevtsova 2013). Improvisational leeway was also given to the main editor, who had access to both the original and edited material and could weave these effects in and out during the actual performance.

Overall this created an extended metaphor of the 'ghosting' effect, the performance became a representation of the ghosts of performances past and their imprint on the spectator's mind. At times this kind of fragmentation had symbolic significance, which for the most part was fortuitous and depended on the spectator's concentrated effort. For instance at the end of Act 1 Scene 5 where Hamlet makes Rosencrantz and Guildenstern swear upon their swords, only the hands and the swords were visible on screen, creating a sense of symbolic fragmentation within the image itself. Another beautiful metaphor emerges when Hamlet says 'And yet, to me, what is this quintessence of dust?' in Act 2 Scene 2, and Burton's image on film slowly fades away. The eerie sound design with frequent speech distortions and reverberation effects together with the blue-green tint of the film image further emphasised this ghostly quality on the figurative level. However the effect of effacement had presentational, indexical functions which often transcended its metaphorical, iconic and symbolic features. As a spectator I often felt that it drew my attention towards the staged performance.

The constant disappearances and appearances of the actors on film made their filmed presences unstable. This heightened the effect of parataxis by undermining the screen presence of the actors, which is one of the key carriers of meaning and identification in film. Again this thwarted the possibility of a stable perspectivist identification with the filmed characters and drew attention to the elements of 'support' that are normally hidden, concealed and made 'invisible' within the representational frame.

Libidinal archaeologies

Having established the overall framing devices of the production and the effects of parataxis, the second question to ask is how does this aesthetic recuperate *jouissance*? And in what ways does this particular re-framing of the spectator's experience as the focus of the piece heighten *jouissance*, recuperating what is lost and concealed in a direct encounter with the film.

For the director LeCompte, one of the intentions behind working on this project was to re-create the experience she had of watching the original Burton production on Broadway back in 1969. Since the rest of the cast had not seen that particular production the only point of reference became its filmed version, which, as we have seen, also became the main component of the devising methodology adopted during the creation of the piece. Hence the spectator's experience addressed by the show is that of the film – which has been watched by the actors – rather than the director's personal memories of the original staged production. Following this we should ask: what kind of 'experience' is being recreated here? A 'spectator's experience' of a film is a very broad concept since it is constituted by a multiplicity of aspects and influenced by a multitude of factors varying from person to person and the time and space in which it takes place. However if we consider the intermedial parataxis inherent in the Wooster Group's *Hamlet*, we can discern that the production was creating a performative aesthetic that emphasised the formal, rhythmic or even musical qualities of the film as opposed to its dramatic content.

In this sense it satisfied some of the conditions of Lyotard's conception of an abstract film in 'Acinema', a cinematic experience whose emphasis lies not so much in the return of narrative, representation and normalised pleasures but in the expression of 'sterile' (in Lyotard's sense) enjoyment: *jouissance*. As was explained in the previous chapter *jouissance* is a form of enjoyment which consists in a diversion from meaning (Lyotard 1989: 171). The methodology and treatment of

Hamlet employed by the Wooster Group seemed to be designed to divert the spectator's attention from a dramatic apprehension of the film to that of its formal qualities. By focusing on the artefacts, technicalities and cinematic aspects of Burton's film, *Hamlet* foregrounded the *jouissance* of the filmic experience. However this experience is complex and compound, comprising of an oscillation between the pleasures of drama and the *jouissance* of the formal and technical elements that comprise the libidinal journey through the film.

Lyotard's critique of mainstream cinema can be helpful here. Lyotard sees classical realist montage as a way of eliminating undesirable movements 'in order to protect the order of the whole (shot and/or sequence and/or film) while banning the intensity it carries' (ibid.: 170). The purpose of direction is thus to 'eliminate aberrant movements, useless expenditures, differences of pure consumption' (ibid.: 172). Lyotard then calls for a cinema that could recuperate some of these lost intensities beyond the structural confines of realist montage that are designed to preserve and protect 'the whole'. He argues for a 'libidinal economy of the cinema [that] should theoretically construct the operators which exclude aberrations from the social and organic bodies and channel the drives into this apparatus' (ibid.: 176). Arguably *Hamlet* offers such an apparatus[2] designed to foreground these cinematic aberrations. There are lots of moments throughout the piece where visual aberrations such as jolts and white-noise image distortions are being performed and/or emphasised through performance by the actors on stage. These stage images of aberration and film artefacts are then intensified through sound and visual effects so that they become instances of charged sensorial effects – foregrounded libidinal intensities in their own right.

Lyotard argues that these intensities do not emerge as mere representations of pleasure or 'representations which imitate pleasure' but as a 'kinetic problematic' a 'composite of decompositions' (ibid.: 171). The enjoyment of staging aberrations does not come from the fact that they in themselves represent pleasure. White noise and jolts are seldom representations of pleasurable moments during a spectator's experience. On the contrary they are the undesirable movements and instances that one would rather edit out, clean up or re-master. In many ways they are suggestive of the ageing and decomposing processes that affect old tapes, obstructing the clarity of the image. *Hamlet*, through its performance, creates a composition out of these decompositions. The kinetic problematic is emphasised through the set movements and part of the *jouissance* effect comes from the meticulous alignments of the set and actors on stage with the filmed image. When discussing ways of instilling a libidinal economy of cinema Lyotard calls for the mobility not of the model (representation) but of the support itself. He claims that this mobility is the opposite of cinematographic movement; 'it arises from any process which undoes the beautiful forms suggested by this latter, from any process which to a greater or lesser degree works on and distorts these forms. It blocks the synthesis of identification and thwarts the mnesic [*sic*] instances' (ibid.: 179). By mobilising the stage set and putting props in motion *Hamlet* creates a choreography that often distracts from dramatic representation. The stage set needs continuous re-adjustments in relation to the film and every such moment is a bit of a puzzle for the performers to solve, a self-referential 'kinetic problematic'. This technically oriented methodology for performance is what Valk refers to as the 'system': 'it is something that gives kinetics to the space so that things happen, and maybe collide, and people have a way to ambulate and to speak, and set the text on its feet right away so that it can run around and get articulated that way' (Valk in Shevtsova 2013: 131)

The 'system' is not subservient to the text (plot) but vice versa. In classical realist cinema (and theatre) the set and the filmic technicalities are part of what Lyotard calls the 'support'. These technical frameworks are the 'support' that underpins representations and the delivery of the screenplay (the main carrier of meaning both verbally and visually) whilst all the technicalities are held in 'invisibility'. In the Wooster Group's *Hamlet*, the expectation to interpret the dramatic functions of props and set is being postponed by the constant performative emphasis of the 'support' system. The same dynamic seems to apply to the actors' movements and actions. Let us consider Act 4 Scene 5, the scene in which Laertes, having returned from France, storms into the main hall determined to avenge his father Polonius. Claudius and Gertrude attempt to calm him down, proclaiming their own innocence, but the scene is interrupted by Ophelia who enters behaving in a manner that indicates insanity. Ophelia's madness, which Laertes blames on the death of their father, infuriates him still further, leading him to swear revenge on whoever was responsible for the murder of Polonius. He proclaims: 'Where th' offence is, let the great axe fall'. One of the striking features of this intense scene in the Wooster Group's production are the movements and gestures of the actors. They are abrupt, jerky and impulsive, as though to reflect the abrupt changes in shots and camera movements on the film. In many instances Casey Spooner playing Laertes walks backwards in order to assume specific positions in relation to the film images. At times Kate Valk playing Ophelia has to speed up her lines so that they fit the speed of the film. There are also distortion sound filters applied to Valk's vocal performance to emphasise this effect further. On a metaphorical level this kind of treatment gives the scene a delirious quality that can be easily related to the scene's thematic. On a presentational level the scene diverges from its dramatic content and works as a means of emphasising the formal aspects of the 'support' evident in the film. The actors' performances are not primarily guided by a psychological construct as would be the case with a Stanislavskian approach (also referred to as the 'system' in Shevtsova), which can be identified as part of the 'invisible' support in traditional theatre/realist cinema. Instead their physical and vocal performances are subservient to Burton's film, with an emphasis on all its glitches and technical trappings. Ari Fliakos who plays Claudius in the production sums up this approach and the relationship between 'acting' and sourcing film for performance material: 'we use the video and this particular film, to take attention off of ourselves, which is a difficult thing to do as a performer. It takes it outside of us' (Fliakos in Shevtsova 2013: 128). This distraction from the performance is what instils a reflexive stance. In these moments the aim and goal of the performance seems to be to foreground the perceptual process of seeing the film rather than encouraging a dramatic identification with a character and subsequently its dramatic content.

Thus the aim of the piece seems to be to move away from the staging of the *content* of perceptions to the staging of *forms* of perception. This is achieved through parataxis, mentioned above. It is important to recall that the effect of parataxis does not suggest a total effacement of meaning-making (semiosis), it *postpones* it instead. This is analogous to Lyotard's argument:

> Representation is essential to this fantasmatic; that is, it is essential that the spectator be offered instances of identification, recognizable forms, all in all, matter for the memory: for it is at the price, we repeat, of going beyond this and disfiguring the order of propagation that the intense emotion is felt.
>
> (Lyotard 1989: 178).

The Wooster Group's *Hamlet* does not do away with representation. The original Burton production is screened in more or less its full dramatic shape. However as a result of the continuous disfigurement of Burton's production the experience of *Hamlet* oscillates between the pleasures of character identification, narrative and representational drama and the *jouissance* of technical fetishes. This is further exemplified in the conversation between Hamlet and Horatio in the final act, which is followed by Osric's invitation to the duel. The screen is filled with mpeg compression artefacts – pixilation and other visual interruptions – making the film mostly unwatchable. The conversations are frequently distorted and manipulated through sound filters (Figure 4.4).

This scene comes towards the end of the play where the plot is approaching its climax and it marks an important instance in the overall emotional journey of the piece. This dramatic momentum intensifies the possibility of character identification. However by emphasising the technical artefacts the scene moves beyond a representational framing. There is a sense of parataxis where the clarity of the representational frame is being sacrificed for the exposure and emphasis of technical artefacts. This parataxal reversal of aesthetic hierarchies – from the representational level to the support level – 'reverses the order of propagation' of meaning-making forms, thus emphasising the libidinal charge: 'the intense emotion is felt' (ibid.: 178).

By performing these disfigured instances of the film the piece also focuses on the materiality of the medium. Not only the support structures such as actor's presence, speech and gestures are rendered opaque

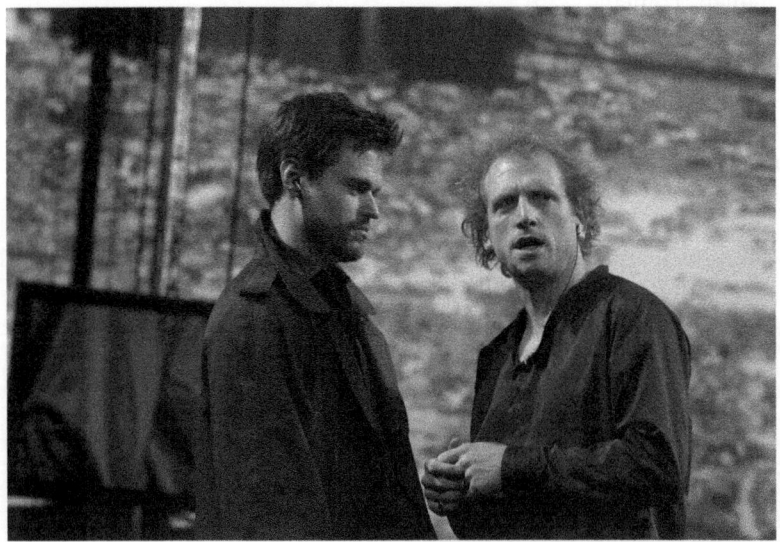

Figure 4.4 *Hamlet,* The Wooster Group. Pictured (l–r): Judson Williams, Scott Shepherd. Photo © Paula Court

but so is the film itself. When discussing his concept of libidinal cinema Lyotard proposes that: 'The film strip is no longer abolished (made transparent) for the benefit of this and that flesh, for it offers itself as the flesh posing itself' (ibid.: 179). In one instance a specific moment from Kenneth Branagh's movie *Hamlet* is rehearsed over and over again until the stage actor gets it right. This is the speech of the player followed by an interjection from Hamlet. In the movie clip we see the speech scene which is mostly an extended close-up of the actor followed by a cut to a close-up of Branagh playing Hamlet. The actor on stage asks for the moment to be repeated until he gets the entrance just right. The presentational *opaque* nature of this scene is further emphasised by the fact that the clip is played in a QuickTime window, which re-emphasises the hypermedial presence of the 'support' technology and the artificiality of cinematic construction. Thus the 'flesh' of the film (the digital clip) is extrapolated and posed as the 'flesh itself' on stage. To use Boenisch's term the presence of the film clip on stage becomes an '*ai*sthetic' effect, as it is no longer a transparent frame through which the audience may immerse themselves into an imaginary world of the movie but a presented object on stage in its own right. Perhaps it is in moments like these that 'the represented ceases to be the libidinal object while the screen itself, in all its most formal aspects, takes its place' (ibid.). Again it is important to problematise this since scenes like these establish an oscillation between the immersive, immediate framing of the action and the hypermediate, self-referential framing. Appropriately enough, this concerns the scene that immediately precedes the famous play-within-the-play. Therefore despite the presentational aspects of this scene, it can also be read as a metaphorical representation of a rehearsal before the performance of the 'Mouse-Trap'.

Conclusion

Lyotard remarked that '[c]inematography is the inscription of movement, a writing with movement, a writing with movements' (Lyotard 1989: 169). In many ways the Wooster Group's *Hamlet* becomes the opposite of this, an inscription with effacement. The constant effacement of the actors on film is a constant creation of a negative space, a perpetual erasure of presence. This erased dramatic presence 'materialises' on stage in the context of the live performance. An interesting way of looking at this notion of 'materialisation' is to consider Burton's production as a document. Thus we can ask what is at stake in the transition from the document to the stage? If we think of Burton's film as a document, a parallel can be drawn between its relationship to the original Broadway production and the relationship between the signified and what Jacques Derrida called the 'supplement'. For Derrida the 'supplement' was a sign or a collection of signs standing in for an absent presence (signified) in a mode of constant deferral. The 'supplement' in this case will be Burton's filmed production, and the absent presence will be the original 1964 Broadway production. The presence of Burton's staged Broadway production in the Wooster Group's *Hamlet* is thus dependent on the presence of its filmed version. Derrida argued that the supplement is a 'terrifying menace', because it points to the lack and the absence of the original. At the same time, however, it is also 'the first and surest protection [...] against that very menace. This is why it cannot be given up' (Derrida 1976: 175). On a thematic level this sense of menace pervades the story of *Hamlet*, based as it is on the loss, the lack, of the father and the undeterminable identity and inability to act of the protagonist. The balance between the menace of loss and Hamlet's desperate attempts to recuperate and re-enact/materialise his father's presence is central to the play. Hamlet's inability to act becomes his identity crisis. The ghosting effect of the Wooster Group's performance can be seen as a metaphor of this loss. However instead of becoming a stable 'supplement', which safeguards against the menace of the loss, the production seems to explore this sense of menace by rendering even the supplement unstable.

As the piece reaches its end there is a sense that the 'surface' of the film is becoming progressively corrupted, turning 'little by little, into a negative, [...] a progressive passage from visibility to invisibility' where the 'representation is self-destroyed, on its surface' (Arfara 2008: 137). By doing so the production undermines the sense of security provided by representational sense-making frames. One of the things that classical cinema does is to provide its audiences with a sense of security and stability when it comes to the sense-making frames. Cinema offers organised signs and representations that can be decoded by the spectator and through that it creates an illusion that one can gain 'access' to the signified. In this sense the cinematic image functions as a supplement standing in for the absent signified. Wooster Group's *Hamlet* takes the 'supplement', the filmed production, and subjects it to theatre's unstable ontology, foregrounding the insecurities behind unstable perceptual processes. By creating that sense of perceptual oscillation between the *jouissance* of the technical artefacts of the film and the dramatic content of Shakespeare's play, the production renders the filmic 'supplement' as unstable. As Arfara points out: 'Once the continuous perception of the so-called classical representation becomes impossible, the spectator is compelled to articulate the different elements of the scenic picture by herself or himself' (ibid.: 135). This instability prompts a reflexive stance on how one may apprehend and experience films. By prompting a removal from the securities of realist filmic illusions *Hamlet* creates a provocative experience of what constitutes cinematic spectatorship. By denying the illusion of direct access to the signified, the production foregrounds the 'politics of perception'. Instead of attempting to implicate the spectator in the narrative of the piece, the production tries to foreground the spectatorial experience prompting the spectators to reflect on the forms of perception that condition it.

5
The Ethics of Perception in
Wunschkonzert

In Chapter 3 I argued that the intermedial deconstruction of realist montage conventions in two pieces by Station House Opera had the potential to induce a state of reflexivity and engage the audience with a 'politics of perception'. There are many factors at play during an experience of cinema and art in general, all of which have a part in influencing and, potentially, guiding our perceptions. Politics can be broadly understood as the management of people's resources. But it also concerns the management of people's freedoms and this is where the ethical considerations come in. These can concern freedom of identity and freedom of thought but also freedom of interpretation and perception of reality. Hence this chapter will concern ethical sentiments which condition our perceptual choices. Much as was the case with aesthetic pleasure in the experience of mainstream cinema, the structures that elicit ethical sentiments may be concealed from spectators; detached as they are from the place of production of images, these structures are not necessarily brought to the forefront of the spectators' attention. There is a sense of detachment in realist cinema that can work to limit perceptual possibilities as well as the possibilities of a more active ethical engagement, and that may induce a comparatively passive and mono-perspectivist mode of spectatorship. Mainstream cinema has the capacity to induce moral and political perspectives and modes of readability precisely because the audience's participation in the construction of meaning is limited, as is their involvement in the perceptual choices they make. Much of the post-theory criticism discussed earlier was concerned with these issues and the socio-political implications of the 'cinematic apparatus' which was seen as limiting the spectator's freedom of response and political agency. This sense of detachment of the audience from the realities of production and the de-responsibility which accompanies it is a significant feature of our contemporary cinematised culture and is also conditioned by ethical sentiments. The effacement of the 'real' effectuated by realist cinema has serious implications for the ways in which we relate ethically to each other, precisely because ethical relationships that would normally arise out of real-life situations are being mediated through cinematic illusions. Thus, this chapter looks at Katie Mitchell's, *Wunschkonzert* (2008), a poignant post-cinematic production of a play by Franz Xaver Kroetz about solitude and suicide, which can be seen as a reaction to the conventional dynamic of realist cinema, which induces perceptual limitations for its audiences. The analysis below focuses on ways in which the exposition and live staging of a film production can recuperate the broken thread between the site of production and the experience of cinematic illusion. Re-establishing this link emancipates the spectators, broadening their freedom to make their perceptual choices and thus bringing the ethical implications of perceptions back from the shadows and to the forefront of attention. However, before moving on with the analysis it is important briefly to elaborate upon the relationship between the 'politics of perception' and ethics.

Lehmann claims that the 'politics of perception' and aesthetics of 'response-ability' are 'ethico-political' (Lehmann 2006: 186) phenomena, in the sense that the perceptual choices that an audience makes have political and ethical implications that could be brought to the forefront of attention. Categorically speaking, a 'politics of perception' is not so much a 'political' concept as a perceptual concept. It concerns a mode of reflexivity upon the perceptual choices that an audience makes, which implies a certain perceptual freedom and a negotiation of these choices. Hence in this chapter the concept of a 'politics of perception' will be referred to as an 'ethics of perception'. This requires a theory that will articulate the relationship between perception and ethics; a requirement which Lévinas's philosophy of ethics fulfils, articulating, as it does, the ethical as a perceptual phenomenon. The gist of Lévinas's argument is that certain perceptual phenomena create an ethical stance. What is interesting about this dynamic for the study of intermediality in post-cinematic theatre is how this relationship could be reversed or turned into a dynamic polarity. In other words it can also be used to explore the potential of the intermedial, the in-between: to explore the fluid relationship between perceptual choices and their ethical implications but also ethical sentiments and their effect on perceptual choices.

The *Wunschkonzert* is an intermedial, post-cinematic piece, directed by Katie Mitchell and premiered at the Schauspiel Köln on 5 December 2008. Mitchell has created other intermedial pieces such as *Waves*

(2007), based on Virginia Woolf's novel *The Waves*, and *Attempts on Her Life* (2007), a play by Martin Crimp. A recurrent feature in her intermedial work is the use of live performance space to construct, shoot and edit a real-time film that is displayed on stage alongside the live performance. In this sense *Wunschkonzert* shares the strategy with Mitchell's previous work. The performance space of *Wunschkonzert* consists of a wide 'studio space' stage with designated areas for a live real-time production of a film that is displayed above the top right corner of the stage set-up. The designated areas of the film production space include spaces for the filming of different types of shots (outdoor bus stop, indoor apartment space, close-ups of the main protagonist), a mini suite for the production of sound and voice-overs, an editing suite, a small chamber radio ensemble to produce the music in a soundproof glass box and spaces for storage of props. During the performance, performers, technicians and filmmakers move around the stage space producing different aspects of the film which are montaged at a desk at the back of the auditorium and displayed live (Figure 5.1).

The narrative of the film is based on a play without words by Franz Xaver Kroetz, which could be summed up as a study of the psychological states leading a lonely woman to suicide. The title *Wunschkonzert,*

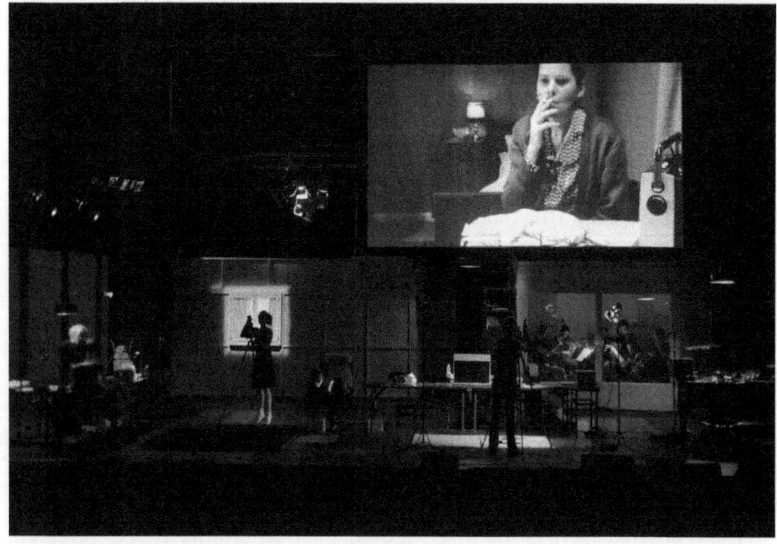

Figure 5.1 Julia Wieninger in *Wunschkonzert* by Franz Xaver Kroetz, Schauspiel Köln, 2008. Photo © Stephen Cummiskey

which was also the title of Kroetz's play, can literally be translated as a 'wish concert', which was the name of a radio programme in Germany where people would phone in and ask for classical music to be played for special occasions such as wedding anniversaries, birthdays and so on. The action of the piece, or more precisely the action of its film component, revolves around a lonely woman sitting in her apartment and preparing for suicide whilst listening to the show on the radio. The mundane actions she performs gain a dramatic significance once they are juxtaposed with fleeting memories from her past or potential alternative pathways that her life might have taken.

Thus in terms of the overall experience of the show, the audience is exposed to an aesthetic film whose psychological realism is reminiscent of Kieslowski's *Three Colors: Blue* (1993), carefully montaged and arguably exemplifying what Lyotard defines as 'libidinal normalisation' – an aestheticisation of 'reality'. At the same time, however, the audience witnesses the production of that film in scenes that are hectic, characterised by excess action and movements that are being effaced or 'discriminated' (to use Lyotard's castigating term) as they make (or not) their way to the film screen. For example, in a scene representing a romantic dream of the protagonist, a messy artificial grass patch is distilled into a stylised flashback of a woman dancing barefoot in a garden at night. The audience witnesses the transition from rubble-laden, 'unaesthetic' studio space into a stylised, gripping, 'well composed' film. They see the 'support' being made transparent and props and actors transformed through cinematic lighting and framing.

As I watched this piece my perception oscillated between the virtual world of the film and the live studio space. Attempts to watch and identify with the character on film and her very personal subjective tragedy were constantly thwarted by the live construction and the constant reminder that it was an illusion being crafted in front of my very eyes. The two worlds of film and theatre were distinctly separated in the *Wunschkonzert*, suggesting that spectators had to choose whether to identify with the main character and her story, thereby ignoring the making of it in the stage space below, or to view the film from a more critical and distanced perspective, which is what the post-cinematic set-up invited its viewers to do. In an interview about the piece, the video designer Leo Werner talks about the freedom the audience is given when watching the piece. He says: '[w]hen you talk to spectators, you realize that they go through completely different experiences. That's really fascinating. It tells you a lot about how people see' (Warner in Thiele 2008). This simultaneous exposition of theatrical and filmic space allows the audiences to choose their own experience of the piece, but it also foregrounds this choice, potentially enabling them to reflect on how they perceive and what is important for them.

Thus the opportunity exists either to repress the live action and identify with the film fiction or vice versa. It could be argued that there is something almost Freudian in the choice to repress reality and yield to the fetish of the filmic illusion. From a thematic perspective this choice might reflect the fact that the film portrayed a realistic issue despite it being obvious that it was an illusion whose construction could also be seen. The witnessing of the live construction could both amplify the need to follow the fictional narrative and at the same time intensify the dilemma as to where the focus should be placed. Adopting a more distanced critical stance and focusing on the stage space might imply a disrespect to all of those who die like that every day. But perhaps there is more at stake in the subjective urge to resist a potential critical/cynical viewing of the film story than the thematic of the piece; suicide inevitably carrying a certain emotional weight. What also complicates the matter is that the opposite argument can also be made, since the piece offers its audience the freedom to choose different perceptual perspectives.

This chapter argues that *Wunschkonzert* emancipates its spectators, giving them a greater perceptual freedom and negotiating the significance and importance of ethical sentiments in the making of perceptual choices. It is Emmanuel Lévinas whose theories concerning the role of ethics in art are to provide the theoretical underpinning to the broader discussion of ethics and perception. However, before introducing Lévinas it is useful to clarify the distinction between ethics and morality which should enable a more lucid articulation of Lévinas's theories.

Lévinas and the 'ethics of perception'

According to Jacques Rancière, morality in the old sense can be understood as the difference between fact and law. 'Morality', he argues in 'The Ethical Turn of Aesthetics and Politics', 'implied the separation of law and fact. It implied concurrently the division of different forms of morality and of rights, the division between the ways in which right was opposed to fact' (Rancière 2006: 6). This difference can be arrived at from a critical perspective by evaluating an existing situation in terms of a law that is agreed to govern it. Thus moral choices require judgement: for example, in certain states the death penalty can be deemed as moral since it concurs with the notions of justice laid out by the accepted laws therein – that it is a just punishment for a crime, an eye for an eye. Ethics however, could be broadly defined as concerning the conduct that a subject believes to be right. The ethical is not a discrepancy between fact and law, but it is that which ought to be. The death penalty can thus also be perceived as unethical, since it deprives an individual of the basic human freedom and right to live. This also comes from a humanist notion that the life of another human being is *infinitely* valuable therefore no equivalent can be taken to measure its right for existence. In this context, the notion of the infinite value of human existence renders impossible any attempt to formulate a judgement contesting its fundamental propriety. Judgements are usually based on definable value systems, whilst infinity is indefinable. Here the discrepancy between ethics and moral judgement becomes evident, because moral judgement is usually based upon moral values, whilst the ethical, as Lévinas suggests, can be perceived as concerning the infinitude of the human subject (Lévinas 1987). This notion of the *infinity* of the 'Other' is a keystone in Lévinas's philosophy.

Arguably, and for Lévinas, ethics belongs to the realm of the transcendental and intuitive, whilst morality belongs to the realm of critical judgement. This difference between morality and ethics underlies a number of intractable problems, such as why punishments such as the death penalty remain so controversial; it can lead to a paradox where capital punishment can end up being perceived as both moral and unethical. The conflict between affective response, belonging to the realm of the ethical, and critical judgement, belonging to the realm of morality, is an important aesthetic feature of many films that deal with the issue of the death penalty. Examples of this would be Lars von Trier's *Dancer in the Dark* (2000) or Bennett Miller's *Capote* (2005). This discussion will be revisited in the final chapter below, on *Dogville*. However, according to Lévinas, considerations of ethics in art are problematic since ethical engagement requires a full cognitive, face to face engagement with the 'Other' that art – because of its aestheticisation and spatial/temporal displacement of subject matter – fails to convey. From an audience standpoint films such as those cited above allow for a reflexivity upon matters of ethical conduct, but do not amplify an awareness of ethical perception because the subject matter tends to be specifically framed by the filmmakers, through aesthetics and narrative structures, and these framings are never explicitly challenged. As I will argue this is different in the case of a post-cinematic theatre piece such as *Wunschkonzert* – the result of its *ai*sthetic and intermedial properties.

There are two lines of criticism of Lévinas's approach to ethics that concern the adaptation of his theory to artworks and that will prove crucial in discussing the ethics of perception in *Wunschkonzert*. These are outlined by Edith Wyschogrod in 'The Art in Ethics: Aesthetics, Objectivity, and Alterity in the Philosophy of Emmanuel Lévinas'. First, for Lévinas 'ethics is an unmediated relation to the *Other*' (Wyschogrod 1995: 137, emphasis added), it essentially transcends linguistic and conceptual structures by means of a nonlinguistic access to the 'Other'. She argues that for Lévinas the routes of access or 'interfaces' with the 'Other' are essentially non-linguistic. They include, 'the human face, an idea of the infinite that exceeds any description of it, sensation as a noncognitive relation of sensing and sensed' (Wyschogrod 1995: 137). In itself this approach is often problematised in academia, for example, Jürgen Habermas critiques the notion of placing ethics beyond the realm of language, hence silencing the subject and rendering meaningless the moral norms that are grounded in discursive reasoning. His theory of 'discourse ethics' (Habermas 1990: 195) locates ethical judgements within discursive practices that can be negotiated and cognised by means of propositional language. The second line of criticism is that Lévinas posits art as essentially anti-presentational (that is, as representational). Art divests objects of their forms, displacing them from their original temporal and spatial circumstances and thus the outcome is not present in the way that it would normally be presented to cognition in reality. In reality objects are experienced and cognised within a complex network of relations concerning their function and utility in given circumstances. According to Lévinas, art lifts objects out of these constituent networks, replacing the field of forms with pure abstracted sensations. It is problematic to think of art as divested of forms and this point becomes yet further complicated when it comes to theatre, primarily because of theatre's inherent *ai*sthetic and presentational properties as a hypermedium.

The first line of criticism of Lévinas concerns the fact that ethical engagement lies within an unmediated relationship with the 'Other'. Consequently, the first step in understanding this is to elaborate on Lévinas's concept of the 'Other' and on what is at stake in the ethical engagement with it. It should be noted that the 'other' and the 'Other' are two different concepts for Lévinas, although both denote another human being. The former, 'other', is reducible to discourse and can be apprehended as an entity and thus equated with oneself. The actions of the other can be measured against a law of conduct. Thinking of the other for Lévinas is thus thinking of other human beings from the perspective of values and knowledge systems that one possesses. In short it is about thinking about someone else from one's own discursive perspective. The 'Other' however is irreducible to the first-person 'I'. It is an entity infinitely altered and ungraspable by discursive means, such as language. The 'Other' cannot be objectified or discursively compartmentalised. The very 'strangeness of the *Other*, his irreducibility to the *I*, to my thoughts and my possessions' (Lévinas 1969: 33, emphasis added) is what, according to Lévinas, calls into question the notion of moral and 'ethical' judgement that seeks to equate human beings in terms of their actions. Thus ethics for Lévinas essentially transcends linguistic and conceptual structures by means of a non-linguistic or pre-linguistic access to the 'Other'. This is why his theories are interesting for this chapter since he sees the ethical as emerging and resulting from a 'fuller' perceptual apparatus, which not only includes the rational, conscious, discursive components of perception but also the affective and unconscious ones and hence can be applicable to the full perceptual spectrum that theatre as a hypermedium can offer.

So how do we engage ethically with the 'Other'? Essential to Lévinas's understanding of ethical engagement, the key access route to the 'Other' is the human face. The human face commands responsibility for the 'Other', where an essential component of this compulsion is located before any volition or discursive deliberation can take place. In the chapter titled: 'Nonintentional Affectivity, Affective Intentionality, and the Ethical in Lévinas's Philosophy' (Tallon 1995), Andrew Tallon tells a story to illustrate this dynamic. The story is about a Hawaiian policeman who sees a man in the act of committing suicide about to jump off a cliff, and feels compelled to risk his own life in trying to save the man, charging after him and even drawing another policeman into the attempt in a strange magnetic chain reaction: this provokes the question of why a human being responds like that, in contradiction to all rational decision and volition. It is an instinctual response which Lévinas explains as an acknowledgement of the infinite humanity of the 'Other' or the recognition of the created image of God, which due to its infinitude resists conceptualisation and therefore fails to be fully realised in language. Language cannot explain the self for Lévinas, and within this failure lies the proof of what constitutes the self beyond language.[1]

Surely, however, the human face is not limited to being perceived as an unfathomable expression of the self, the 'Other', whose encounter exceeds conceptualisation and definition through language? It can also be viewed as a sign, or rather a symbol, that produces an excess of meaning due to its very presence. Tallon suggests the following when analysing the significance of the face in Lévinas's philosophy of ethics:

> the reason why the face communicates more meaning than itself is that there is an affective connaturality not between my knowing and the other but between my being and the other. It is what Ricoeur calls an 'existential assimilation,' or what Sartre calls an affective intentionality when he says that 'Heidegger's being-with is not knowledge,' and what I would call an affective connaturality.
>
> (Ibid.: 111)

The engagement with the face, as Andrew Tallon explains, thus has two moments, that of affective intentionality and that of '*non*intentional' affectivity. He maps them out onto a Jungian conflict between the conscious 'ego' and the pre-conscious 'Self'.

> Affective intentionality, as one of consciousness's three intentionalities, is an activity of ego, taking the ego as the center of consciousness. *Non*intentional affectivity, however, is a passivity of the Self, taking the Self as the center of the whole psyche, of which consciousness is a small part. Ego and Self are complementary and connected because both are of the psyche. If we accept that the psyche communicates within itself, namely, between the ego and Self, through symbols, and accept the face as a real symbol, and further accept that the unconscious psyche as unconscious has no intentionalities (for intentions are experiences of consciousness), then we have at least a formal structure for explaining [...] the possible content or quality of the connection as ethical.
>
> (Ibid.: 112)

What is crucial to Lévinas's argument, according to Tallon, is that the Self can overrule the ego – the affective response can overtake logic and critical response. The meeting with the 'Other' towards whom we may feel 'responsible':

> is an event which by transcending the ego calls forth from the Self a response that exceeds and dethrones the ego – precisely by driving it out of the paradise of enjoyment as the center of consciousness back to an anarchic 'past' so remote as to arise from a nonintentional, nonconscious affectivity – and places it into question in such a way that one experiences it as answer-ability, respons-ibility [*sic*].
>
> (Ibid.: 113)

This is essentially a reversal of Freud's approach but also of psychoanalytic approaches to cinema that are based on Freud's theory. In short Freud tried to map out the unconscious by creating an artificial language to describe it and develop a discourse for it. He employed his critical faculties to create an analysis of the unconscious in order to reveal what motivates human behaviour. In Freud's model of the Superego–Ego–Id[2] there is an implicit hierarchy where the unconscious affective drives of the Id are subservient to the decision making Ego, and the Ego is in turn subservient to the ideal, 'raw model' Superego. The Superego overrules the decision-making process influenced by all the different dimensions of the psyche, whilst the input from the Id is mostly repressed. Lévinas reverses this relationship by arguing that the immediate unconscious affective impulse can be a key overruling factor of response capable of overthrowing reason and logic.

So how can we relate this first line of criticism to the *Wunschkonzert*'s intermedial strategies in foregrounding the 'ethics of perception'? This first line of criticism has important affinities with Lehmann's notion of aesthetics of 'response-ability'. The two antagonistic moments of response outlined by Tallon, the 'affective response' and the 'logical and critical response', can be applied to an analysis of film and theatre. These two moments have an affinity with Eisenstein's two moments of the affective 'shock' and critical 'thought' in the experience of the cinematic image. By extension, the coupling of these two moments into what Lyotard defined as 'libidinal normalisation' has often been attributed to classical realist film, and subjected to criticism by post-theory critics. The criticism consisted of how the affective power of cinema justified the represented ideological constructs that would also carry moral and ethical judgements. However, post-theory critics such as Baudry, Metz and MacCabe placed the emphasis on the 'critical', discursive moment, essentially wanting to break away from the affective 'spell' of the cinematic experience and rationalise it. By rationalising this experience the ideology – and hence the moral and ethical implications of what was being represented – would be uncovered and the ethical response could then be reasoned. Contrary to the post-theory critics Lévinas places the emphasis on the pre-linguistic, affective moment which lies beyond discourse and judgement. Ethical responses are thus not subordinate to reason but to unconscious impulses. As mentioned before such an approach to ethics is problematic since it places ethics beyond the realm of language, hence silencing the subject and rendering meaningless the moral norms that are grounded in discursive reasoning. Nonetheless it can make Lévinas appealing to critics trying to explain the alluring ethical power of art. Of course Lévinas's theory is not strictly a theory of ethics in art or cinema, but it has been adapted to this context in the past as it will be below.

Wunschkonzert has the potential to intensify and uncouple the two moments articulated by Tallon, by undoing the structures that bind them together on an *ais*thetic level through the interinvolvement of film and theatre. This in turn creates an experience similar to what Tallon defines as a questioning of these two moments, an experience of 'answer-ability', 'respons-ibility'. One moment consists of immediate affective responses eliciting a particular ethical stance, whilst another consists of an awareness of ethical sentiments as a discourse and a perceptual choice made accordingly. However before analysing the way in which the aisthetic properties of the *Wunschkonzert* potentially elicit this questioning, it is necessary to articulate the ontological status of film and theatre in relation to Lévinas's theories of ethics. This is essential in order to adapt his theory, which rests on the notion of an unmediated, fully cognitive perception, to intermedial theatre, which by its very definition is partially mediated. What will prove interesting in this adaptation is that theatre is not so much a medium but a hypermedium hence potentially more compatible with the parameters of Lévinas's theory than other forms of art. This requires an understanding of the second line of criticism outlined by Wyschogrod.

This second line of criticism of Lévinas's theory is that he posits art as essentially anti-presentational (that is, as representational). As a result the experience of art is 'infracognitive and dangerously nonethical' (Wyschogrod 1995: 138), since the unmediated relationship with the 'Other' is lost. For Lévinas art is a shadow of reality, which neither replicates nor yields the object by presenting it to the spectator. These 'shadows' are not signs that transparently point towards the objects they represent but are images 'of a certain opacity' (Lévinas 1987: 6) in themselves born in the act of resemblance. Resemblance here is understood not as a comparison between an artwork and the original, but as 'the very structure of the sensible as such' (ibid.: 8). In other words, according to Lévinas, art is a structure conveying the sensible experience, one that is essentially estranged from the original.

As a result of this estrangement and withdrawal of the shadow of art from real experience, art becomes atemporal. This atemporality of the shadow renders it trapped and incapable of yielding itself to the world of action. Lévinas seems to talk about an eternally enduring instant of an artwork, an image of movement congealed in a 'quasi-eternal dura-tion' (ibid.: 9). He exemplifies this with reference to the Laocoön:

> Within the life, or rather the death, of a statue, an instant endures infinitely: eternally Laocoön will be caught up in the grip of ser-pents [...] Eternally the future announced in the strained muscles of Laocoön will be unable to become present [...] An eternally suspended future floats around the congealed position of a statue like a future forever to come [...] In this situation the present can assume nothing, can take on nothing, and thus is an impersonal and anonymous instant.
>
> (Ibid.)

In this sense Lévinas's interpretation of the Laocoön is very similar to Eisenstein's, where the latter explained the image of movement, result-ing from montaged elements, of an 'impossible' posture. For Lévinas non-plastic arts, such as music, theatre, literature and cinema, are also incapable of shattering this fixity of images. Characters in novels and films are still prisoners of their own shadowy reflection, 'commit-ted to the infinite repetition of the same acts and the same thoughts' (ibid.: 10). One could draw an analogy here with Pirandello's play *Six Characters in Search of an Author*, where the family of six characters find themselves fatally trapped within the plot of the play. But what does Lévinas's concept of art being a 'shadowy reflection' of life imply for artistic practice and how does an artist essentially go about constructing it? Lévinas sums up that 'what we call the artist's choice is the natural selection of facts and traits which are fixed in a rhythm, and transform time into images' (ibid.: 10). If we were to extend this into film craft, again an affinity with Eisenstein can be found. For Eisenstein the essen-tial component of montage is its rhythm, which enables the creation of a metaphor, a specific selection of movements bound by a generalised rhythmic dimension (for example the shots of Aurora's crew rhythmi-cally montaged with the ship's revolving engine – the beating heart of the revolution). Therefore metaphors in film can also function to trans-form time into images. So even if realist film is capable of conveying an image of movement, this 'movement' is still immobilised and following on from Lévinas it can be stated that this immobilisation is essentially an aesthetic limitation of realist film.

For Lévinas the experience of aesthetics in art, 'both as creation and appreciation of the aesthetic object – is a kind of shamanistic seizure of consciousness by being prior to being's assumption of form' (Wyschogrod 1995: 138), a pure sensation. But nonetheless this sensation is a form of imprisonment, a constructed passivity, allowing for an impersonal mode of being. As a result, representational art such as classical realist film may be deemed as 'non-ethical' according to Lévinas since it cannot offer an unmediated relationship with the 'Other' that would prompt immediate responsive action. It should also be noted that Lévinas's critique of art focuses mainly on the way that art immobilises 'reality' through *aesthetic* means. He does not take into account the *aisthetic* modes which can problematise the aestheticisation of reality and the passivity of its experience. Arguably the *Wunschkonzert* can expose both the aesthetic cinematised representations – which 'trap' and 'freeze' instances of reality like shadows cast on a wall – and at the same time expose the presentational, *ais*thetic nature of the production process of these images. Perhaps in this intermedial exposition and deconstruction of the effacement process that lies at the heart of realist cinema (the effacement resulting from the transition from *mise-en-scène* to *mise-en-cadre*) lies the potential to elicit an ethical dimension of response that is otherwise lost to it?

Lévinas and the post-cinematic

Before answering that question with an analysis of the *Wunschkonzert*, it is useful to articulate in more detail a few of Lévinas's terms in relation to post-cinematic theatre and to see how they apply to the different ontologies of film and theatre components in the piece. First of all, the distinction Lévinas makes between art and reality cannot be easily applied to a piece like *Wunschkonzert*. One can easily develop the perception that, in *Wunschkonzert*, the corporeal theatrical dimension strays towards being deliberately artificial, self-reflexive and critical, whilst the 'aesthetic' realist film attempts to present a 'realistic', affective, illusionary world, dominated by close-ups of the protagonist's face, which could be easily conflated with Lévinas's face-to-face ethical experience. Let us unpick the two ontological dimensions, that of film and theatre in the context of Lévinas's theories, beginning with the film component of the piece.

Realist cinema in general could be classified here as 'art', a shadow of reality, a Freudian fetish substitute, which in fact would be very close to the 'double mirroring' that Metz claims to comprise the experience of film. Following on from this reading, Wyschogrod's remark that art from Lévinas's standpoint could be seen as 'infracognitive and dangerously nonethical' (Wyschogrod 1995: 138) may also apply to realist cinema. This is because in films the subject matter is divested of form in the sense of form presenting itself to cognition in a 'real' setting. Films cannot present the spectator with a full cognitive experience therefore the experience of the ethical is compromised, if one were to follow Lévinas strictly, and thus it is subject to 'augmentation by criticism' (ibid.). The film component of the *Wunschkonzert* shows us discontinuous and fragmented shadows of reality. It shows images of the protagonist and elements of what would appear to be her apartment. These representations only merge into a portrayal of the reality of that person's solitary lifestyle when the spectator brings in external knowledge, employing their critical faculties. Because these film images are essentially disconnected or being made disconnected as the show unfolds they cannot – on their own – offer an ethical engagement in Lévinas's terms. The experience of film here is concealed within a 'realist aesthetic' that perhaps does not have the potential to elicit the type of questioning and reflexivity that Tallon attributes to Lévinas's notions of ethical engagement. From this standpoint realist cinema can offer an experience of perception of ethics (representation of ethical dilemmas) but not the converse, an experience of ethics of perception (the ethical choice to be made in the way that reality is to be perceived). This argument rests on the assumption that realist films replace the ways in which causal chains and networks between objects in reality are perceived and cognised with artificial forms and conventions. In that sense art is not formless, but its perceived aesthetic forms do not correspond to the perceived 'real' forms as cognised in reality. How far that is true is very arguable. Since Eisenstein's early writings cinematic aesthetics have been posited as transcendental and revealing of a philosophy of perception. Further, cinematic aesthetics influence the way people perceive, imagine and experience reality itself. (In Chapter 1 this was considered in terms of Baudry's theory of the 'cinematographic apparatus' and the post-theory postulates, wherein it was argued that mainstream cinema spectators were implicated within a wider ideological context that conditioned their worldview and that the only way to emancipate them was to decontextualise or, as suggested, theatricalise the process of production of these films.) Thus in the analysis below I will be looking at how the *Wunschkonzert* can re-frame and theatricalise the process of production of a realist film.

The other ontology at stake here is that of the theatrical space. Theatre is more problematic in the context of Lévinas's theories since while it can be deemed as an art form, lifting stories, characters and places out of their 'original' constituency into an imaginary world created on stage, it can also be interpreted as creating a world that co-exists with that of the spectator, abiding by the same laws of physics, time and space and contained within the social arena in which the audience is situated. In this sense, theatrical presence can go beyond representation and become a presentation of its own existence. On stage Therese Dürrenberger plays the protagonist as both the character and the actor/performer, and the set-up of *Wunschkonzert* emphasises this ambivalence.

Even though the film component of *Wunschkonzert* arguably remains 'nonethical' in Lévinas's terms when perceived purely as a piece of film, the performance as a whole is evidently not a film. The film in it can offer a representation of a life on the brink of suicide, but it is also an electronic image on stage, derived from a studio space that constructs it as the show progresses, therefore it has its specific presentation. If *Wunschkonzert* was just a film then the reality it attempts to represent would have to be imagined, which would prove Lévinas's point about the 'formlessness' of art and the need for the spectator to fill in the context in order for moral and ethical implications to be assessed. This is still part of what goes on during the performance but the audience is also confronted with the reality from which the film is derived, that is, the reality of a studio space with live performers. The 'ethics of perception' can emerge out of the way in which the audience chooses between the possibilities of experiencing this performance. It can be experienced as a realist representation of a solitary woman's existential tragedy or it can be seen as a critical statement on the way cinema shamelessly claims to dissect people's lives, claiming truth value for the illusion it conveys. Alternatively the performers creating the film on stage can be read as paying homage to the protagonist by sustaining the illusion of her life and thus refusing to let her die, since she dies when the film ends.

How does the interinvolvement of theatre and film work in the *Wunschkonzert* to produce this effect? The piece unfolds as the protagonist prepares for her own death whilst engaging in mundane actions such as eating, washing or going to the toilet. The music of the 'wish concert' played on the radio comes into poignant contrast with a solitary woman preparing for suicide. The detachment of the stage action where the elements of the film are acted out further emphasises this sense of isolation and separation. This becomes very clear in instances where the protagonist's actions on film are performed by other actors. For example, in one of the scenes Dürrenberger walks into the bathroom but her footsteps are performed by someone else. The detachment between the *mise-en-cadre* and the *mise-en-scène* is emphasised by the use of film close-ups which enable an almost face-to-face affective engagement. By contrast the depth of the stage, where the actor is located physically, and the frequent interruption of the audience's view by a descending wall of the apartment set, almost like a tomb closing upon her, can create a distancing effect but also emphasise isolation. The other perspective is that of the stage cluttered with a busy studio space. There are lots of performers and stage-hands performing additional extreme close-ups or filling material which becomes perfectly synchronised on the film. This emphasis on perfection and craft is almost like a forensic reconstruction of the illusion presented on film.

Going back to Lévinas, this piece could be read as teasing the immobility of the narrative to which all the elements of the spectacle are subservient. This is because the film is constructed live as, so to speak, is the 'shadow' of the character's reality. The witnessing of the live construction cannot help but carry an implicit awareness of the potentiality of a theatrical event. Even though the theatrical event is scripted, the audience might crave that perhaps things could have turned out differently and the protagonist could have been saved from her prescribed 'fate'. Fate is what Lévinas ascribes to realist art, the fixity of time in an image. In *Wunschkonzert* there is an ongoing play with this fixity of time, wherein the image created (that of the personal tragedy of the protagonist) retains the potential for change as a result of the 'inter-involvement' of film and theatre. This potential change – a way out, a last minute turn of events – intensifies the drama of a fatalistic suicide. In doing so it can also be read as working against itself by making explicit the fact that an audience invests emotionally in a spectacle that is intrinsically untrue. The relationship between reality (an unknown individual who may have died in a similar way to that performed by the protagonist) and the shadow of reality (the image of time created by the spectacle, the narrative) is constantly dislodged by the production process exposed on stage. This triggers an oscillation between these two perspectives (at least) – one of the realist film representation and the other of the presentational stage action – which can provoke an awareness of one's affective responses to the performance and by extension, within the context of Lévinas's argument, of one's ethical engagement.

In one of the later scenes the protagonist takes out a box of sleeping pills and places the pills neatly in a row on a desk in front of her bed. Earlier scenes have sparked the spectators' imagination, enabling them to fill in the 'traces' of her past life, so this scene has a considerable emotive charge. Cinematically it is a well balanced moment. Both the nostalgic soundtrack, featuring a Mozart serenade, and the film montage give the scene an appropriate weight, which is further emphasised by Dürrenberger's brooding performance. At the same time, on the live production stage, the audience can hear the sounds of the pills being snapped out of the plastic box and the music ensemble playing the soundtrack of the radio. They see the hands laying out the pills being filmed in close-up, but the action being performed by a different actor. We also see Dürrenberger in a different space, performing the appropriate facial expressions, which are montaged with the rest. These kinds of collisions occur throughout the performance and have a slightly comical aspect in the way that they undercut the film. But they can also become frustrating as they undermine the film construction, disrupting identification with the character. This disjunction also raises the question of whether it is wrong to undermine the subject matter of the film? After all the fiction of the film concerns death, which is a serious universal subject, something which ought to be approached with consideration.

Realist film requires an imaginary supplement, in other words the world that the audience imagines that lies beyond the screen depiction. This supplement or imaginary reality beyond the depictions offered by the film becomes juxtaposed or even overridden by the process of production being performed on stage. This is because the out-of-field of the *mise-en-cadre* is materialised and presented in the theatrical space. The unity of the image which arises out of discontinuous montaged fragments becomes thus interinvolved with the reality of the production process, experienced live. As a result affective engagement with the film, with the power of the face conveyed through close-ups and montage, is undercut by the stage reality which works against the truth of the film by triggering a critical faculty. In this situation, the 'ethics of perception' do not emerge out of the film material itself but out of the choice that a spectator is compelled to make between the fiction created on film and the staged process of its production. It is like shifting emphasis between Freud's critical approach and Lévinas's notions of dominating affectivity. By Freud's critical approach I mean a dynamism where emotions stimulated by the spectacle would be reinstated into thought, into a discourse that would explain their origins and implications and give them a context. In the case of *Wunschkonzert* this would mean identification with the filmed fiction and the acceptance of it as a fetish, a shadow of reality, or a mirror, to use Metz's terms. To feel pity for the protagonist could thus be explained by all the associations and possible contexts that the film triggers discursively. But what could be at stake is the shift of emphasis, from the critical 'at the back of my head I *know* this is just an illusion' perception, to what Lévinas claims is a dynamic dominated by affectivity. In the moment when the choice is made to indulge in an affective engagement, the image of the film no longer becomes knowable but is instead deeply affective, overruling the possibility of a critical stance. The story of the suicidal woman thus becomes compelling and affective, demanding that the spectator repress the reality of the stage production in order to identify with it. Surely this effect can also occur during the experience of a standard realist film – but then the perception is prone to be yet again justified by the logic of the fetish. The difference here is that a withdrawal from the film's fiction occurs as a result of the post-cinematic set-up, where the film itself becomes an ontologically distinct interface. Thus the spectator is put in a less passive and more active position where they constantly have to make a choice, a response, a decision as to the way in which they wish to engage. Following Lévinas's logic it is the unknown nature of these affective responses, which in the case of the *Wunschkonzert* may result from the particular defamiliarisation of the film fiction, that brings about the ethical dimension of this perceptual choice.

Also key to this amplification of ethical perception are the temporal dimensions of the piece. As noted above, the romantic fantasies of the protagonist are represented on film by a shot of two pairs of feet dancing in what seems to be a garden at night to the accompaniment of music played on the radio. These shots are constructed live by separate performers in the studio space and juxtaposed with moments when the woman is pondering suicide. The temporality of these scenes is complex. There is (1) the time of the performance which constructs the film, (2) the time of narrative arising from the fragmented performance on stage, (3) the time of the narrative of the film, (4) a separate flash-back time of the romantic fantasies within the film and (5) the time of juxtaposition between the film and the representations derived from the stage action. At least two temporalities that are significant for this analysis become immanent: the temporality of the film fiction, which constantly affixes the action, and the temporality of the live present of the performance. The experience of film fiction could be what Lévinas terms the 'meanwhile', the interval which is traversed in this case by the spectator. This 'meanwhile', despite enabling the spectator to inhabit and identify with an illusion is nonetheless posited as a prison, a fate. Lévinas describes it as an instant of 'eternally suspended future [... where...] the power of freedom congeals into impotence' (Lévinas 1987: 9). It is the experience of this frozen interval of time, the image of movement and the anticipation of cinematic suture which eventually becomes eternally affixed on the celluloid that according to Lévinas makes art 'irresponsible'.

> Art brings into the world the obscurity of fate, but it especially brings the irresponsibility that charms as a lightness and grace. It frees. To make or to appreciate a novel and a picture is to no longer have to conceive, is to renounce the effort of science, philosophy, and action. Do not speak, do not reflect, admire in silence and in peace – such are the counsels of wisdom satisfied before the beautiful.
>
> (Lévinas 1987: 12)

But the experience of *Wunschkonzert* is not solely made up of experiencing the potentially frozen temporality of film fiction, which as Lévinas argues leads to a particular detached form of 'irresponse-ability'. The live performance that constructs and underscores the fictitious world can potentially negotiate 'response-ability'. The 'meanwhile' of fiction is constantly juxtaposed with the live performance, causing the spectator to reflect upon the construction of the film. The film fiction in the piece relies on aesthetics and metaphorical structures congealing to describe the fate of the protagonist. One of the extended metaphors in the story is waiting. It finds its picturesque epitome at the end of the piece with a shot of a clock face that catches the first sunbeams of approaching morning. This could be read as an image of fatality, of the protagonist's death. It is an expression of an inevitable fate that one may accept as a spectator and ultimately indulge in while appreciating the final catharsis. In this sense the film represents an ethical issue, a chain of events whose consequence is to lead a socially isolated person to suicide. But this film image constantly collides with the live manifestation of its own construction. The metaphors in the film images are constantly thwarted and undone by the actuality and the presentness of the live construction of these very images. As Lévinas claims: '[b]eyond all metaphor, such would be the voice of ethical conscience' (Lévinas 1998: 151).

This oscillation between the temporality of the sealed fate and the potentiality of its construction can stimulate the audience to reflect upon the 'ethics of perception', their 'ethical conscience'. For instance, this temporal disorientation can juxtapose the moments of affective response and critical judgement and interrogate them beyond any metaphorical function. Consequently as spectators we may be posed with an ethical dilemma as to our choice of perception of the piece. On the one hand, the poignant dramatic film demands identification and empathy even though it is constantly rendered as a lie through an exposition of its live construction. On the other hand, the critical stance unmasks the inner working of a 'cinematic apparatus' which seeks to unify and simplify a social problem, but it can also easily be perceived as cynical, inappropriate and disrespectful. Is it ethical to portray – in what is interpretable as a potentially voyeuristic way – the intimate choices that might lead an individual to suicide? Or is it ethical not to represent them at all, and pretend that these problems simply do not exist?

This interpretation of the interinvolvement of the live performance and film in this piece assumes that the live performance is read as cold and forensic, essentially inhuman, whilst the film is the space which invites a more empathetic and affective engagement. This polarity finds confirmation in Lehmann's distinction between the warmth and coldness of a theatrical image. He claims that:

> [f]or someone who expects the representation of a human – in the sense of psychological – world of experience, [postdramatic theatre] can manifest a *coldness* that is hard to bear. It is especially alienating because in the theatre we are dealing not just with visual processes but with human bodies and their warmth, with which the perceiving imagination cannot avoid associating human experiences.
>
> (Lehmann 2006: 95)

We could bifurcate the filmic space and the live performance space into a space of warmth and a space of coldness. In fact Katie Mitchell makes a similar remark in the interview with Rita Thiele: 'You can have hot, emotional experiences when you watch the woman in the film output. But you can also cool down by watching the actors below who organise the detail shots and produce sounds such as footsteps in curious ways' (Mitchell in Thiele 2008). The psychological realism of film and its allure would play an important part in defining the film as a humanist, warm space. However the matter is once again complicated by the fact that we are not just dealing with film but with a post-cinematic piece of theatre. As Lehmann suggests, the bodies in postdramatic theatre (and one could read the live performance aspect of *Wunschkonzert* as post-dramatic) invite the expectation of a humanist reading because of their warmth. However, this expectation of warmth may clash with the 'de-psychologization' (Lehmann 2006: 95) of a postdramatic performance and it could be argued that the forensic quality of the live performance in *Wunschkonzert* is inhuman in comparison to the film. This is very similar to an expectation that one may have of realist cinema which quite often exhibits a warmth and a 'psychologization' in terms of how identification with characters is elicited. However, in *Wunschkonzert* the warmth of the live action can also reverse this polarity. The live performers can be read as sustaining the character's life. This is in a way derived from an aesthetic strategy adopted by Kroetz and maintained by Mitchell. Throughout the piece the protagonist performs simple daily tasks. She goes to the toilet, eats supper, brushes her teeth and listens to the radio, placing it opposite herself on the table as if it were a friend. Katie Mitchell suggests that the logic behind the performance of these mundane tasks is that of clinging to life:

> I believe that this woman struggles to hold on to life, and that little bit she can hold on to are these objects. Those are the only relationships that she has: with cups, fish, her cigarette pack and her handbag. She has no other relationships or things that hold her in life. I love the scene in which she puts the radio on the opposite side of the table as if she were talking to a friend. It is extremely desperate. When your life is reduced to the relationship with a piece of cheese or a teacup then it is very hopeless.
>
> (Mitchell in Thiele 2008)

In *Three Colors: Blue* Kieslowski uses a comparable strategy. The story deals with a character in a similar situation – a woman on the brink of suicide after having lost her husband and daughter in a car accident. In *Wunschkonzert* all these vital little moments are created on stage by the live performers. If they stop performing, the film character will die. There is a depressing sense of solitude surrounding the character on film and the lively stage performers can offer a refuge from this. The shift to perceiving the live performance as warm can thus be stimulated in this piece by the juxtaposition of the temporalities of the sealed fate of the protagonist on film and the inherent potentiality of the film's live construction. That is because the potentiality of the live performance suggests, at least on an unconscious level, that her life can still be saved.

Again this reading carries an 'ethics of perception'. This is because the live performers can be seen as a group of people paying homage to the protagonist and respecting her existence by doing everything in their power to keep her alive, almost saving her life. It is the right thing to do: according to Lévinas human life, is 'the ultimate value, the unassailable value' (Lévinas 1998: 203) and therefore to attempt to save a life lies beyond judgement. Even though we are discussing the life of a filmic representation, the live theatricalisation of it complicates the ethical sentiments. The post-cinematic setup of *Wunschkonzert* brings the filmic reality to the realm of the live, and beyond all metaphor. Thus the ethical perception greatly depends on the mode of engagement that the spectator adopts during the piece. It is the simultaneity and the exposition of the process of production of a realist fiction that allows for this emancipation, and stimulates the spectator to be active in the perceptual choices they make, inviting them to be reflexive of these choices.

Conclusion

This chapter has looked at the ways in which the interinvolvement of theatre and film in *Wunschkonzert* plays out a tension between immediate ethical sentiments, which influence perceptual choices, and ethical and moral judgements that may condition and provoke reflection upon these choices. Through its intermedial strategy it recuperates and stages the relationship between the *mise-en-scène* and the *mise-en-cadre*, broadening the spectrum of perceptual choices for the spectator. By doing so, *Wunschkonzert* can be seen as effectuating a post-cinematic reaction to the fact that realist cinema conceals its modes of production, hence removing and/or limiting the audience's engagement with the process of production of meaning and consequently also with the ethico-political considerations that may arise out of such participation. Like the pieces by Station House Opera in the earlier chapter it effectuates a certain resistance to the notion of a passive, mono-perspectivist mode of spectatorship.

The piece can also be seen as a reaction against the cultural efface-ment of the real effectuated by the classical realist tradition in cinema. I have touched upon the concept of perception of reality arguing that the post-cinematic strategy in *Wunschkonzert* can make the realist film fiction appear sometimes as more real or at least more true than the stage reality and vice versa. This destabilisation of the notion of real-ity in *Wunschkonzert* is interesting because it can illuminate something about the culturally dominant grasp of realist cinema over our percep-tions of what is real or not. If we were to follow Lévinas's argument that the ethical emerges out of perceptual and cognitive mechanisms and is based upon immediate sentiments such as affect, not yet mediated by language and critical thought, what is ethical is, therefore, closer to the Lacanian 'real' or to the truth. This immediate relationship with truth then becomes deconstructed through critical discourses in the higher realms of consciousness. If we accept this chain reaction of immediate impulses creating an ethical attitude which leads to an in-depth spiritual comprehension of truth, then we can question and potentially reverse this dynamic. Perhaps preconceived ethical and moral assumptions may lead to perceptual choices and experiences which one would perceive as more true. This is of course following Lévinas's argument which essentially claims that our cognitive apparatus is designed to establish an immediate ethical relationship with the 'Other', one that commands infinite respect and value. Reversing this means that choosing to perceive a representation as ethical from the polarity of critical thought (or moral in this case since morality is the critical correlate of the ethical in Lévinas) may lead to a re-calibration of the cognitive apparatus in such a way that what is perceived as more moral will be perceived as more truthful. In other words believing that one representation is more right than another may make it seem more true and more real.[3] This is similar to Tallon's distinction between 'affective intentionality' and 'nonintentional affectivity'. In this case 'affective intentionality' would be an ethical thought leading to and producing affect. In this sense the long tradition of realist cinema, which concealed the process of production of its representations and in doing so limited the ethical engagement and responsiveness of the spectator, may have posited its constructions of reality as credible.

Playing upon moral and ethical sentiments in order to make fiction seem more real and plausible is a strategy long pre-dating realist cinema. Perhaps this is part of why Shakespeare's strategy to use plays-within-plays in order to enhance the reality of the outer theatrical world is so successful; it is not only because of a stylistic mismatch and meta-theatrical framing but because these mini plays usually concern moral and ethical dilemmas and are revealing of moral truths. A good example is the 'Mouse-Trap' scene in *Hamlet*, which dispels Hamlet's ethical doubts. The new moral stance[4] that emerges out of it in the final act, that of punishing his uncle and avenging his father, becomes a pursuit of truth and indeed adds a potentially new truth value to the unfolding of the play.

Realist cinema has a long tradition of aligning constructions of reality with what can be perceived as moral and ethical in order to add credibility to them. A contemporary example of this effect is the meta-structure found in James Cameron's *Avatar* (2009). The film is built around a clash between two worlds, an impressive CGI rendering of native aliens on a planet called Pandora and the filmed world of human mercenaries who seek to exploit them. The protagonist is ex-marine Jake Skully, employed by the mercenary company to conduct diplomatic relations with the natives. In order to communicate with the Pandorans he uses a virtual reality apparatus to control a genetically engineered avatar body of one of the natives. He soon becomes involved with them and renounces his affiliation with the human world in order to guide the exploited natives to freedom. In short a cowboys and Indians story reminiscent of *Dances with Wolves*, but what is interesting in this film is the way in which, as the story progresses, the artificial CGI world of Pandora seems to become almost more real than the photographic reality of the humans. As in *Hamlet*, there are numerous meta-levels and remediations of reality in *Avatar*. But the ethical and consequently moral arguments behind the choices made by Skully and his group of dissidents (research scientists led by Sigourney Weaver) played a vital role in enhancing the truth value and 'reality' of what was clearly a CGI artifice.

The *Wunschkonzert* is very different since it deliberately plays with and confronts the audience with these potentially differing modes of perception. *Hamlet* and *Avatar* work by exposing different levels and perceptions of reality. The succession of these expositions dictates an empathetic journey for the audience wherein ethical sentiments play a role in validating the truth value of subject matter. In *Wunschkonzert* these layers are exposed simultaneously. And it is the un-designed-for freedom to shift between the spaces of film and theatre, with their different ontologies, that invites the spectators to actively reflect on the 'ethics of perception', making this reflexivity an integral experience of the piece. However with *Avatar*, and even *Hamlet*, it is more a case of a critical retrospective afterthought, since their makers took great care to guide their audiences' perceptions. This notion of guided perceptions and carefully weighed out sympathies and moral agendas is one of the properties of realist cinema and its often salient montage structures. Thus by broadening the perceptual choices and re-calibrating sensibilities through intermedial strategies the *Wunschkonzert* can be said to challenge this tradition, by bringing a new sense of ethical consideration to the assessment of perception of realist fiction.

6
Disorienting Landscapes in *Hotel Methuselah*

Imitating the Dog's *Hotel Methuselah* is very different from the pieces discussed in the previous chapters. The main difference being the balance between live theatrical performance and the cinematic projection which accompanies it. On a spectrum with theatrical and cinematic elements at either end, *Hotel Methuselah* lies much closer towards the cinematic end than any of the previous pieces. The stage is dominated by a huge film projection to which all live action is subjected and the plot, together with its filmic representation, is heavily stylised and reliant on cinematic convention. The apparent dominance of the cinematic stylistic in *Hotel Methuselah* is an interesting starting point for this chapter's theoretical enquiry into the 'politics of perception' because it starkly addresses the expectations and perceptual habits inspired by realist cinema. We live in a culture that is saturated with cinematic modes of representation that also constitute forms of perception, modes of framing and perceiving representations and what one may call expectations of a 'cinematic gaze'. Where the previous chapters have investigated the ways in which post-cinematic theatre can make spectators aware and reflexive of pleasure and ethical stances that affect their perceptual choices in relation to cinematic/filmic representations, this chapter will focus on the more formal aesthetics of film and cinema in the context of an intermedial deconstruction. That is, on the way in which the interinvolvement of cinematic and theatrical spaces in *Hotel Methuselah* potentially deconstructs or, rather, disorients the specific cinematic forms and conventions that the piece addresses. The space of the intermedial between theatre and cinema investigated here will be a space of disorientation. The next question is how this disorientation of cinematic perceptions emancipates the spectator and foregrounds the 'politics of perception' at play.

Imitating the Dog is a Leeds-based theatre company working in close collaboration with director Pete Brooks. They use a wide range of media in their pieces and their more recent work can be classified as post-cinematic and/or heavily influenced by cinema culture. Among their recent productions are *Kellerman* (2008) and *Tales from the Bar of Lost Souls* (2010). If one was to try to contextualise their work in relation to theatre that aspires towards cinematic spectacle, then at first glance Imitating the Dog's work might be seen as stylistically reminiscent of Robert Lepage's *Opium and Needles* (1991) and *The Far Side of the Moon* (2001). For instance, both Lepage and Imitating the Dog use back projection juxtaposed with live action in order to create composite cinematic/theatrical images. Such spectacular images always carry a tension between the potential of being perceived as an immersive whole or as a dialectical opposition of the live and mediated. Lepage and Imitating the Dog share other stylistic affinities, such as the use of widescreen letterbox masking, the cinematic look and the use of various mobile scenic elements such as moving panels. What is also interesting about the work of Imitating the Dog here is that it uses the tension between cinematic and theatrical modes of representation to interrogate what is philosophically and politically at stake in our perceptions. Despite the company's substantial 'magical realist' aesthetic, Imitating the Dog's work is also influenced by the Wooster Group. Even though their work is not at all presentational, there seems to be a far greater emphasis on the exposition of the ways illusion is constructed both in theatre and film than in, for example, Lepage for whom it never really constitutes the foreground. Other companies sharing a similar approach to the use of cinematic representations in their work might be Forkbeard Fantasy, Mark Snow and to some extent the Builders Association. With this in mind, we can take a closer look at *Hotel Methuselah*.

Hotel Methuselah is a contemporary ghost story which uses a mixture of film and live performance stylised in the manner of British post-war cinema and the French New Wave to suggest a circular disjointed narrative. The story focuses on Harry, a night porter working in a hotel in a city under siege somewhere in Europe. Harry is the focus of identification for the audience from start to finish of the piece throughout which he encounters various hotel guests, people from his past, and figures that might be from his past or that might represent character archetypes that prompt the fact that he is unable to remember his past and thus define his existence in the light of a possible future. The piece becomes a riddle for the audience who attempt to reconstruct Harry's past, working backwards and forwards – a riddle that denies a conclusive chain of events. In many ways Harry is a stereotypical film noir hero, a subject lost amidst an overwhelming landscape of war that threatens to invade and disperse any little hope of security or stability that he may seek.

What is intrinsic to the spectacle is a clash between the formal aspects of film and theatre. *Hotel Methuselah* is a theatre piece containing live action and video projection as its main set-up. The audience faces an unusually wide letterbox frame behind which all the live action takes place with video projection as a backdrop (Figure 6.1).

The letterbox is a visual structuring device which here blocks off the view of the actors' heads as it does the rest of the theatre machinery. What is central to the concept of the piece is the interinvolvement of the live theatre action and the film material. The piece constitutes a film that has been made part of a theatrical set and a live performance that has been made cinematic. It is almost as if the boundary between the film and the live action has been reduced to a minimum but never quite effaced.

Thus the initial impression of *Hotel Methuselah* might be that it is alluringly cinematic, more of a film than a piece of theatre. In this sense it might be argued that it alludes to a contemporary culture where visual representation is heavily influenced by cinematic aesthetics. These

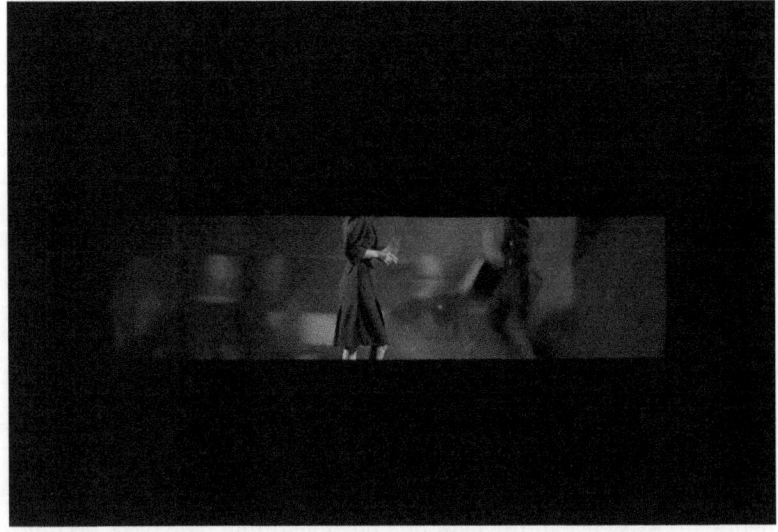

Figure 6.1   Letterbox framing, *Hotel Methuselah*. Photo © Ed Waring/Imitating the Dog

forms of cinematic representation and the expectations that they trigger are an important part of *Hotel Methuselah's* intermedial strategy, which essentially refers to a set of expectations stemming from these forms.

Hotel Methuselah potentially unsettles and disorients the dominant cinematic framework through which the audience is initially invited to 'read' the piece. In this sense *Hotel Methuselah* is an experiment, transforming what often can be a closed reading of a cinematic experience into a more open, writerly and active one. *Hotel Methuselah's* intermedial strategy can also be seen as reaction against culturally dominant realist cinematic aesthetics and the modes of spectatorship that they inspire. The analysis below will demonstrate how *Hotel Methuselah* disorients and complicates the experience of its alleged cinematic frameworks and by doing so encourages a mode of reflexivity that foregrounds the 'politics of perception' behind the cinematic experience it presents. Lyotard's concept of a 'disorienting landscape', a phenomenological perspective developed in his essay 'Scapeland', will provide the methodological basis for an exploration of this disorientation.

In 'Scapeland' Lyotard describes an encounter with the landscape as one in which our capacities to form a description are challenged. He describes it as a 'matter that offers itself in a raw state before being tamed' (Lyotard 1991: 186), a 'landscape which abolishes limits' (ibid.: 182). The landscape is conveyed as an 'open whole' extending beyond our capacities of formal synthesis. He argues that often when encountering any event or phenomenon (matter) we attempt to impose a structure through which that matter can be understood, organised, predicted and so on. Lyotard also relates this encounter to the notion of visual perspective, 'mountainous landscape sketched from an aerial perspective calls forth a quite different judgement when it is viewed from the plain' (ibid.). He goes on to argue that it is essentially a question of matter:

> Matter is that element in datum which has no destiny. Forms domesticate it, make it consumable. Especially visual perspectives, and modes and scales of sound. Forms of sensibility which have come under the control of understanding without difficulty.
>
> (Ibid.: 185)

Andrew Quick elaborates on this concept by relating it to the subject. He describes the encounter with the landscape as disorienting, causing:

> [an] inability to create a stable framework through which the landscape can be addressed and experienced and the landscape's capacity

to seize and displace readable notions of space and time debilitate the process by which a subject may try to define their own boundaries.

(Quick 2005: 147)

Lyotard's concepts and Quick's interpretation of the 'disorienting landscape' (ibid.) as metaphor will be used in this chapter to explore the aesthetics of disorientation in the post-cinematic spectacle of *Hotel Methuselah*. The encounter with the 'landscape' will be interpreted as an encounter with a spectacle which often resists and escapes attempts at the imposition of formal systems (narrative and dramatic conventions, visual conventions, soundscape) that would render it 'knowable' or predictable or allow the audience a sense of orientation within the piece. This disorienting encounter in *Hotel Methuselah* can also be argued potentially to challenge the perception of representations of war, which is the subject matter at the heart of the piece.

Hotel Methuselah is not a landscape piece as such since most of the action represented on stage and film takes place indoors, however it is a piece where an audience could be said to witness the deconstruction of a cinematic landscape, or more specifically the deconstruction of cinematic modes of representation. Thus Lyotard's concept of the 'disorienting landscape' will serve here as a metaphor for disorientation and deconstruction of these cinematic modes of representation. Arguably by creating this 'disorienting landscape' *Hotel Methuselah* attempts to convey an experience of the threat of meaninglessness, formlessness, incomprehensibility and loss – all in all a disorienting cinematic experience. In his article on *Hotel Methuselah*, 'Time to be Responsible', Quick suggests a similar line of argument:

> The haunting in *Hotel Methuselah*, I would like to suggest, is not just about, or by, people, it is directly connected to the ways in which different modes of representation operate; how cinema and theatre work (and fail) to make their representations hold fast in the world. Although we observe Harry's failure to command the trajectories of time and memory, we are always made aware that it is the placing of the theatrical alongside the cinematic and the way in which each haunts the other, that brings his disorientation and ultimate disintegration so vividly to life.
>
> (Quick 2006: 9)

In this context the argument below will focus on the analysis of how this sense of haunting and disorientation is conveyed through an interinvolvement of theatrical and cinematic space in the piece. Disorientation is mainly conveyed through a series of disruptions of an expected filmic logic that comprises the cinematic. These interruptions occur on many levels within the piece: narratives and character formation, visual composition of film and stage elements, de-synchronicity and soundscape. By creating a disorienting cinematic experience, *Hotel Methuselah* emancipates its audience, prompting them to find their own way to perceive the world represented in the piece.

The 'knowable machine'

One of the key questions here relates to the expectations associated with cinema and its medium, film, that potentially come into play with the disorienting aesthetics of *Hotel Methuselah*. But before moving on to the analysis it might be helpful to revise some earlier debates concerning the nature of cinematic experience. The previous chapters have articulated at length the mechanics and effects of dominant forms of cinema aesthetics, mainly focusing on classical realism which has been heavily criticised by post-theory. There are obviously many other forms of film and cinema to draw upon and indeed *Hotel Methuselah* has its own specific filmic intertexts. However Imitating the Dog often describe their style as magical realism. This is a realism-plus, and the realist aspect of it is heavily dominated by cinematic realism. What could be defined as a mainstream film grammar is often instrumental to the devising process of both the film and stage elements in the work of Imitating the Dog. Cinematic aesthetics are the keystones supporting the architecture of their pieces at all levels of production. The magical aspect of the realism in their work consists of the interinvolvement of theatrical and cinematic forms which foregrounds a 'politics of perception'.

So, to return to the question of the generic expectations of the cinematic that are relevant to the theme of disorientation and loss in *Hotel Methuselah*. These expectations amount to the fact that cinema can be viewed as a 'knowable machine', a spectacle that has the formal means for organising and representing readable knowledge about human experience. This is important for Lyotard's notion of a 'disorienting landscape', which is essentially concerned with an encounter that challenges expectations and frameworks commonly used to make sense of experience. But it is also a metaphor for a process of perception, of setting the perception in motion to explore and experience the 'unknown' beyond the confines of subjective frame formations. The generic expectations with which I will deal here are mainly derived from a kind of cinema that falls under the category of 'mass art' or mainstream culture. Noel Carroll states as one of the crucial characteristics of 'mass art' that it:

> is intentionally designed to gravitate in its structural choices (for example, its narrative forms, symbolism, intended affect, and even its content) toward those choices that promise accessibility with minimum effort, virtually on first contact, for the largest number of (or relatively untutored) audiences.
>
> (Carroll 1998: 196)

One of the generic expectations in question is that cinema is perspectivist. In other words it can provide a logically coherent framework for human experience. This has already been discussed earlier in relation to classical realism. For example as an audience watching *Hotel Methuselah* we might expect to gain a perspective and form a system of knowledge and description of the illusory world we will experience/imagine in front of us. The characters and environments will be bound together by a cinematic aesthetic that will act as a map guiding us through the wartime landscape of the *Hotel Methuselah* plot. Vivian Sobchack puts forward a more phenomenological approach by arguing that cinema presents its spectator with an introceptive image. It is already a viewing done by someone else, a subject in itself. The experience of viewing a film is one of seeing someone else's seeing. She claims:

> [t]he frame provides the synoptic centre of the film's experience of the world it sees; it functions for the film as the field of our bodies does for us. That is, as does every lived-body, the frame literally provides the premises for perception as expressed experience.
>
> (Sobchack 1992: 134)

Sobchack goes on to argue that there is freedom in the act of perceiving a film to the extent of there being a constantly changing and unfolding 'out of field', but this sense of an introceptive image of film and consequently the 'body' of film (the image supposedly embodied by the camera) may nonetheless create an expectation of guidance. The choices and selections made by the filming apparatus do not quite belong to the spectator. Someone has done the selecting and viewing for us, so as an audience we can sit back and enjoy the unfolding narrative. Consequently one could argue that there is a tendency to perceive mainstream cinematic experience as implicitly safe, secure and predictable. After all, no matter what takes place on the screen, as spectators we are removed both spatially and temporarily from the actual sites in which the representations were produced. This detachment, as both Lyotard in 'Acinema' and Lehmann in *Postdramatic Theatre* have argued, creates a sense of de-responsibility. Even though the spectator always partakes in the creation of meaning to some degree, the responsibility for the construction of meaning in mainstream cinema is heavily weighted towards the pole of the filmmaker.[1] Ultimately the filmmakers are likely to be responsible for the spectator's interpretation of their work, no matter what meandering process different individuals might choose to take whilst reading the film.

Another expectation which contributes to the knowable nature of cinema is its use and re-use of well-known formulas, styles and conventions that establish means of organising communication and locating the signs used in wider networks of meaning. There are a wide variety of film conventions and genre dependent stylistics that have been in operation long enough to have acquired significant popularity and proficiency. In short, conventions concern conceptual, structural and aesthetic elements that have been used repeatedly and over a long enough period of time to have been labelled as conventional, even as being unoriginal. Even films that try to subvert the already established conventions can be seen as relying heavily on their respective intertexts. For example the twists and turns in Sergio Leone's *The Good, the Bad and the Ugly* rely heavily on audiences' implicit knowledge of the classical Western conventions. Every film is haunted by the past and the practices that precede it. The use of literary tropes, as in MacCabe's contention (see Chapter 1) that nineteenth-century Victorian novel narrative structures were applied to mainstream Hollywood film,[2] exemplifies the way in which an awareness of cultural tropes influences the readability of film. The use of Western classical painting and photography, both as superficial intertexts and as inspiration for compositional techniques, can also contribute to the knowable aspect of cinema. Also film scores, which to this day heavily rest on rewritings of nineteenth-century romantic music and early twentieth-century modern, impressionistic styles, are a powerful means of establishing meanings and dramatic relations between moving images. Another example would be the regurgitation of popular culture such as pop songs and MTV-style editing.

These cultural tropes can make the experience of film more knowable because they act as intertexts or references to concepts and ideas that require prior knowledge in order to be understood. They can also be seen as containing generic logical structures that are designed to generate specific meanings. Conventions become games with specific rules of meaning-production that generate representation. As with all communication, the formalities of a medium allow for redundancy of meaning to occur. In other words they allow for a prediction and expectation of content based on an experience of and identification of formal patterns. One could bring to mind Leibniz's theory of the mathematical formula, where a formula – a reduced concept containing little information – can be expanded to generate a wealth of data external to itself. This implicit knowledge of how to expand and interpret convention, joined with a high cinematic literacy is what creates the image of contemporary cinema and film as a 'knowable machine', a machine that by means of editing, camera angles, image composition, lighting and so on establishes a knowable basis for the communication of meaning. This is also true of theatre where the use of structure, patterning and scenography carries redundant implicit meaning even in the most experimental shows. An example would be the work of Forced Entertainment who often re-use structures and conventions from their past shows (for example, routine introductions of performer's personas, 'upstaging' dynamics, stand-up comedy numbers, exhaustive repetition of actions and so on). However contemporary audiences are likely to be more exposed to filmic than to theatrical conventions simply because they are generally far more exposed to television and cinema than to theatre.

Another contribution to the knowable nature of cinema is that cinema can be perceived as a 'time machine'. Film is always viewed in retrospect; it is a performance that has taken place and cannot be undone. We can safely anticipate watching something that will not become anything other than that which it was at the time of filming and editing. Film never leaves a mark in the reality of the viewer, since it is an illusion of movement created by a sequence of instantaneous frames. In theatre on the other hand there is always an element of improvisation as performance unfolds in real time. Something can always happen that was not accounted for. Despite the audience's trust and attempts to suspend disbelief this unpredictability adds an element of uncertainty to the theatrical experience. Performers swap roles, sweat, breathe and experience a change in the 'real'; live performance offers a qualitative change in movement, a change 'in duration or in the whole' (Deleuze 1983: 8).[3] This is an ontological distinction, which makes the framing devices of the theatrical apparatus far less stable than those of film. It also implies that every theatrical performance is more or less different from previous performances.

Films can come across as overly descriptive, they can give the impression that they are able to show us every single facet of the reality that they construct. Films rely on photography to make claim for the realism of their representations. Photographs can be heavily constructed representations, but they always draw attention to the object that is being photographed. Photographs are always processed representations of something that was there at the time of shooting. On the other hand, a theatrical image or a figure on stage often points beyond itself. It points towards a virtual reality whose boundaries are not yet visibly present or defined. As Lehmann points out 'the other in theatre [that which a theatrical figure represents] always has a reality only of *arrival,* not presence' (Lehmann 2006: 172). This expectation of the arrival of representation relates to the directing outwards of theatrical images: essentially it means looking out for the potential arrival of representation. With film, photographs and electronic images (which Lehmann contrasts with the theatrical image), the dynamic is to 'bridge the emptiness, fulfil the wish' (Lehmann 2006: 172), enable a direct representation. Hence the cinematic image could be said to be pointing inwards in the sense that it fills in the gap, the emptiness at its heart with a direct representation. These notions of pointing inwards and outwards can lead us to outline two complementary dynamics – the centrifugal and the centripetal – through which an image stimulates our perception. Bazin also makes this distinction between theatrical and cinematic imagery in those terms. For him the screen is not so much a frame as a 'mask which allows only a part of the action to be seen' (Bazin 2005: 117). The screen becomes a device for focusing and picking out elements from the surrounding universe. The cinematic image could be said to have a centripetal dynamic because it focuses the surrounding imagery on the screen, much like a flashlight 'moving like an uncertain comet across the night of our waking dream'. The theatrical image on the other hand, is like a refraction from a chandelier, 'which refuses to let itself be captured' (ibid.: 118). The theatrical image points beyond itself, it is always in the process of dispersing and becoming something else. In this sense it can be defined as centrifugal. This possibly somewhat artificial and binary distinction highlights two complementary dynamics which can be at play within the perception of theatrical and cinematic imagery. It also points to a potential for tension when cinematic expectations are being addressed within a theatre piece, because two different perceptual dynamics are at play.

These then are among the generic expectations of cinematic experience that can make it knowable. The next step will be to analyse in detail, by using Lyotard's notion of a 'disorienting landscape', how *Hotel Methuselah* can be seen as unsettling these expectations and deconstructing the conventions from which they stem. The disorientation and instability of perception evoked through this deconstruction, foregrounds the 'politics of perception' at play in the piece. The analysis is presented in three sections: dramatic conventions, visual filmic conventions and soundscape.

Dramatic conventions

This section considers two aspects of the dramatic composition of *Hotel Methuselah*. The first is the concept of narrative within *Hotel Methuselah* and the way in which its post-cinematic features can be seen as disorienting narrative structures. The second is the narrative orientation (in spatio-temporal terms) in relation to character and, by extension, subject constitution, with a particular focus on character and the environment.

Narratives in classical realist cinema can be said to be perspectivist. As with the use of perspective and the vanishing point in classical painting the realist aesthetic in film, for the most part, works to establish a clearly readable relationship between the subject and the landscape environment that surrounds them. In this sense, a cinematic narrative can be classified as a spatio-temporal map and there is an expectation of guidance associated with it. The Aristotelian model offers a good starting point for analysing the way in which *Hotel Methuselah* can be seen as destabilising and disorienting mainstream notions of cinematic narrative. Even though Aristotle developed his poetics in relation to dramatic tragedy, his theory can and has been applied to cinema. In Aristotelian terms a linear sequence of events produces definable and comprehensible consequences. The events in a plot leading to the peripety (*peripeteia*) or discovery, he claims, 'should each of them arise out of the structure of the plot itself, so as to be the consequence, necessary or probable, of the antecedents. There is a great difference between a thing happening *propter hoc* and *post hoc*' (Aristotle 1940: 29). *Hotel Methuselah*, in contradiction to this, shows distinctly postdramatic traits in so far as narrative structures are concerned. It has a circular, repetitive narrative structure that does not evolve in a traditional consequential sense that might allow for a more formulaic comprehensibility. Lehmann quotes Aristotle to convey Aristotle's concept of what a definable and comprehensible plot should be. He calls it 'surveyability', an 'intellectual processing unclouded by confusion' (Lehmann 2006: 40).

Interestingly Aristotle sees narrative as being in need of a certain magnitude, a scale that will provide boundaries and limits so that it can be comprehended:

> For this reason no organism could be beautiful if it is excessively small (since observation becomes confused as it comes close to having no perceptible duration in time) or excessively large (since the observation is then not simultaneous, and the observers find that the sense of unity and wholeness is lost from their observation, e.g. if there were an animal a thousand miles long). So just as in the case of physical objects and living organisms, they should possess a certain magnitude, and this should be such that it can readily be taken in at one view [*eusynopton*], so in the case of plots: they should have a certain length, and this should be such that it can readily be held in memory.
>
> (Aristotle in ibid.)

It is important to add that for Aristotle plot and character are interdependent. For Aristotle, characters carry the audience through the journey of the plot but in doing so they also generate and create the plot. From this theoretical standpoint, an audience watching *Hotel Methuselah* might expect to identify with the main protagonist, Harry, and try to discover why he is in the situation as presented, and what his past and future relationships might be to the characters he encounters. It quickly becomes evident, however, that both Harry's past and his present situation are unclear and dislodged. This conundrum is triggered from the very beginning by a voice-over describing the status quo. The voice-over is a conventional narrative device that is usually used to locate the action in space and time. This notion is played upon but not fully realised. We are told that the action takes place in a European city under siege, 'a Stalingrad of the soul', but no specific reference is ever made. The World War II set, the film noir aesthetic and the soundtrack echoing Shostakovich's *Stalingrad Symphony* offer contextual suggestions. Thus the piece establishes itself in a dangerous, ambiguous and not easily definable realm of war. The soundscape at the opening of the piece also creates a temporal disorientation. It is a sound collage of a series of repetitive phrases whispered in different languages. The multiplicity of these sounds and their random cultural/national identities do not convey any coherent sense of a real place or state of things. The very title – *Hotel Methuselah* – encapsulates this disorientation, conjoining 'Hotel' – an international 'non-place', or space – and the name of 'Methuselah', the oldest man in the Bible, implying a notion of timelessness.

Narrative can often be perceived as framed, cut out and artificial. Following Aristotle's metaphor, it is an animal appropriately shaved, with a shortened tail and elegantly cut whiskers so it attains the right magnitude. It is an interesting metaphor here because it is a spatial metaphor. Narrative forms in realist cinema often reduce life experience into a consequential, formulaic narrative chain, where real life is reduced into a series of dialectically linked scenes. These film narratives can also be insular in the way that they attempt to resolve and reconcile most or all of the narrative strands. By doing so they also define a journey through a landscape, and to a significant extent classical realist montage is concerned with defining and setting up limits to the represented spaces. Surely there is pleasure in wondering what lies beyond the confines of montage? Possibly a fetishistic pleasure, as Metz points out, likening the wandering film frame to an act of 'permanent undressing, generalised strip-tease' (Metz 1982: 77). But this process is nonetheless marked by 'censorship', to use Metz's term, which implies an attempt to limit and subdue any potential *jouissance* of the image. On the other hand the metaphor of the 'disorienting landscape' can be read as something that lies beyond the possibilities of narrativisation, beyond an argumentative structure. It is continuous, never-ending, open, and offering, in theory, an infinite set of possibilities for narrative consequences. One way in which *Hotel Methuselah* evokes this metaphor of a disorienting landscape type narrative is by interinvolving rigorous filmic structures with the theatrical machine, which at times echoes much looser rehearsal type structures. Returning to Aristotle's notion of a tragic plot, there might also be something here in the relationship/difference between tragedy and trauma. According to Aristotle, as an audience we may expect the guidance and development of dramatic (tragic) structure but instead we only get the repetitive structure of trauma. Trauma and traumatic memory are the themes of *Hotel Methuselah* and central to Harry's character and thus perfectly account for its disorientating and circular plot.

The play is structured in three acts. Every act begins with the arrival of a mysterious widow (Amy) who asks the night porter Harry for a room. It seems that they know each other from before but Harry cannot remember and the woman is incapable or does not wish to specify what their relationship is. A recurrent theme of Harry's amnesia is established; he speculates that this might be the result of some past war injury. Subsequent scenes show conversations between Harry and the Weird Man and Weird Woman. None of the scenes establish much about character, since they comprise a series of questions and insinuations directed towards Harry to which he does not respond in any reasonable way. Every act ends with Harry and Amy fantasising about a future after having made love to each other. There are many hints along the way that Amy was somehow related to Harry in the past or that Amy suspects Harry to be her absent husband. We also get many hints that Amy is pregnant. This is clear from innuendo in the dialogues but also from images and metaphors of procreation such as a visual effect of sperm scattering on Harry's notebook page (projected on the film). At the very end of each act we hear a loud shot. It is also made clear at the end of the third act that Amy commits suicide. Every act becomes a traumatic 'rehearsal' for retelling Harry's story, an attempt to find a definition for the character. Each act fails in doing this and is obliged to repeat itself.

However, every time the cycle repeats things change slightly. It is as if the dramatic form were trying to accommodate the landscape, rehearsing the way to a resolution. Lyotard claims that the disorienting landscape presents the beholder with 'a place without DESTINY' (Lyotard 1991: 183). In that sense there is no resolution in *Hotel Methuselah*, and the landscape becomes a mark that could be thought 'as an erasure of support' (Lyotard 1991: 189). The dramatic structures (the support) that shape and guide the audience through a plot are systematically 'erased' through the mechanical, repetitive structure of the piece. Audiences tend to trust and read into dramatic conventions as vehicles and schematics for understanding, and orient themselves within the realm that is presented. For example, one of the expectations in dramatic and cinematic texts is for the conversations between characters to move the story forward. In *Hotel Methuselah* this expectation is challenged in the bedroom scenes in which Harry and Amy expose more of a personal dimension, hinting at their past, but where it nonetheless remains difficult to work out what exactly their relationship is, particularly as what occurs dramatically within *Hotel Methuselah* is a series of conversations that do not go anywhere. Vehicles that set out into the troubled landscape get lost, break down and disappear without losing their concrete substance.

On many occasions this can be also illustrated by a clash between a routine and the opportunity of transcending it. This is often the case in Harry's relation to other characters. He follows a very minimal routine which often clumsily protects him from any attempt to open up a conversation or progress into a substantial action. For example, there is a scene in which the Weird Woman is trying to get Harry into bed but he keeps on clumsily resisting by falling back on routine:

> WEIRD WOMAN: [...] So, what do you charge?
> HARRY: Sorry?
> WEIRD WOMAN: For the drink. Drink makes people talk. Loosens tongues. And I like a loose tongue. Why don't you join me, Harry, you seem a bit tense.
> HARRY: I don't drink on the job.
> WEIRD WOMAN: Then why are you so fucking irresponsible? You're just like all the other fucking men I know. Pant. Pant. Pant. And then empty it all out into the dust bag. Without a care in the world about what might happen next.
> HARRY: It's on the house.
> WEIRD WOMAN: What is?
> HARRY: The drink.

Any attempt at sparking a relationship or opening a real conversation is cut short by Harry. All that remains is just speculation on the spectator's part. The repetitious nature of the narrative creates the sense of a series of traumatic rehearsals that will culminate in Amy's suicide. Every time the story repeats, more details of Harry's past are revealed until eventually Amy kills herself. This could be interpreted as indicating that Harry is in limbo, forced to see over and over again his wife's suicide (a story structure reminiscent of Stanislaw Lem's novel *Solaris*). However there is no resolution to this plot in a classical sense, since the story restarts after she dies. As a result it is difficult to grasp any consequential chain of events. Harry's past and his character remain an enigma. He no longer has any role as a dramatic agency that might enable the audience to reflect and project upon the fictional world, since the notions of past and future are being constantly interrupted or, as in Lyotard's 'disorienting landscape', the 'self is left behind' (Lyotard 1991: 187). Unlike Aristotle's tragic hero, Harry has no moment of *anagnoresis* – of insight into his situation – indeed, he is a ghost. Harry's lack of insight, which might involve developing a perspective or a framing of a given situation, means he has no basis on which to act or to form a response. In spatial terms he has no coordinates. Thus Harry's journey becomes a constant displacement of the 'vanishing point [...] a vanishing of a standpoint rather' (ibid.). Harry is not the guiding agent within the narrative that one might expect in realist cinema, but a blank canvas – a displaced enigma.

It is important to emphasise here that character and plot in *Hotel Methuselah* are interdependent. Events cannot unfold without an agency bringing them about and their being acted upon. Likewise, a character has to be defined in space and time by acting and reacting to some environmental stimuli. Thus what is at the heart of the constitution of the subject within a landscape is the relationship between the subject and the environment. Traditionally films work by defining the environment and placing a subject in relation to it. In *Hotel Methuselah* the environment outside the eponymous hotel is presented as a threat. There is a war raging and people are being killed. However most of that can only be deduced from Harry's behaviour in that he is afraid to leave the building and venture into the landscape as he fears an unhappy ending. Harry's character refuses opportunities for movement in many ways. He is a largely static character, enjoying the safety of his desk, usually standing behind the counter. The filmic close-up distances him from the other characters and even when he moves he moves on the spot. Simon Wainwright playing Harry is actually situated on a moving tape that shifts him onto the stage and out, he hardly ever moves. In scenes where he is walking, he walks on a moving tape, and the film background behind him creates an illusion of movement. Harry's character literally stands for order or at least attempts to:

> HARRY: I'm supposed to keep an eye on things. To make sure that...
> WEIRD WOMAN: Nothing untoward is going on...
> HARRY: No, that everything is in order, is how it should be...

A potentially insightful approach to Harry's constant refusal to engage with the environment is Julia Kristeva's theory of the abject. Kristeva describes abjection as a fear of venturing into a territory that 'disturbs identity, system, order [...] does not respect, borders, positions, rules. The in-between, the ambiguous, the composite' (Kristeva 1982: 4). To Kristeva abjection is a safeguard from a territory which is untamed, dangerous and beyond rules of conduct: 'On the edge of non-existence and hallucination, of a reality that, if I acknowledge it, annihilates me. There, abject and abjection are my safeguards' (ibid.: 2). The outside could be seen as an abject territory for Harry; however, there is an important difference between Kristeva's theory and the dynamic of Harry's character. Kristeva's theory concerns the constitution of the subject through a definition of that which the subject is not, or does not want to be part of (the negative set of elements). However a definition of the negative set requires some kind of engagement with it in order to arrive at a negative judgement. The difference here is precisely that Harry does not even try, therefore he cannot arrive at a definition of what is truly abject to him in the world that surrounds him. Harry's problem is almost mechanical, he is trapped within an aesthetic structure, a 'cine-theatrical machine' that does not allow him to grow as a character – again much like one of Pirandello's characters trapped in a play, and much as in Pirandello's play this awareness is made explicit.

Consequently the audience never sees what is beyond the hotel; Harry for the most part evades any potential interaction with the environment and other characters, and the plot hardly ever moves forward. In that sense *Hotel Methuselah* denies the traditional realist cinematic expectation of a plot constituted of character responses to the challenges and stimulation of their environment. Instead the narrative structure of the piece stays in one spot, like a chimerical 'cine-theatrical' machine being wound and rewound, back and forth, with all of its ghosts inside – a dynamic reminiscent of some of Beckett's dramas, such as *Waiting for Godot* or *Endgame*. There is no narrative spatio-temporal orientation in a traditional sense and the audience are not offered the continuous journey of a character through a world but a series of fragmented scenes. From these narrative fragments the spectator has freedom to trace a plot, play the 'detective' as it were. In this sense *Hotel Methuselah* emancipates and stimulates the audience to become more active spectators, precisely because the traditional cinematic mechanisms that would set a more definite plot in motion have been short-circuited. An audience that expected to be guided through a narrative structure would be left disoriented, prompted only to find their own way out.

It is not only the 'cine-theatrical machine' of *Hotel Methuselah* which traps Harry's character on a formal level and destabilises the possibility of character formation and consequently a perspectivist cinematic experience; it is also the way that the theatrical 'live' presences are dealt with. In dramatic theatre the actor is usually perceived as the centre of the character's subjectivity. They are the page from which character development can be read during a play. The actors must be in control of the temporality of the piece in order for a convincing organic representation to occur.[4] Harry's paradoxical fear of liveness and activeness is reflected in the formal interruptions and disruptions of live performance. The 'beheading' of the live actors by the letterbox conceals the faces of the actors – vital central elements of character representation. The result of this is the destabilisation and de-centring of an important element of performance that takes with it key possibilities for identification and thus character constitution. Instead, the faces appear as close-ups on film, which also works towards a sense of disorientation. (This will be further discussed in the next section.)

The lack of centrality of character is further reinforced by the acting styles. Michael Kirby has coined a term called 'non-matrixed representation' (Kirby 1972: 8). Philip Auslander describes this style of non-matrixed acting as a performance that does not embody a fictional character but 'merely carries out certain actions' (Kirby in Auslander 1999: 28) that nevertheless can have 'referential or representational significance when inserted into a sign system of a show' (Auslander 1999: 28). Auslander goes on to claim that film acting is essentially 'non-matrixed acting' since the very nature of filming and performing on the set implies carrying out actions that are pulled out of context, that are repetitive and discontinuous. The live performance in *Hotel Methuselah*, which to a great extent remediates filmic conventions, can be defined as 'non-matrixed'. The film is like a blueprint for the live performance, it dictates cues, movement, gesture and facial expression; even the speech is pre-recorded and played back with the film. This re-appropriation of the live creates a tension between the live and the filmed performance. There is a fatalism about the acting in *Hotel Methuselah* which manifests itself on a meta-theatrical level but also on a narrative level. Both performers and characters are trapped within a 'cine-theatrical machine'. They are trapped by the text, they are trapped by the framing (film and letterbox), they are trapped within visual convention, soundscapes and an overlaid soundtrack that puts words into their mouths. It is a repetitive cine-theatrical trauma, where the discomfort comes from the inter-involvement of the live and the mediated. No definite closure can be assigned to Harry's story precisely because the de-synchronicity and the openings towards the landscape are potentially a way out. The tragedy in a classical sense can never be satisfactory or reconciled. The inter-involvement of theatre and cinema in *Hotel Methuselah* thus un-frames and destabilises the perception of potentially cinematic narrative.

Finally, how does this move away from the perspectivist structuring of a subject foreground and amplify the 'politics of perception'? Despite the ambiguous and disorienting nature of its dramatic structures, there is a narrative to be teased out of *Hotel Methuselah* when all the puzzling elements are put together: Harry was a soldier in wartime, and perished, leaving his pregnant wife Amy behind; unable to come to terms with his death Amy commits suicide. The action of *Hotel Methuselah* can be interpreted as a vision of purgatory where Harry is trapped and forced repeatedly to witness the traumatic moment of his wife committing suicide, always being too late to react or respond. The other two characters may be interpreted as part of Harry's consciousness. The important thing however, is that the audience do not know any of that when they come to see the play, nor does the play really offer any clear revelation of this interpretation. Instead it plunges the audience into a series of games and repetitive structures which form the disorientating aesthetic of the unfolding narrative. But as in the pieces discussed in the previous chapters, these disorientations make the audience reflect upon the moral implications of the perceptual processes at play during the experience of cinematic material. Quick, in 'Time to be Responsible' claims that the disorientation inherent in *Hotel Methuselah* was intended to make the audience 'responsible':

> By inviting the spectator to participate in the act of piecing together, [...], we have always presumed that the audience would begin to take on the very weight of responsibility that Harry is seen to shun. [...] If Harry is damned because he is unable to step out of time in order to face up to the consequences of his actions, then redemption must lie in our ability to find the time to respond and be responsible.
>
> (Quick 2006: 11)

The story of Hotel Methuselah does not provide the audience with answers, political judgements or specific historical framings. Instead it shows a character who refuses to act or engage with the world around him to the point where, as a character, he cannot drive the story forward, and an artificial cine-theatrical machine has to take over to keep it in motion. His lack of activity and engagement results in a repetitive process that serves to emphasise the erasure of the past. Arguably this deconstructive dynamic prompts the audience to become more active and fill in the empty canvas, the empty signifier that Harry has become. The act of filling in this empty signifier may be revealing of political attitudes. For instance Quick elaborates on the dangers of political apathy and historical ignorance: '*Hotel Methuselah* can be seen as giving us a warning as to the dire consequences of ignoring history, of the terrible price we might have to pay when we submerge ourselves into the active erasure of the past that appears to mark so much of contemporary culture' (ibid.: 11). This could be seen as a call for a more politically active mode of spectatorship, a reaction against the passive modes inherent in the cinematisation of our contemporary culture. And if we as spectators do not take responsibility for our interpretations, as Harry refuses to take responsibility for his actions, then someone else might do it for us. The history of war films for instance is filled with interpretations of real events that have constructed the way in which many perceive the historical reality of past wars. Often, specific ideological and political agendas underlie these interpretations, and in that context the dramatic structures of *Hotel Methuselah* can be seen as inspiring the spectator to be more 'response-able' in their interpretation and aware of what is politically at stake in their perceptions.

Dis-*play*-cing visual filmic conventions

So far this chapter has looked at how the interinvolvement of the filmic and theatrical in *Hotel Methuselah* disorients potential perspectivist narrative structures. Let us consider now how *Hotel Methuselah* deconstructs cinematic expectations and conventions through the formal aspects of the visual spectacle it creates. As discussed in Chapter 3 above, one of the ways in which realist cinema orients and manipulates the perceptions of its audience through the reality it constructs is by means of a phenomenon called cinematic suture. This mechanism of identification with the cinematic image is heavily ingrained in our culture hence it is an expectation of cinematic experience that will be interesting to look at in terms of the disorienting aesthetics of *Hotel Methuselah*. First of all I would like to quickly look again at the notion of a realist cinematic discursive. Deleuze argues along the lines of Bakhtin and Pasolini, for a free indirect discourse in cinema:

> an assemblage of enunciation, carrying out two inseparable acts of subjectivisation simultaneously, one of which constitutes a character in the first person, but the other of which is present at his birth and brings him on to the scene.
>
> (Deleuze 1986: 75)

Deleuze claims that an oscillation takes place between the notion of objective and subjective image, 'a correlation between a perception-image and a camera-consciousness which transforms it' (ibid.: 76). He then expands that theory by giving a Bergsonian definition of this oscillation:

> a subjective perception is one in which the images vary in relation to a central and privileged image; an objective perception is one where, as in things, all the images vary in relation to one another, on all their facets and in all their parts.
>
> (ibid.: 79)

It is this process of 'settling' a subjective perception in film that is referred to as cinematic suture. With reference to Lacanian terminology, Jacques-Alain Miller defines suture as the moment in which the subject inserts himself into the symbolic order in the guise of a signifier, filling an absence or a lack.

> Suture names the relation of the subject to the chain of its discourse [...] it figures there as the element which is lacking, in the form of a stand-in. For, while there lacking, it is not purely and simply absent. Suture, by extension is the general relation of lack to the structure of which it is an element, in as much as it implies the position of a taking-the-place-of.
>
> (Miller 1978: 25–6)

A simple example of this would be a shot of a landscape, followed by a close-up of a character staring into the distance. The first shot has an absent subject/beholder, which may suggest the following question: to whom does this perception belong? The following shot provides a subject with whom the spectator may identify and establishes a discursive link between the perception of the landscape and the beholder of that perception (the character in the second shot). The establishment of this discursive dependency is termed as suture. Thus suture is a way of achieving narrative continuity through interlocking shots. The shot relationships can be seen as the equivalent of syntactic relationships in linguistic discourse. It is an agency through which meaning is constructed and a subject position is set out for the viewer. To return to *Hotel Methuselah*, how, in this instance, does the interjection of live theatricality work to destabilise the effect of cinematic suture?

Audiences to *Hotel Methuselah* witness a theatre piece which contains a film within an exaggeratedly wide landscape letter-box. What is striking about the piece is the literal breadth of visual material with which the audience can be faced. According to Lyotard the landscape is always in 'excess of presence' (Lyotard 1991: 187), it 'always requires something that is TOO' (Lyotard 1991: 187). In that sense the 'disorienting landscape' emerges here as an excess of visual material. This notion of 'excess' also emerges when live and film action double each other. The spectator is constantly obliged to make decisions as to what elements of the spectacle to focus on in order to construct a continuous narrative. Thus, the usual expectations of watching a film, which edits, breaks down and organises the action for the spectator's apprehension, as well as directing sympathies and identification towards particular characters, are challenged. The audience is prompted to 're-edit' the material to find a cinematic form for the theatrical landscape with which it is faced. For example, it is a convention in *Hotel Methuselah* to show two characters' faces in close-up on screen, but with one at the extreme right of the screen and the other at the extreme left, as shown in Figure 6.2. The letterbox is so wide that it is difficult to grasp both of the close-ups with one look and hence spectators have to 'edit' the shot with their gaze. In that sense *Hotel Methuselah* creates a space for a visual experience beyond cinematic form, an intermedial space, in-between the live and film image. Another example of this effect is in the scene where Harry is being approached and tempted by the Weird Woman to have sex with her and the screen is filled with her close up. On stage the desk has been turned on its side and a special apparatus set up to hold the actors in place so as to give an illusion of an overhead shot. The audience sees the live action as if it were looking from above but the long close-up shot is also visible on film (Figure 6.3).

The gaze of the spectator may oscillate between these perspectives. The audience might tend to look for details and clues in the live performance in an attempt to get more insight into the unfolding relationship between the two characters and to understand the already ambiguous dialogue. By presenting the audience with an excess of material *Hotel Methuselah* makes them potentially more involved and aware of the process of the production of meaning. A landscape of perceptual choices is being opened up before the spectator. This lack of any clear implicit

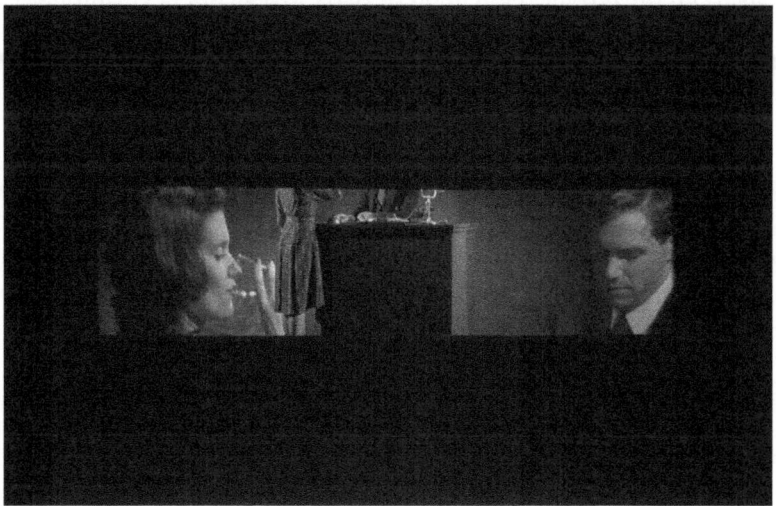

Figure 6.2   Amy's arrival at the Hotel, *Hotel Methuselah*. Photo © Ed Waring/ Imitating the Dog

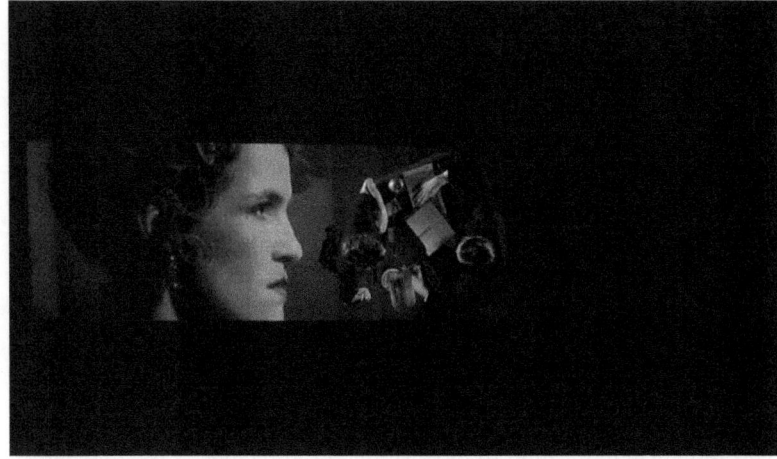

Figure 6.3   'Overhead' shot, *Hotel Methuselah*. Photo © Ed Waring/Imitating the Dog

perspective and the excess of visual material spilling out beyond the cinematic frame may foreground the 'politics of perception'. To give a concrete example, the ambiguity of perspective in the 'overhead' scene opens up the possible perception of Harry as a victim of circumstance, haunted and threatened by entities unknown to him. Equally, he could be read as a misogynistic narcissist who believes that every female figure in his imagination wishes to offer herself to him whilst he contemplates the state of his indecisiveness. Thus, for example, the way in which a spectator chooses to perceive this scene may become reflexive of their attitude towards gender politics. The way in which *Hotel Methuselah* is composed gives the spectators a greater sense of freedom to become more active in piecing the film and stage material together; more so than they would be whilst watching a realist film where the above reflexivity would not be foregrounded. Spectators are enabled to pick out hand gestures, body positions, personal space, proxemics and so on in order to seek additional nuances within the scene and develop their own particular viewpoint on a situation that is thematically morally ambiguous and carries varied political implications behind the modes of perception it offers.

Some of the most disorienting aspects of *Hotel Methuselah*, which also challenge realist cinematic expectations, are the moments of juxtaposition between the screen close-ups of characters and their live performers. These moments complicate the potential for character identification and represent a notable post-cinematic stylistic within the piece. They also displace a more conventional cinematic discourse that hinges on the montage of close-ups. Deleuze's notion of the cinematic close-up, which he often relates to what he calls the 'affection-image' (Deleuze 1986: 105), is useful for an analysis of these moments. For Deleuze the 'affection-image' is a 'power-quality', like the 'brightness of the light' on Jack the Ripper's knife or 'Lulu's compassionate look' (ibid.). Affection-images are always somewhat detached from the state of things from which they arise, 'taken all together they only refer back to themselves, and constitute the "expressed" of the state of things, [...] As Balázs says, however much the precipice may be the cause of vertigo, it does not explain the expression it produces on the face' (ibid.). Of course these affects often prepare the spectator for an event that will take place soon after, be it the slash of the knife or a fall from the precipice, hence they play an anticipatory role; but the argument is that they are detached events in themselves, loose 'power-qualities' with a potential to unfold into action. Deleuze claims that close-ups often function as and are of the order of 'affection-images'. In contrast with the popular psychoanalytic reading of the close-up, Deleuze argues that the phenomenon of the cinematic close-up lies not so much in presenting us with a fragmented, partial object which has to be re-assembled with the rest of the film so as to achieve continuity but that it 'abstracts [the object] from all spatio-temporal co-ordinates' (ibid.: 98). The close-up is an affection-image, 'abstracted from the spatio-temporal coordinates which would relate it to a state of things, and abstracts the face from the person to which it belongs in the state of things' (ibid.: 100). He supports his claim by quoting Balázs: 'for the expression of a face and the signification of this expression have no relation or connection with space. Faced with an isolated face, we do not perceive space. Our sensation of space is abolished. A dimension of another order is opened to us' (Balázs in ibid.: 98).

In other words, according to Deleuze, the close-up does not stand as a part which can be inscribed back into the whole, it is a deterritorialised entity. The close-up becomes a primary expression of power-quality; it does not have to be reconstituted into a 'state of things' in order to function within a film.[5] The 'face of a fleeing coward, as soon as we see it in close-up, we see cowardice in person, the feeling thing, the entity' (ibid.). In fact, Deleuze argues that any attempt to find reconciliation would simply reveal an inherent discontinuity within the medium of film, an 'impossible reality' that lurks between the construct and the 'real'. The experience of a close-up within a film thus has the privilege of isolation and abstractedness. Essentially Deleuze argues for the *integrity* of the cinematic close-up. I would also like to add that the cinematic frame can impose its own set of rules, in which partial objects and set elements will function exclusively within the dimension of the close-up. Gestalt psychology terms this phenomenological experience as 'global precedence', a tendency of the human mind 'to blend the elements into an integrated whole rather than isolating separate elements' (Robinson-Riegler 2004: 79). The famous credo here being that the 'whole is greater than the sum of its parts' – we always see the forest before the trees. In the case of the close-up the principle of 'common region'[6] visually overrules any need for the closure of an incomplete human figure. Deleuze argues that the close-up retains a certain degree of purity: a primary enunciation, as opposed to a secondary enunciation that is in relation to an external 'state-of-things'.

In *Hotel Methuselah* this effect of integrity and gestalt perception is challenged by the introduction of live space and time in juxtaposition with the cinematic frame. The close-ups are contested by live performers who represent their bodies. This lack of synchronicity between the two dimensions might stimulate a desire to synchronise the elements and match them up. The film frame no longer feels isolated, and the tendency to seek a gestalt might prompt the spectator to seek closure within this collage of the live and the mediated. In many ways the close-ups in *Hotel Methuselah* lose their sense of imaginary integrity and deterritorialisation as a result of the contact with live action. Or at least a perceptual tension develops in this respect. The disproportionately huge faces gain a landscape quality. This is very effective in scenes where the front projection is used for extreme close-ups, such as the example shown in Figure 6.4.

The face, which normally would be a trope for identification in realist cinema, here gains the potential to become a 'disorienting landscape'. A psychoanalytic interpretation could also be made to explain this phenomenon. Lacan states that the reconciliation of the real, the imaginary and consequently the symbolic is impossible. The link with the real has been severed at the 'mirror stage'. Thus the real is beyond mediation (Lacan 1991: 102). One could argue that *Hotel Methuselah* plays on this notion of the 'real' present body, whose head is only present within the virtual, imaginary-symbolic dimension of film. This stimulates a desire to 'link' the imaginary head with the rest of the body and establish continuity. The impossibility of reconciling these phantasies lies at the basis of how a subject attempts to constitute itself. Normally in films

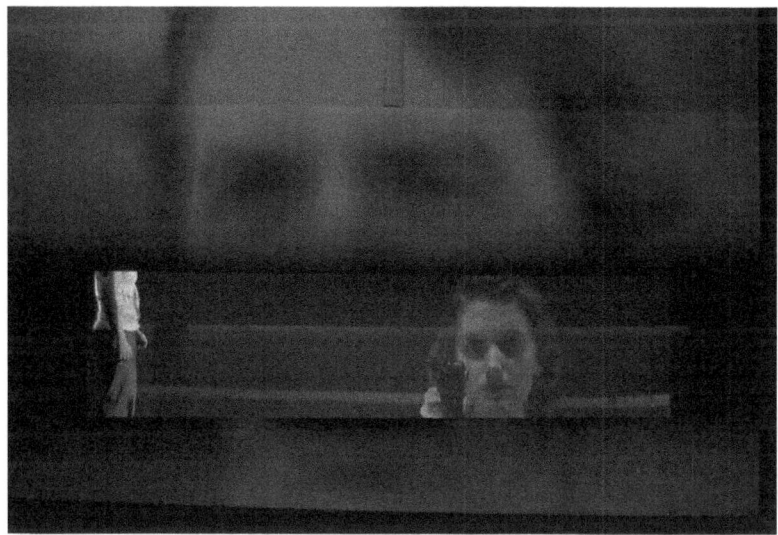

Figure 6.4 Extreme close-up of Harry on front projection, *Hotel Methuselah.*
Photo © Ed Waring/Imitating the Dog

the operations of suture hide this discontinuity and the imaginary constitution of the subject is achieved as an illusion. *Hotel Methuselah* disrupts these operations by juxtaposing filmic close-ups and live bodies.
By highlighting this discontinuity *Hotel Methuselah* disrupts a potential
illusionistic (cinematic) constitution of the subject. In many ways this
'*ai*sthetic effect', works well with the theme of Harry not being able
to define himself as a stable subject and the perpetual limbo of his
undecidability. Thus this undecidability of subjective constitution is not
only exposed thematically but also formally, as it may oscillate between
the identity of his film representation, the stage representation and also
the identity of the actor playing on stage. The modes of perception and
character identification are no longer tightly controlled by a cinematic
convention wherein the responsibility for meaning lies mainly with
the filmmaker. Instead responsibility shifts towards the audience, thus
negotiating the notion of 'response-ability' and making the spectators
more actively aware of the perceptual process and choices involved in
the constitution of the experience of cinematic images.

The emancipation and reflexivity resulting from the lack of a 'guided'
cinematic gaze is further enhanced by what I described above as the
desynchronicity between the live and the cinematic images. The

audience is prompted to map the live onto film in order to satisfy the expectation of visual forms and conventions, enabling them to find a visual continuity, a sense-making frame. An example of this would be the scene where Amy and the Weird Woman are walking down a corridor and the suggestion that Amy is pregnant is brought up. This dialogue brings in the notion of responsibility but also the consequences that follow in life. This scene can be perceived as a representation of yet another of Harry's fantasies or as an attempt to introduce a new dimension of the victimhood that wars bring with them. But again the disorienting interinvolvement of theatre and film adds an interesting critical commentary. On screen we see a tracking shot through a hotel corridor, whilst on stage the actors stand in one place and pretend to be walking forwards (Figure 6.5). Their conversation is overshadowed and displaced by the incongruity of the film and the live action, which is never quite right nor properly synchronised. This displacement becomes a way of theatricalising the broken thread between the *mise-en-cadre* and the potential *mise-en-scène*. Even though the film material has been clearly pre-recorded, a scene like this exemplifies the broken thread between the site of production and the virtual images formed. This clash and tension between modes of representation, past/present, fantasy/reality, but also the temporalities of film and live action accentuated by their interinvolvement, are significant in reflecting upon the context of the conversation, which deals with the issue of pregnancy. Whether the spectator believes that the pregnancy is, or was, real or

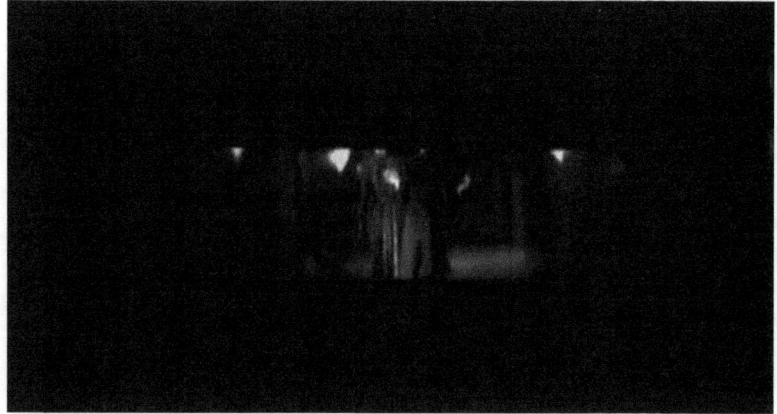

Figure 6.5 Amy and the Weird Woman walking down the corridor, *Hotel Methuselah*. Photo © Ed Waring/Imitating the Dog

simply only a fantasy depends on the way that they may choose to perceive this scene.

Finally, *Hotel Methuselah* utilises a number of filmic intertexts and it is useful to consider the way in which their film grammar is interinvolved with the theatrical elements of the piece. The visual and dramatic language of *Hotel Methuselah* – in terms of both the film and stage components – is heavily influenced by French New Wave and film noir stylistics. This choice of stylistic models immediately relates the piece to a period in which cinema explored the possibilities of ambiguity and developed a language suited to it. In that sense it already exemplifies a break with the realist cinematic conventions. For example in David Lean's *Brief Encounter* (1945), the short relationship between two married people that is at the centre of the film develops primarily in the in-between space of a railway station. The filmic palette of the film material in *Hotel Methuselah* is heavily derived from film noir and it is exploited to heighten the sense of ambiguity and disorientation within the piece.

One of the characteristics of film noir cinematography which was extensively used in *Hotel Methuselah* is that of low-key lighting.

> The ratio of key to fill light is great, creating areas of high contrast and rich, black shadows. Unlike the even illumination of high-key lighting which seeks to display attractively all areas of the frame, the low-key noir style opposes light and dark, hiding faces, rooms, urban landscapes – and, by extension, motivations and true character – in shadow and darkness which carry connotations of the mysterious and the unknown.
>
> (Place and Peterson 1974: 30)

Most of the close-ups in *Hotel Methuselah* are heavily shadowed. This not only conceals facial expressions but also makes the image of the face uncanny and resistant to identification.

The elimination of fill light to produce areas of total black is yet another feature of the film noir genre, the overwhelming darkness or abyss encroaching on a helpless subject. In *Hotel Methuselah* this is best captured in the bedroom scenes, where Amy and Harry occupy the lower diagonal of the screen and are set against a pitch black background (Figure 6.6).

They speculate upon a future that they might share. The blackness, Amy's war stories and distant sounds of shell explosions convey a sense of claustrophobia, of the inevitable destruction and their approaching

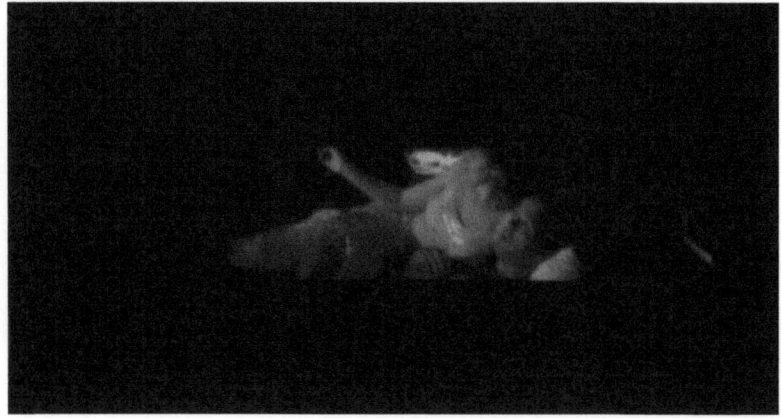

Figure 6.6   Bedroom scene, *Hotel Methuselah*. Photo © Ed Waring/Imitating the Dog

deaths. They also convey a sense that the characters are in the dark about their past. All hopes for a solution, a way out of the state they find themselves in, are engulfed by the formless, all-consuming blackness, the landscape of war seeking to displace any notions of a structured existence.

This sense of the meaningless of the human subject within the land-scape is further intensified through the occasional use of large depth of field to increase the amount of detail in the frame by putting all in focus. In film noir the idea of this effect is that the environment becomes distracting and disorientating. It also creates a sense that the 'environment will exist unchanged long after [the characters'] death' (Place and Peterson 1996: 67). Such characters are only elements of a greater overwhelming landscape. A similar effect is achieved in *Hotel Methuselah* in scenes where excessive detail is exposed in the projected film. This is especially effective when front projections are used to fur-ther discompose the viewer and accentuate Harry's disorientation (see Figure 6.7).

The key to creating such a powerful sense of disorientation and dis-placement is the use of film noir *mise-en-scène*, which was 'designed to unsettle, jar, and disorient the viewer in correlation with the diso-rientation felt by the noir heroes' (ibid.: 68). In *Hotel Methuselah* this disorientation is achieved via the excessive details doubled on screen and on stage. The film noir convention of a balanced two-shot of a character and a mirror reflection, to indicate the notion of a fragmented

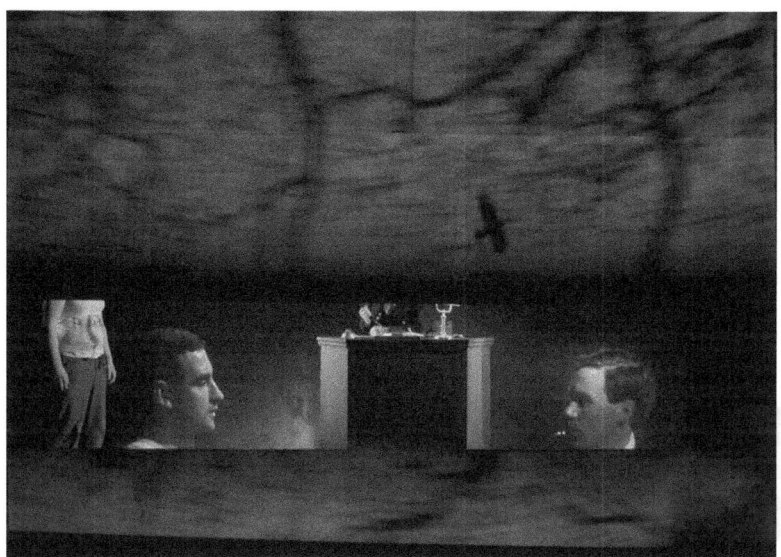

Figure 6.7 Weird Man and Harry, *Hotel Methuselah*. Photo © Ed Waring/ Imitating the Dog

ego, further defamiliarises our attempts to see Harry as a guide. This is inherent in the two-shots in *Hotel Methuselah* in which the characters speaking with Harry can be read as facets of his fragmented ego. Just as in film noir, the makers of *Hotel Methuselah* have avoided establishing shots. Withholding shots that would clarify the location of the action provides the 'the viewer with no means of spatial orientation' (ibid.: 68). High angle shots – often used in film noir – convey a sense of an 'oppressive and fatalistic angle that looks down on its helpless victim to make it look like a rat in a maze' (ibid.: 68). In *Hotel Methuselah* the hotel itself is presented as a labyrinth of endless corridors and unnumbered rooms. From the film's tracking shots à la *The Shining* to the puzzling swastika-like patterns on the floor the audience is provided only with fragmented information that requires re-ordering.

Apart from reinforcing the themes of the piece and locating them within a framework of potential references, the use of film noir aesthetics also alludes to a time when cinema tried to redefine itself formally and establish an aesthetic to convey the themes of ambiguity and loss. Arguably *Hotel Methuselah* further explores these formal aspects of film noir. It is not only the filmic representations of the characters who are trapped within the claustrophobic aesthetics of film noir, their live representations on stage are also confined within the letterbox framing. Films belong to the past. Once they have been recorded they can only be reproduced. Theatre, no matter how rehearsed or mechanised, always carries the potential of the unexpected, of unfolding into the future and breaking any framework imposed. Even though the stage action never leaves the letterbox the potential is always there. This constant reminder of a different form of perception that is not cinematic implies a subtle resistance. But through it the audiences are reminded formally that their perceptions and interpretations do not necessarily have to be trapped within cinematic aesthetic, in this case specifically in that of the film noir. Harry is not only a character trapped within the circumstances of his story, he is also held within the cinematic machine as a representation. By exaggerating and formally alienating the film noir aesthetic *Hotel Methuselah* invites the audience to be reflexive but also to take more 'response-ability' for the production of meaning.

Soundscape – visionscape

Hotel Methuselah further disorients perceptions of the cinematic and offers a more reflexive perceptual standpoint through the soundscape. The soundtrack of *Hotel Methuselah* could be split into two strands, the musical filmic soundtrack and the ambient soundscape. The former serves a dramatic function, mainly that of providing leitmotifs for the characters, making the piece sound 'cinematic' and underscoring emotions. In conjunction with the music we have a more disorienting industrial soundscape which jars our perception in terms of its dissonance with the visual environment and its interaction with the musical dimension. Cinematic soundtracks of the operatic/symphonic type are designed to guide, narrativise and underscore the audience's emotional involvement with a film. In that sense, the audience may have an expectation for the soundtrack to lead and underscore their emotional journey through *Hotel Methuselah*, too. A lot of film music is designed to reinforce the emotional blueprint of a film that Lyotard calls 'libidinal normalisation'. Thus classical film soundtracks often function as metaphors. They are not usually illustrative or depictive as tended to be the case during the silent movie era and early talkies, but rather offer different angles or perspectives on the images of the film. Hence, despite its inherently fragmentary nature, film music usually functions to offer a perspective of some kind: be it rhythmic, emotive or atmospheric, it essentially creates a montage that is parallel to the film. In the case of *Hotel Methuselah* the potential of Neil Boynton's cinematic music to be perceived as 'organic' and 'perspectivist' comes into tension with the 'industrial' ambient soundscape. The 'organic' is disrupted by the 'industrial' dimension. This tension displaces and disorients the conventional experience of a montage-driven soundtrack. This break with the guiding role of the cinematic soundtrack stimulates a more reflexive stance, allowing the audience to reflect upon the role that music plays in the act of perceiving cinematic images and also giving them more freedom and agency to correlate sound and image that is not necessarily strictly bound by the soundtrack.

In order to analyse this disorientation, and consequently the emancipatory quality of the soundtrack that to a great extent emerges as a contrast between the two dimensions, this section will first look at what the 'organic' cinematic musical dimension provides. Overall it can be argued that the experience of the cinematic dimension of *Hotel Methuselah's* soundtrack is one which seems to promise a sense of integrity. A promise that is phantasmagorical and ultimately dissolves into the broader soundscape.

One way in which this promise of integrity is achieved is through formal aspects of the 'organic' soundtrack. The musical motifs are generally classically composed using fairly simple harmonic structures. Both of the French songs used in the piece, *J'ai deux amour* and *D'amour*, and the love theme written by Neil Boynton, which was derived from these two songs, are very conventional in terms of their musical structures. This formal simplicity allows for an easy comprehension of these musical structures, thus creating a feeling of familiarity. This is further reinforced by the dramatic implementation of these themes, since they are used to underscore scenes between Harry and Amy, hence functioning as standard love themes.

Another way in which music gives a sense of integrity in *Hotel Methuselah* is through the use of familiarity and intertextuality. The songs can be perceived as familiar both for the characters and the audience. They also suggest a location of the action in time since both songs are from the 1950s.

> AMY: I like this song.
> HARRY: Do you? I think I've heard it before.
> AMY: It's a very popular tune.

The fact that the love song keeps returning like a ghost theme and often underscores scenes between Harry and Amy implies a nostalgic reminiscence of an integral relationship that once was, which is always there like a phantom in Harry's world but which he is unable to name.

There is another more austere, desolate musical theme. It comes up during the bedroom scenes when Harry and Amy try to talk about the ghosts from their past. Nonetheless the theme is still conventional and recognisable, it is a familiar 'uncanny theme' so to speak, made up of a series of cascading augmented triads.[7] It sounds familiar because augmented triads have often been used in popular film music in order to conjure up a desolate, uncanny atmosphere or landscape. Similar motifs could be found in Bernard Herrmann's soundtrack for *Psycho*, or in John Williams's the *Dune Sea of Tatooine* from *Star Wars* or Ennio Morricone's desert theme from *The Good, the Bad and the Ugly*.

On the other hand the industrial soundscape, made up of repetitive machine sounds, abrupt shell explosions and aeroplane noises creates an immersive chaotic experience. It often disrupts the 'organic' dimension of the soundtrack and is used to disorient a more perspectivist engagement with the piece. It is filled with sounds of things that are inhuman, fragmented, threatening, uncanny and sometimes discontinuous with the action taking place on film or stage. For instance the initial sound sequence of a fragmented collage of whispers in different languages creates an early sense of disorientation. The way the sounds were edited is mechanical and fragmentary. Repetitive machine sounds or sounds of human breathing looped in mechanical patterns produce a sense of fragmentation in relation to the organic nature of their source sounds.

This sense of the uncanny is emphasised through technological mediation. For example the sound of wind that whizzes through hotel corridors is a processed televisual noise. Even though this is common practice in sound design for cinema, the large amplitudes and uncanny use of the surround system expose its falseness. Another example is the sound of unusually loud rat screeches. The use of loud volume itself can dislodge the audience's orientation. For example one of the ways in which we usually identify the location of sound is through what is known as inter-aural intensity difference, that is, the 'difference in a sound intensity as it enters each ear' (Robinson-Riegler 2004: 77). The use of stereo and quadrophony allows the production to dislodge that sense by changing channel intensities. This mismatch of intensities was purposefully created in the opening and the closing sequences of *Hotel Methuselah* where loud sounds come in from all directions.

The other disorienting effect is the excess of sound information which resists the easy perceptual grouping enabled by the simple harmonic structures of the songs. For most of the piece, however, the soundscape is kept far in the distance, only occasionally threatening the more contrived atmosphere of the interior with occasional outbursts of gunfire or shell explosions. Some of the sounds are also discontinuous with the action taking place, as for example footsteps that are not in sync with the performers walking on stage. The love themes themselves become overlaid with industrial sounds which create tension and compromise their musical clarity.

Even though sound effects combined with a musical soundtrack are commonplace in cinema, there seems to be a deliberate disruption of organicity in the montage of the soundtrack in *Hotel Methuselah*. It is to a great extent an aesthetic operation but the use of extra loud volume makes the sound palpable, almost excessive to the image. There is a hierarchy of elements within classical cinema when it comes to scoring and soundtrack design, which defines the overall composition. This hierarchy follows the logic of montage, and serves the plot by providing dramatic tension; on the whole it is a part of the construction of a perspectivist cinematic experience. In *Hotel Methuselah* the potential of the soundtrack to endorse a perspectivist experience is disrupted at many points during the piece through moments of disorientation.

Conclusion

This chapter has explored the disorienting processes underlying post-cinematic performance which stimulate the audience to reconstruct a narrative from the disconnected elements conveyed by the spectacle. It has also explored the way in which the formal interplay of cinema and theatre questioned representations of war trauma in *Hotel Methuselah* in performances that took place at a time of heated debate and considerable scepticism surrounding the Iraq war and arguments in the media about the political apathy surrounding these debates. In many ways the piece provoked its audiences to be more active and reflexive of how they perceive the issue of war in the media and cinema, and the political implications of their perceptions. The experience of watching *Hotel Methuselah* can be characterised as an oscillation between binary oppositions of orientation/disorientation, passivity/activity, comfort/risk and safety/danger. This experience is essentially disorienting and somewhat confusing, but within it lies the potential for stimulating an active form of responsiveness, a 'response-ability'. Consequently there is also a potential to stimulate a political awareness. At times of conflict and profound disagreement, the public media and film can induce political apathy by presenting a distant, detached world and by creating a specific perspective on it that does not necessarily do justice to the complexity of the phenomenon. These perspectives are promoted to the general public whose perception narrows to a response to the information that they are given access to. This is not to say that there aren't any films that challenge singular or supposedly consensual mainstream perspectives on war. If we consider some comparatively recent blockbusters however, such as *We Were Soldiers Once* (2002), *Pearl Harbor* (2001) or *Black Hawk Down* (2001), films which clearly promote American wartime actions in an uncritical fashion, one could easily argue that there is a mass 'manufacturing of consent' at play, to use Noam Chomsky's term. An interesting feature of these films is that they usually represent the tactical and strategic mastery of their protagonists in a glorifying light. This focus on war as a strategic competition is nicely illustrated by films such as *Midway* (1976), where most of the action is structured around the strategic deliberations of generals. This approach may send a message that war can be controlled and designed for, whilst superior means of warfare somehow justify its ends. It also implies that the superior side (in the case of the above examples, the US Army) can be trusted to do the right thing and that it is their responsibility ultimately to resolve the conflict. The formal aesthetics of these movies work towards enhancing and inducing such perspectives.

Hotel Methuselah offers a different take on war, not only because the perspective of the protagonist is that of an anti-hero, lost in the middle of chaos, but also because of its formal disorientation. There is no overarching master viewpoint, nor is there any suggestion of a clear direction or strategy that could be taken by Harry to resolve at least his personal situation. There is no specific political message being put forward. Instead the complete lack of direction in Harry's life, together with the show's disorienting aesthetics work to stimulate the audience to become more active, whilst negotiating meaning, and also to become more aware of how cinema may shape their perceptions. In that sense the next time they watch a one-sided blockbuster they might step back and reflect upon what is at stake in the way cinematic forms induce political perspectives or even work as propaganda tools. Thus, like the pieces analysed in the earlier chapters, *Hotel Methuselah* recalibrates cinematic sensibilities by deconstructing culturally dominant cinematic conventions and the perceptual expectations associated with them. There is a certain form of resistance and reaction to dominant cinematic culture at play here. This is not a specific political resistance but a resistance against the passivity of the audience in relation to the perceptual choices they are able to make. By emancipating the audience and giving them a greater sense of perceptual freedom, *Hotel Methuselah* foregrounds and negotiates the 'politics of perception', inspiring the audience to become more 'response-able' for the perceptual choices they make.

7
Pedipulating *'Footage'* in Duncan Speakman's *As If It Were The Last Time*

In a seminal lecture, Peter Greenaway (2010) outlined what he called the tyrannies of classical realist cinema: the tyranny of the camera, the tyranny of the actor, the tyranny of text-based, literary narrative and the tyranny of the screen frame. To that list I would add the tyranny of realist montage, which, as we have seen so far in this book, percolates the majority of mainstream cinematic productions. Greenaway calls for a cinema that does away with all of these tyrannies. It is a provocative call in many ways, and it is not easy to conceive a cinema which does not use cameras or actors, has no narrative element or exists beyond the screen frame.

This chapter is concerned with *As If It Were The Last Time* – a 'soundwalk' created by Duncan Speakman and Circumstance. Duncan Speakman is a Bristol-based artist who creates various forms of site-based performance seeking to connect audiences with public spaces. Amongst his disparate body of work, he has produced a series of sound-walks that are heavily influenced by cinematic culture and its conventions. Like the work of other sound artists, such as Graeme Miller, Janet Cardiff and Platform, Speakman's pieces are performed by the audience, who carry portable sound equipment and wear headphones through which they can listen to a soundtrack with music, instructions and story-lines. He calls this type of performance practice, the 'Subtlemob'. For Speakman, the Subtlemob is a 'cinema made without cameras. We have all the elements, e.g. the script, the soundtrack and the location, but the audience is in the middle of it rather than watching it play out on a screen' (Speakman in Davies-Crook 2011). What makes his work – such as the *Opening Scene* (2009), *As If It Were The Last Time* (2009) and *Broken Voices* (2011) – so distinctive is that it specifically sets out to create cinematic experiences of, and in, public spaces. In Speakman's pieces, participants are invited to imagine, or montage, their own 'film' from the environment they experience. They have no film editing equipment apart from their imaginations and perceptions.

What is fascinating about this piece is that it manages to move beyond all of the tyrannies defined by Greenaway and create a novel post-cinematic experience. Greenaway's tyrannies will be used here as a mode of structuring the analysis that follows; an exploration of the ways in which the post-cinematic aesthetics of *As If It Were The Last Time* refashion and deconstruct culturally dominant conventions of realist cinema, thus locating the piece itself as a site of cultural difference. Four elements will underpin the analysis: camera, montage, narrative and framing. This substitutes Greenaway's 'actor' with 'montage' but while the notion of the actor as participant will percolate throughout most of the analysis, the aspect of montage, which for the most part is participant driven, is one of the key features of the piece. The analysis will mainly focus on the function of the soundtrack. Instead of providing a set path with clearly defined goals, the piece creates a framework for participant trajectories in which participants are given an MP3 with the soundtrack and instructions in order to create a performance for themselves by walking through a city. It will be argued that this kind of audio theatre offers a categorically different degree of participation and audience emancipation from the pieces analysed so far, whilst still embedding itself heavily within cinematic culture. The chapter will use intermedial theory – mainly stemming from Gabriella Giannachi and Steve Benford's research on 'mixed-reality performances' – supported by site-specific performance theory in order to explore the 'politics of perception' arising from the piece's post-cinematic aesthetic. Finally, the chapter will explore the relationship between the 'politics of perception' and neo-situationist philosophy – namely Guy Debord's concept of *dérive* – which can offer interesting insights when considering the site-specific soundwalk character of the piece.

However, it might first be useful to contextualise this specific 'cinematic' soundwalk in a broader field of intermedial practices. Since *As If It Were The Last Time* encompasses a multiplicity of art forms, such as site-specific/site-generic performance, music, audio theatre, cinema, interactive performance (flashmob) and storytelling, this discussion will locate it within the broad field of what Giannachi and Benford call 'mixed-reality' performances.

Mixed-reality performances

Giannachi and Benford define mixed-reality performances straightforwardly 'as the staging of theatrical performances in mixed reality environments' (Giannachi and Benford 2011: 2). They use Paul Milgram and Furni Kishino's continuum of mixed reality in order to outline a taxonomical framework in which mixed-reality performances can be located. At one end of the continuum we have 'purely physical, real environments' (ibid.), and at the other we have purely virtual environments. At the centre of the spectrum lies 'augmented reality', which comprises real, physical environments overlaid with digital data, and virtual environments underpinned by physical data (ibid.). This model provides a good taxonomical framework for the classification of interactive performances that use technology in live environments and site-specific contexts (Figure 7.1).

Mixed-reality performances can broadly be described as hybrid performances that combine instances of the real, virtual, augmented reality and augmented virtuality. Duncan Speakman's *As If It Were The Last Time* sits well within this paradigm since it incorporates a guided soundwalk, a cinematic soundtrack and performance elements staged in particular areas of a city. Thus, it can be classified as a type of augmented reality where the soundtrack, with its instructions, augments the experience of the real city.

An important concept in mixed-reality performances, which will prove useful in the analysis of *As If It Were The Last Time*, is the concept of 'trajectories':

> Each participant may follow his or her own routes or trajectories, which intertwine and interweave in different ways to create social structures. Trajectories emphasize aspects of journey, continuity, future and past, perspectival points of view [...] Unlike routes or journeys, trajectories embrace both embedded and emergent narratives, thus representing not only a direction or path, but also a way of experiencing and performing mixed reality environments.
>
> (Giannachi and Benford 2011: 15)

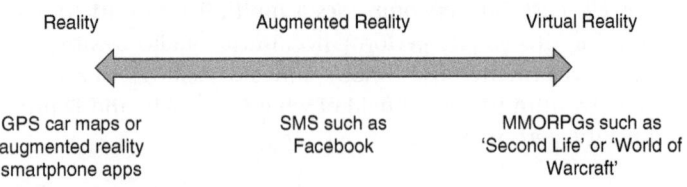

Figure 7.1 Mixed-reality continuum

Source: Based on Steve Benford's diagram in Giannachi and Benford (2011: 3); examples at the lower level added.

In order to analyse the post-cinematic qualities of *As If It Were The Last Time* by using this concept of trajectories we have to ask how these trajectories relate to the experience of mainstream cinematic works? Does a cinema spectator also engage with a trajectory – a perceptual journey through the world of a film? How are cinematic trajectories constructed and how do they differ from trajectories in mixed-reality performances? It will be important to look at these differences because from a post-cinematic perspective the kind of perceptual trajectories that a mixed-reality performance, such as *As If It Were The Last Time*, evokes can be seen as a deconstruction of realist cinematic aesthetics which are used to guide and frame a spectator's experience in mainstream cinematic works. This does not mean that a spectator cannot read against the grain or feel sufficiently emancipated to construct their own perceptual trajectory. Jacques Rancière has argued for that in his book, *The Emancipated Spectator*, which will be looked at more extensively in the next chapter on *Dogville*.

Perceptual trajectories in cinema

How can we understand the function of perceptual trajectories in film and cinema? As we have seen in previous chapters, Eisenstein has written extensively on the ways in which cinematic montage in classical film can guide the spectatorial gaze. When discussing the ways in which spectators perceive films, he claims that 'the word *path* is not used by chance'. It is 'the imaginary path followed by the eye and the varying perceptions of an object that depends on how it appears to the eye' (Eisenstein 1989: 111). The design of the perceptual path or the trajectory is central to his thesis on montage. Eisenstein's analysis of Renaissance painting is worth noting here. He argues that lines in Renaissance painting were utilised to visualise 'the character of movement' (Eisenstein 1986: 148). One of the methods was to use roads as graphical lines amongst which 'events that the artist wished to portray in particular sequence' were distributed. He gives the example of Domenico Ghirlandaio's *The Adoration of the Shepherds* (1485), where 'the infant surrounded by the shepherds occupied the foreground, and on [the road] that twists forward from the background appear the Magi; so that the road ties together events which are, in subject, thirteen days apart' (Giannachi 2011: 18). Giannachi recounts:

> In a subsequent period, Eisenstein points out, the road is replaced by a 'path of the eye', marking the change from a sphere of 'representation

to one of composition' that, once perspective started to be used, often included the viewer into the journey. He notes, 'there is usually something in a painting which attracts attention before all other elements. From this point the attention moves along that path desired by the artist'.

(Giannachi and Benford 2011: 18)

Eisenstein applies these notions to the composition of shots in movies. Camera angles and tracking shots, as well as internal graphical structures within frames, can be used to guide an audience's perception and establish a perceptual trajectory. In an interesting early essay he extends the idea to architecture, citing the Acropolis as a careful design which guides and structures the visitor's experience in ways which he claims exemplify proto-cinematic montage:

The Greeks have left us the most perfect examples of shot design, change of shot, and shot length (that is, the duration of a particular impression). Victor Hugo called the medieval cathedrals 'books in stone' (see Notre Dame de Paris). The Acropolis of Athens has an equal right to be called the perfect example of one of the most ancient films.

(Eisenstein 1989: 112)

This trans-historical notion of cinematic montage and cinematic experience beyond the medium of film is very telling when approaching Speakman's work. It exemplifies the possibility of creating cinematic experience beyond the medium of film – beyond the limitations outlined by Greenaway.

Nonetheless, it is important to stress that for Eisenstein the technology of film was perceived as an ultimate tool, the 'highest form' (Eisenstein 1949: 48) of art, which allowed the filmmaker the opportunity to create a singular perspectivist experience rather than offering a multiplicity of trajectories. The aim was not to create an open text,[1] within which different interpretations and trajectories could be contemplated, but rather to create a guide and manipulate the audience towards specific meanings. Thus, film montage for Eisenstein was an 'opportunity to encourage and direct the whole *thought process*' (ibid.: 62). The trajectory thus became the intellectual journey of the spectator through the world of the movie, heavily influenced by the montage.

In this book, we have looked at various ways in which cinema can guide and influence our perceptions, including montage, conventions and programmability of meaning, narrative structures, the temporality of cinema, camera perspectivism and actors' performances. In many cases, these concerned domains, strategies and techniques through which thought and perceptual patterns could be manipulated. Whereas perceptual trajectories in classical cinema are contingent and related to a fixed audiovisual structure that has been designed in consonance with these parameters, perceptual trajectories in mixed-reality performance arise from a partially desynchronised design which is categorically different to that of a classical film. Consequently, a mixed-reality performance such as *As If It Were The Last Time* has the potential to deconstruct mainstream cinematic design in a post-cinematic fashion.

Perceptual trajectories in mixed-reality performances

Mixed-reality performances, such as *As If It Were The Last Time*, are essentially site-specific (or site-generic) performances. Therefore, the outcome of such a performance and, consequently, the trajectories it will elicit are the result of a complex negotiation between the participants, the author and the site. In stark contrast to mainstream cinema, a site-specific work, and in particular a guided audio-tour, is more about designing a framework to facilitate the active engagement of the participants than it is about designing a specific trajectory for a more passive spectatorial experience. As Walter Heim observes, in the context of site-specific work: '[t]he artist asks the instigating question, listens, sets a context for action, creates an aesthetic milieu in which an event is mutually created' (Heim 2006: 203). When considering perceptual trajectories in site-specific performances, we must also take into account the unpredictable effects of the environment. Misha Myers – an artist working in the area of site-specific performance, and famous for her 'conversive wayfinding' (Myers 2006) projects – defines some of the aspects and challenges of designing a site-specific guided tour in this respect: 'there are conditions which the artist may create space for, but cannot predetermine, such as weather, transformations of the landscape, walker's corporeal rhythms, capacities, desires and mood' (ibid.: 104). In cinema, most of these effects can be edited out, erased or manipulated by the filmmaker. In site-specific performances many layers of meaning and stimuli may arise fortuitously. There is always a tension between the material that is brought to the site, that is the soundtrack, and the site itself. Nick Kaye argues that the meaning of site-specific performances 'is to be discovered in an encounter with that which lies beyond the obvious elements of the piece, through intrusion of the "found", *in looking,* into the incompletions of the "fabricated"' (Kaye 1996: 66). Contrary to Eisenstein's theories of montage, which advocate the orchestration of multi-layered aesthetic superstructures as carriers of meaning, the emphasis here lies on incompleteness, on the fissures and cracks that emerge from the tensile relationship between the fabricated soundtrack and the experience of the real city environment.

One of the main distinctions between cinematic and mixed-reality trajectories is the distinction between those that are author-led and those that are participant-led. Giannachi and Benford define this as a distinction between 'canonical' and 'participant' trajectories (2011: 230). In their analysis of the design of mixed-reality performance, they claim that canonical trajectories are optimal, those that the designers/artists have anticipated in advance. Participant trajectories are the ones chosen by the participants, which may very well deviate from the planned or assumed original trajectory. A similar dichotomy can be applied to the experience of film and cinema. After all, while Eisenstein's methodologies of montage can be classified as attempts to design for canonical perceptual trajectories, a spectator may wish to read against the grain and therefore effectuate something akin to a participant trajectory.

So, to some extent, the difference between cinematic and mixed-reality trajectories can simply be related to their positions on a spectrum between author-led and participant/spectator-led trajectories – between what might also be called the 'writerly' and the 'readerly'. However, there is still a categorical difference between the two. This is best explained if we consider McLucas's model of a site-specific performance. For this model, McLucas comes up with an interesting definition of the structure of site-specific performances. According to him, site-specific performances have three components: 'the host, the ghost and the witness' (McLucas in Kaye 2000: 128).

The 'host' is the site itself, with all of its intricacies: the physical space, its geography and climate, the architecture, communities of people who live there, passers-by, events that take place there and so on. The 'host' also brings its history with it, the memories and recollections of its past. In the case of *As If It Were The Last Time* the first host of the piece was Covent Garden in London. The 'ghost' describes both the material and the performance/presence of the participants brought to the site. In relation to *As If It Were The Last Time*, this would be the soundtrack – with its music, poetry and instructions – but also the performances of the participants, including the simple fact of their presence at the site. Thus, the 'ghost' intrudes upon and modifies the perception of the site ('host') and/or modifies the site itself. Finally, in this model, there is the 'witness', the participant/spectator. The witness is a spectator but might also become an active participant. These components interact in complex ways in order to constitute the final trajectory through the piece.

It is interesting to try to apply this model to a more traditional cinematic experience in order to see how it might influence the formation of some kind of trajectory through the world of a film. What would the 'host' be in the case of cinema? One way of looking at it is that a traditional/orthodox experience of a movie (that is, watching it in a cinema) will have both a 'real' and a 'virtual' host. The 'real' host in this case is the cinema. The interiors of cinemas are usually designed to provide as little distraction as possible from the film itself. A blacked-out interior, soundproof walls and comfortable chairs that make spectators forget about their physical presence are central elements in this design, which is supposed to create an immersive experience, minimise distractions and focus the audience's perceptions on the film.[2] Thus, the physical host, the place and its effects are minimised and made negligible in the composition of the experience.

The 'virtual' host could be understood here to be the filmed environment – that is, the *mise-en-scène* of the movie – the set, props and the actors that were filmed and fixed on the celluloid. The *mise-en-scène* was once a physical host, of course, offering all the possibilities for exploration that a physical site might offer – specific and contingent upon the type of set-up it was (for instance, a set in a studio or an outside location). The 'ghost' is the film itself, a time machine that engulfs the virtual host. The 'witness' – the spectator in this case – cannot interact with the virtual host as it has been permanently fixed on the celluloid. The virtual host can only be viewed through the 'ghostly' cinematic apparatus. The real host – the cinema – is insignificant and ideally is forgotten altogether. If *As If It Were The Last Time* was a movie about a city, like Wim Wenders's *Lisbon Story* for instance, the city would be a virtual host, completely subsumed into the inner workings of the ghost that is the movie machine itself. By following McLucas's model, then, we can conclude that a conventional cinematic experience (screening) contains the element of the 'host' fully incorporated into, and absorbed by, the 'ghost'. Thus, the spectator's freedom to form a perceptual trajectory in the case of cinema is always limited by the effacement of the host, or what Jean Baudrillard has called the repression of the real. This distinction places a piece like *As If It Were The Last Time* in an interesting position, as it has the potential to re-frame most of the aspects that are culturally associated with realist cinema, making it a post-cinematic piece par excellence. Below, the chapter will look at the ways in which

As If It Were The Last Time challenges traditional notions of cinema and expectations of cinematic experience. It will also investigate the ways in which the soundtrack sets up expectations for cinematic trajectories and their relationship to the participant-led trajectories that emerge from the myriad of possibilities offered by the host site.

In the first performance of *As If It Were The Last Time*, the participants were given an MP3 player containing a soundtrack with instructions to be followed as they walked through the streets of Covent Garden. The participants were split into two groups and coupled into pairs, with each group having a different MP3 track. The composition of the soundtrack consisted of three registers: a monologue by a narrator describing sensations and memories of city life, a voice describing a scene performed by members of the other group, and a series of instructions to be performed by the participant and their partner. The piece was designed in such a way that when one group was performing the other was spectating. Then the roles would alternate. Both action and speech were underscored by a continuous musical soundtrack varying in pace and composition. Here is a short extract from the script to show how this worked. Participants in Group 1 are spectating while those in Group 2 are performing.

Group 1:
the camera zooms in to a couple
standing in the glow of a shop window
it's hard to tell their age
they could be lovers
there are decisions to be made
they're thinking about their parents
about how she is going to break the news to her boss
about each other
and they just keep looking in the window...

Group 2:
ok, so now it's time to start playing your part
with your partner you should
find a window that 'you' think looks interesting
maybe a shop or a restaurant
i'll give you a moment to find one

now go up to the window and stand right next to your partner
in front of it

think for a moment about why you picked this one
can you see inside?
can you see your own reflection right now?
look at yourself for a moment
and just think about your day...

(Speakman 2009)

Cinema without cameras

As If It Were The Last Time invites its participants to take an active role in the performance, inspiring them to transform their visual apparatus into a 'living camera'. In his lecture, Greenaway called for a cinema without cameras, defining the camera as a blunt instrument which does more to limit visual experiences than to allow for an exploration of the visual field and its experiential plethora. The camera is the main recording instrument in filmmaking. As a technological device, it allows for the documentation and preservation of moving images in a fixed spatio-temporal matrix: the celluloid. The camera itself has a long history of development worth briefly noting here. The photographic camera developed from the camera obscura – a pinhole camera device dating as far back as the cultures of ancient China and Greece. Some of the key developments of this device were made by the instrument maker Reiners Gemma Frisius, in 1544, for the purpose of watching a solar eclipse, a method he later published in *De Radio Astronimica et Geometrico*, and Giovanni Batista della Porta, in 1558, who used the pinhole camera as a device to aid drawing. Since then, the camera obscura has been used as a device for the fixation of images on a screen. It has been used by artists across many media, ranging from drawing, painting, sculpture eventually to photography per se. Thus, one of the main uses of the camera obscura in Western culture was in facilitating the creation process of fixed, static imagery; recall that the movie camera also records static images, twenty-four static frames per second. Only by playing back a sequence of these static images is an illusion of movement created. This brief historical account is important because it accounts for the camera's role in aiding the artist to create a fixed representation of reality. If we then ask why is an aid required at all, we can arrive at an insight into the difference between experiencing the world through a camera and experiencing the world through our eyes. This difference becomes quite apparent in *As If It Were The Last Time*.

In *As If It Were The Last Time*, the participants were given instructions that included explicit references to cinematic techniques. They were asked to look at the world around them through close-ups, camera zooms, pans and so on. Yet they had no cameras. It was as if they were supposed to film the city with their own eyes. What became quite apparent in this for me, as a participant, was the clash between the cinematic expectations of a fixed shot and the experience of trying to perform a shot. Framing some of the images that the instructions suggested was complicated. For instance, trying to catch a reflection in a shop window at the right angle can be awkward. At one point, staring through the glass of a clothes shop, I managed to frame my own reflection and align it with the figure of a mannequin. By shifting my virtual image across the mannequin gallery and the clothes racks I created what McLucas called a 'ghosting' effect on the 'host'. I brought my own presence and visual image into the context of the host – the actual city. In the case of the clothes shop display, it became a playful recognition of the fact that I was not only a spectator but also a performer – free to assume different roles. This effect was shared by the participants from the other group, who were watching me at that time. However, this was not only ghosting the place, it was also ghosting oneself. The instruction *'look at yourself for a moment and just think about your day...'* made that explicit. The instructions on the soundtrack emphasised this further by prompting me to tidy my hair, and to judge whether my outfit needed straightening and so on. There was a constant shift in focus between the external and internal experience. This could also provoke a degree of dissatisfaction with the fact that it was not easy to frame the assigned image accurately. Human visual perception is fluid, and our field of vision has no boundaries. In cinema, it is the fixed nature of the photographic image, with its set boundaries, which enables spectators to identify compositional dialectics and contrasts – for instance, making them appear as explicit and meaningful. In the case of *As If It Were The Last Time*, the spectator's perceptual trajectories do not encounter a fixed artefact, but are rather in a constant mode of rehearsal – in a reiterative state of searching and adjusting to an ever-changing reality.

By foregrounding the liveness of the visual apparatus, the piece also drew attention to the participants' own presence in the space – unlike the conventional cinema experience in which one is asked to forget about one's own presence and invited into an immersive reality. Cinemas are dark and acoustically isolated so that audiences are better able to focus and immerse themselves into the cinematic illusion on screen. The camera's look is an invisible omnipresent eye, and the spectator is invited to assume its transparent position. A cinematic version of the above sequence would create a perspective on the event, or even a series of perspectives, but it could not involve the spectator in an active, reiterative process of constructing images of that event.

Films have been theorised as 'mirrors' – reflecting identities, images of society and social relationships – with the screen as the mirror's reflective plane. For instance, Lyotard argued that 'film acts as the orthopaedic mirror analysed by Lacan in 1949 as constitutive of the imaginary subject of *object a*; that we are dealing with the social body in no way alters its function' (Lyotard 1988: 176). This concept of a film-mirror posits film as an unalterable image of the social body and its reality. Film is seen as an unchangeable work of art that does not respond to nor change in relation to spectators' reactions. Mirrors, on the other hand, enable the viewer to alter and adjust his/her appearance in relation to the virtual image. Mirrors are instruments for the rehearsal of identity and thus an effective prop in the process of identity construction. A film is a mirror reflection constructed by a third party with which its viewers may or may not resonate. In the case of *As If It Were The Last Time*, this dynamic is different. It can become a 'mirror', but it is one that enables the spectator/performer to construct or readjust their own self-image. It is through this deconstruction that participants in this performance were freed to negotiate the politics of the personal in the public space. Unlike cinema spectators in the theoretical context of Jean Baudry's cinematic apparatus, participants were not implicated in an ideological/political framing. Instead, they were allowed to negotiate their own 'politics of perception' by staging their identities within the live environment of the city.

Cinema without montage

Montage is a key concept in cinematic works and Greenaway refers to it throughout his lecture. It is a methodology by which representations of events are organised and displayed. It is thus an essential way of creating and designing canonical trajectories. Even though the soundtrack of *As If It Were The Last Time* itself was edited, the overall cinematic experience of the piece was by no means fixed. Unlike a conventional cinema audience experiencing a montaged *mise-en-cadre*, an end-product, the participants here were directly involved in the process of the production of images. They were positioned between the *mise-en-scène* and the cinematic experience conjured by the piece. Participants were given a part of the cinematic construct and asked to perform/improvise the other part. They received the music, instructions and elements of the script, information about locations, and the general structure of the piece (the macro montage of the different scenes). By contrast, the direction of the gaze (camera movement), perceptual choices (lateral montage) and the specifics of the action were their choice. They become partial witnesses but also partial creators of the piece, filling in the initial framework suggested by the soundtrack. The instructions tended to be quite generalised and non-specific so that the participants could creatively seek out images of their choice. The following section from the piece exemplifies this:

> and the camera pulls back to reveal a street
> people
> some moving, some pause
> one unaware of the other
> a man speaks into his mobile phone
> a woman turns to look over her shoulder
> a couple wait expectantly
>
> (Speakman 2009)

The images in the instructions had to be generalised enough to fit with what was happening in the real city. This is a very different process to realist cinema where images are carefully selected and salient. As was discussed in earlier chapters, there is a methodology of structuring images of movement in realist cinema by moving from the general image of movement to the specific. In some sense, by providing a generalised framework, Speakman initiates this process. Generalised images of movement, such as 'and the camera pulls back to reveal a street / people / some moving, some pause', are an example of this shift in focus. A more general image of the street, with all its movements, shifts to that of the movements of specific people. However, there are also specific interjections that do not necessarily match what is going on around the participants. For instance, when I performed this scene there was no woman turning to look over her shoulder in sight.

As a result, there are no canonical trajectories here, because there is no way of predicting or controlling the environment in order to montage it to the soundtrack. There is no structured correspondence between what is heard on the MP3 and the visual and material experience of the city. Instead, the whole performance becomes an aesthetic adventure. Even though the piece is structured around certain canonical routes (in the sense that there are checkpoints and places that one has to reach on time in order for the performance to progress) there is a lot of space given for the participants to wander off and develop their own participant trajectories – their very own 'participant montage'. As a result, there is a sense of openness and potentiality of what can occur, which is not the case with a standard cinematic experience. In order to emphasise this further, the participants were often asked to take risks. For example, at one point the participants were instructed to separate from their partners:

> so now is the moment where you both need to be a little brave
> you're going to have to fend for yourself for a moment
> one of you is going to stay exactly where you are
> decide who is going to stay
> so the other one of you should get out of sight
> I'll give you a moment to separate
>
> (Speakman 2009)

Moments like these were conceived to create a sense of disorientation, but also to allow for moments of reflection. The narrative would stop and participants were given time to wander about and experience the surroundings at will without any guidance.

This space for reflexivity outside the temporal framework, imposed by the soundtrack preceding such moments, brought forth an alteration in duration. Shot durations in realist montage are usually dictated by the pace of the editing and the shot sequences. The temporal construction tends to be built in such a way as to create an illusion of an organic construct – one that can convey a coherent subjective position and thus establish a canonical trajectory through the world of the film. In 'Acinema', Lyotard argues that '[t]he diegesis' of film 'locks together the synthesis of movements in the temporal order', much as 'perspectivist representation does so in the spatial order' (Lyotard 1989: 172). This locking and fixity is what creates a perspectivist perceptual trajectory by design, but it also engenders a system of values by selecting those images that are perceived to have value. Also, images tend to be tailored towards time frames which can hold the audience's attention and interests. Any montage that challenges these temporal conventions and perceptual tempos can be considered, from a mainstream standpoint, to run the risk of becoming tedious and losing the audience's attention. Many directors who have challenged these conventions, such as Werner Herzog, Andrei Tarkovsky, David Lynch and Michael Haneke, have commented on this phenomenon and the creative potential opened up by expanding the temporal frame. Their experiments with temporality became a way to allow the audience to explore and investigate the world of the film beyond these initial cultural expectations. For instance, Sean Martin comments on Tarkovsky's treatment of temporality:

> Tarkovsky proposed that if a take is lengthened, boredom naturally sets in for the audience. But if the take is extended even further, something else arises: curiosity. Tarkovsky is essentially proposing giving the audience time to inhabit the world that the take is showing us, not *watch* it, but to *look* at it, to explore it.
>
> (Martin 2005: 49)

He then gives an example from Tarkovsky's film *Mirror*. The action is set in the Soviet Union in the mid-1930s, and the protagonist Maria works as a proofreader for a daily newspaper. In one of the scenes, she runs from her home in the pouring rain concerned that she has not corrected a misprint of Stalin's name which was misspelled as 'Sralin' (meaning 'shitter'). Martin recounts that the emphasis of this scene is not so much on the narrative and Maria's worries, but rather on her physical beauty, and this is achieved through the extended temporality of the shot:

> It is as if Tarkovsky were content just to watch Margarita Terekhova running through the rain, down steps, across yards, into corridors. Here, Tarkovsky reveals the presence of beauty in something that is apparently mundane and, paradoxically (given the period), also potentially fatal for Maria if the mistake she thinks she's made has gone to press.
>
> (Martin 2005: 135)

The notion of *watching* seems to engender a perceptual methodology here. One watches and reads in a certain way according to specific rules and expectations. The freedom to look and explore is evocative of Nick Kaye's remark about site-specific performances which prompt the participants to take their time and investigate and discover. Due to the fixed nature of montage in classical film, this freedom is still framed and controlled by the editor/director. In the case of Tarkovsky's films, it is still a formal dialectic – an avant-garde aesthetic set in relation to popular fast-paced montage engendering a different mode of temporal perception. In other words, it becomes a way of substituting one canonical trajectory for another. However, in *As If It Were The Last Time*, the temporal experience is cut loose from these constraints and the gaze is allowed to wonder more freely and encounter the unexpected. For instance, one may focus on a street musician imposing his own tempos and rhythms or a cyclist dashing through a nearby park.

This effect is heightened by the fact that different participants have different rhythms when they walk around the city and perform the assigned scenes. This is well exemplified by a scene in which participants were asked to dance with their partners. One set of participants was asked to dance in pairs while the other set watched. Once the dance was complete, the groups would swap roles. This dance felt like an extended shot. It is difficult to say whether the temporal frame was adequate or not in terms of maintaining interest since it greatly depended on what the dances were like and on the specific perceptual choices made by the onlookers. Quite often, as spectators, we find certain temporal frames more appropriate than others. Tarkovsky's reference to boredom can be read as implying that spectators have certain expectations, a blueprint or a sense-making frame that they bring to their expectations of experience and what is of value to them. If the scene fits those parameters, it may be deemed as interesting, if it fails it runs the risk of coming across as boring. These preconceptions may include a political point of view. By confronting the participants with the real dimension of the host, the piece potentially questioned what was politically at stake in the temporality of realist cinematic montage. To explain this, let us evoke the famous example of Henri Bergson's reflection on the melting of the sugar cube:

> If I want to mix a glass of sugar and water, I must, willy-nilly, wait until the sugar melts. This little fact is big with meaning. For here the time I have to wait is not that mathematical time which would apply equally well to the entire history of the material world, even if that history were spread out instantaneously in space. It coincides with my impatience, that is to say, with a certain portion of my own duration, which I cannot protract or contract as I like. It is no longer something thought, it is something lived.
>
> (Bergson 1911: 10)

The shift in the experience of duration is a shift from the thought to the lived. But what exactly does thought constitute for Bergson in this instance? It is a particular frame of meaning-making and a particular frame through which one can make sense of reality. This notion of thought has a direct affinity with temporality in classical realist montage, since montage affects viewing habits and ways of looking at reality by organising images in time. We may choose to value what we perceive as important and significant, and choose not to see what we prefer to ignore or marginalise. As Lyotard argued in 'Acinema', mainstream Hollywood often discriminates against those movements that will not return a certain level of excitement and pleasure or a clear sense of narrative meaning. This can have an effect on the way we end up perceiving the world around us.[3] By exposing participants to a multiplicity of durations and speeds, in their concurrent simultaneity, *As If It Were The Last Time* points towards the Bergsonian notion of the lived – as far as that can be read as an experience outside preconceived notions and perceptual expectations. Also, by allowing the participants to be performers and spectators at the same time, the piece deconstructs the position of the judging spectator/voyeur and questions the durational aspects of performance. For example, a spectator's choice as to how to allocate attention during the piece might reveal that behind the management of perception lies a value system that allocates more interest and importance to some images than to others. Different 'politics of perception' come into play in the choice of whether to look at one's fellow participants, a street musician, a beggar or a couple looking through a shop window. The value system underlying these perceptual choices was – in my case – partially constructed as a result of my exposure to cinematic culture and its political agendas. In effect, the piece foregrounded the 'politics of perception' by exposing the participants to different rhythms and durations of images and by making the differences between them explicit.

Cinema without narratives

It is difficult to conceive of a film without a narrative – after all, any sequence of visual patterns or sounds can be interpreted as telling some kind of story. When Greenaway refers to the notion of narratives in classical cinema in his lecture on the post-cinematic, he is referring to something very specific: a realist mode of structuring and shaping film narratives based on literary traditions as a means of creating perspectivist discursive positions.[4] *As If It Were The Last Time* has no storyline as such, instead it is structured around reminiscences of everyday life in the city, which the narrator shares with the participants. There are lots of brief fragmented narratives, short episodes concerning non-specific, fairly generic characters that serve as narrative concepts to be 'projected' on to the random passers-by encountered during the performance. We may call these bursts of storytelling the embedded narratives. These embedded narratives, when projected onto a participant's situation, may in turn form emergent narratives – narratives that are developed by participants. Embedded narratives tend to follow a classical lateral progression – in the sense that there is a certain story and some sort of linear, sequential development to them. Emergent narratives can be classified as being vertical in nature – in the sense that they require the participants not to perceive laterally but to investigate the world around them in depth, 'vertically', in order to connect the embedded narrative fragments with the surrounding context.

As far as classical realist film is concerned, Eisenstein often spoke of the verticality of montage, where the dramatic, visual and audio elements were combined to create an aesthetically pleasing correspondence or image. He compared this type of montage with orchestral practice:

> Everyone is familiar with the appearance of an orchestral score. There are several staffs, each containing the part for one instrument or a group of like instruments. Each part is developed horizontally. But vertical structure plays no less important a role, interrelating as it does all the elements of the orchestra within each unit of time. Through the progression of the vertical line, [...], the intricate harmonic musical movement of the whole orchestra moves forward.
>
> (Eisenstein 1947: 64)

Nonetheless, this notion of verticality is elusive in his example since it serves to 'move the whole orchestra forward'. In other words, we are dealing with 'depth' designed to propel a lateral movement of narrative. In site-specific performances, such as *As If It Were The Last Time*, the notion of depth and verticality provides a different understanding. Depth is no longer a support system for the creation of canonical trajectories but rather a dimension for exploration and discovery of the specificities of place. Mike Pearson gives a good account of the concept of depth in site-specific performance:

> This might resemble what Michael Shanks and I called a *deep map:* an attempt to record and represent the substance, grain and patina of a particular place, through juxtapositions and interweaving of the historical and the contemporary, the political and the poetic, the factual and the fictional, the academic and the aesthetic [...] depth not as profundity but as topographic and cultural density.
>
> (Pearson 2010: 32).

The realities of the place (host) and the potential to navigate and explore it enable the participants to form their own narratives. According to the American anthropologist Kathleen Stewart, who has worked extensively with coal-mining communities in West Virginia, attempting to narrativise 'a local cultural real' (Stewart 1996: 3), the place itself is an essential ingredient in the creation of stories and narratives. She claims that the experience of a place:

> Tells its story through interruptions, amassed densities of descriptions, evocations of voices and the conditions of their possibility, and lyrical, ruminative aporias that give pause. It fashions itself as a tendon between interpretation and evocation, mimicking the tension in culture between the disciplinary and the imaginary.
>
> (Ibid.)

This is very similar to Speakman's work, in which the emergent narratives arise from personal reflections and explorations. As in most site-specific performances, the narrative effect depends greatly on the interaction of the participants/audiences with the actual environment. *As If It Were The Last Time* is often narrated in the second person, which addresses the participant directly:

> I'd ask you what you'd take back
> and when your mouth opens a wind would rise up
> carrying unsaid words that became choked in your chest case
> and it would blow out from between kissed lips
>
> (Speakman 2009)

There are short interludes where themes about moving and searching for a new home and a place to live are being explored – hence most of the script revolves around searching for a place one could somehow identify with. The piece becomes a form of cinematic archaeology, a vertical investigation into the personal and the public. These narrative segments function like a series of springboards for emergent narratives:

> and this moment passes with 6 beats of your heart
> with the beat of a moth wing,
> with a birth,
> with a football in the neighbor's garden,
> with the balloon you let go, the glasses in a toast,
> the car you crashed, the door you left unlocked,

the food you left out, the loan you repaid,
the first pet, the lost wife, and the husband found

(Speakman 2009)

It is easy for most people to recall an unlocked door, or perhaps a car crash, the food left out, a loan and so on. These suggestions function as starting points for the participants to run with the idea, to embody the suggestions imaginatively and to give them existential consistency. Much of the narrative progression in this piece relies on the way the participants interact, but it is also in how they choose to perceive the environment. Therefore, the landscape in this case becomes what Ingold terms a 'taskscape'. Yet these reminiscences never quite fit with the experience of the surroundings. The piece may thus become a search for metaphors, and an attempt to find personal connections with the otherwise unfamiliar city. Thus, one could see it as 'a work-in-progress, perpetually under construction [...] a matrix of movement, with distinct places as nodes bound together' (Ingold cited in Pearson 2010: 15) by the actions of the participants.

There are some themes which carry a certain political weight and, in a sense, position participants within an ideological perspective. For instance, lines such as 'and watch the flag that we refuse / to stand under as it's raised by a national party' (Speakman 2009), with the explicit use of 'we', seem to be an attempt to implicate the participants politically. Also, there are attempts to draw attention to a side of the life of the city that is perhaps marginalised: 'you stumble in moonlight / hoping the streetlights are maintained by / the unknown workers we rally against' (Speakman 2009). There were also references made to immigration. For instance: 'Someone turns up to fix your boiler and speaks in broken English. You feel apart but strangely close.' These kinds of statements function differently here than they would in a film. Pearson claims that in site-specific performance '[m]oving between places, *wayfinding*, more closely resembles story-telling than map-using' (Pearson 2010: 15). In realist film, the host is always mapped onto the ghost. One can read against the grain, but the film remains unchanged. In *As If It Were The Last Time*, this is different since it is possible to ignore the instructions and stand underneath the flag. This would not automatically indicate any kind of sympathy with nationalist parties, but it might indicate that political stances depend on forms of experience or, in this case, on forms of perception. The line 'You feel apart but strangely close' is also very telling. Meta-discourses in classical cinema have the potential to frame sub-discourses such as those referring to social minorities.

They can elicit identification with particular characters or induce a sense of distance. By evoking an oscillation between closeness and distance, this line exemplifies how the piece deconstructs the meta-discursive position of a cinematic narrative by positioning the participant in a place of tension and undecidability in relation to their surroundings and potential ways of perceiving them. Whether a spectator/participant feels close or apart in this case is a result of individual perception and mapping of the narratives to the host site. Thus, by allowing the participants to find their own way through the narratives and stories, the piece foregrounds the fact that the way we choose to see and perceive may be bound to some political choice or activity, which in the end might influence the way we integrate and identify with the places we live in and the people we come across.

Cinema without frames

Greenaway argued for a cinema that challenged the concept of the screen frame. He saw the screen frame as a limiting boundary, a rectangular restriction imposed upon the visual material of film, limiting the multiplicity and overabundance of potentially visual experience. When considering the screen frame, Chion argues along similar lines:

> Why in the cinema do we speak of 'the image' in the singular, when a film has thousands of them? The reason is that even if there were millions, there would still be only one container for them, the frame. What 'the image' designates in the cinema is not the content but the container: the frame.

> (Chion 1994: 66)

As If It Were The Last Time has no frame or container for the images; they are experienced as they would be in reality. The piece itself exists in the audio dimension, which to some extent becomes its only framing device. It is thus worth looking briefly at the ways in which a cinematic soundtrack can function as a frame in this piece. Chion claims that sound does not have a container in a way that images do. One can record sound, but the aural experience is never bound by a frame as is the case with the visual experience of film:

> We can pile up as many sounds on the soundtrack as we wish without reaching a limit. Further, these sounds can be situated at different narrative levels, such as conventional background music

(nondiegetic) and synch dialogue (diegetic) – while visual elements can hardly ever be located at more than one of these levels at once.

(Chion 1994: 67)

If there is no frame or container for sounds as such, how do they function in film in relation to the visual frame?

[sounds] dispose themselves in relation to the frame and its content. Some are embraced as synchronous and onscreen, others wander at the surface and on the edges as offscreen. And still others position themselves clearly outside the diegesis, in an imaginary orchestra pit (nondiegetic music), or on a sort of balcony, the place of voiceovers. In short, we classify sounds in relation to what we see in the image, and this classification is constantly subject to revision, depending on the changes in what we see. Thus we can define most cinema as 'a place of image, plus sounds', with sound being 'that which seeks its place'.

(Chion 1994: 68)

In *As If It Were The Last Time*, the sound seeks its place as the participant seeks out connections between the cityscape environment and the soundtrack, but there is no longer any restricting frame. For example, in the opening scene participants are told to look down and focus on their feet. As the music builds up into a crescendo, the instruction changes to looking up and out onto the cityscape. This is obviously a take on the classical establishing-shot convention, but without the boundaries of a frame holding the images in place – this ghost does not frame and contain the host. Instead, there is a sense of overflow and excess. Like sound in cinema, perceived images in *As If It Were The Last Time* are allowed to wander off, suggesting opaque and inaccessible spaces beyond that which is immediately visually accessible. Random details – such as people sitting at a bus stop, cars speeding through the streets, flags waving, people running, parents arguing with children – compete for the participants' attention during the piece. The emphatic disconnectedness between the images and the soundtrack, can provoke a compulsion to investigate and question the surrounding reality. The instructions can act as a prompt to question the identity of the people on the streets and imagine potential stories and scenarios. There were no definite statements, only invitations to imagine and indulge in potential narrative constructs. For instance, one story was about a couple who were looking for a new home and uncertain about their future. There was no way of knowing if a couple spotted on the street would fit that narrative. Therefore, there was always a tension between the way the instructions were attempting to frame a reality – potentially explaining it in a way as to make it more transparent – and the very opaqueness, or inaccessible mystery, of the real.

This tension, resulting from the split between the seen and the heard, created the effect of 'acousmatization'. In his seminal work on sound in film, *Audio-Vision*, Michel Chion defined 'acousmatization' as the dissociation between a sound and the image of its source. It is 'an effect of the mediation that marks the absence in ostension of an immediate connection between sound and its source' (Chion quoted in Verstraete 2010: 92). If we extend this notion to *As If It Were The Last Time*, 'acousmatization' defines the relationship between the sounds we cannot see and the images we cannot hear. This effect works on many levels within the piece. It works in relation to instructions for gazing at things which aren't there. It works in relation to diegetic sound effects interspersed throughout the soundtrack. For example, at one point on the soundtrack a man is heard running through the street and shouting 'Sally'. For most participants this will be a ghost effect since the chances are that there will be no one running at the time in the vicinity to match this sound clip – making it fully diegetic. This effect also works in relation to music that is overlaid on the performance and does not necessarily punctuate the reality in conventional cinematic ways. Thus, there is a sense of fluid coexistence between the visual/material and the aural accompanied by a sense of tension. Slavoj Žižek, following Chion's theory, talks about the relationship between the voice and the image, which can very well be extended to the relationship between the soundtrack of *As If It Were The Last Time* and the visual experience of the city. He claims that the relationship between voice and image 'does not simply persist at a different level with regard to what we see, it rather points towards a gap in the field of the visible, towards the dimension of what eludes our gaze' (Žižek 2012: 670). By being prompted to search for connections between the visual and the aural, as Kaye has argued, participants explore the incompleteness within the unresolvable relationship between the host and the ghost. In that sense, *As If It Were The Last Time* enables the participants to seek out those elements which escape the cinematic apparatus and elude the cinematic gaze – the often 'unimportant' details which lie beyond the canonical cinematic framings. These may range, for instance, from dogs running through the street, to the looks on people's faces, to the full plethora and richness of the visual field.

This disconnectedness between the visual and the aural, and the recurrent effect of 'acousmatization', foreground the fact that no interpretations are obvious and that there is a 'politics of perception' at play in the way one chooses to perceive and interpret reality. In that sense, *As If It Were The Last Time* offers a sense of framing that could be seen in opposition to the stability of the cinematic frame – not only in its role as a container of images but also as a structural container of cinematic and canonical trajectories – by allowing the participant trajectories to find lines of flight and to investigate the unfathomable real around them.

'Politics of perception'

Finally, I would like to reflect on the broader political significance here by considering some affinities between the post-cinematic aesthetic strategies discussed above and the situationists' concept of *dérive*. *Dérive* can be translated into English as 'drifting' and it can be defined as an unplanned journey through a cityscape, where the traveller is guided by the aesthetic contours of the surrounding scenery with the aim of experiencing the city in a new and authentic way. Situationist theorist Guy Debord defined *dérive* as 'a playful-constructive behavior' (Debord 1958) with the awareness of 'psychogeographical effects' where 'one or more persons during a certain period drop their relations, their work and leisure activities, and all their other usual motives for movement and action, and let themselves be drawn by the attractions of the terrain and the encounters they find there' (Debord 1958). Thus the practice of *dérive* consists of disregarding any structures and frameworks imposed by urban culture that motivate our actions and consequently construct our identity in order to explore new possibilities of perceiving the city and the self within it. It is also about exploring attractions and pleasures that are not necessarily prescribed by the established urban culture. There is an affinity here with Speakman's concept of the Subtlemob. Much like in the case of *dérive*, *As If It Were The Last Time* enables the participants to reframe their experiences of the urban landscape, except in this case the focus is on the rediscovery of daily life in the context of cinematic culture. As *dérive* necessarily included the awareness and reflection upon 'psychogeographical effects' and the impact they have on the construction of our identities, the Subtlemob becomes a way of reflecting on how cinema culture forms our perceptions of reality and consequently plays a role in constructing our identities and aesthetic sensibilities. The piece can also be seen as a way of liberating the individual from the fixed perceptions induced by the cinematic apparatus.

This is similar to the way in which *dérive* was meant to liberate the individual from the socio-political fabric of his/her urban environment, which masks potential new ways of experiencing the city. As I pointed out earlier, this sense of liberation is contestable because the piece does impose structures, give instructions of where to look and how to behave at specific moments and, in some instances, there is a sense that it has a leftist political agenda. However, the relationship between the host and the ghost is not fixed, and the piece negotiates the 'politics of perception' by creating frameworks and turning the cityscape into a form of perceptual *play*-ground.

Thus, the political significance of *As If It Were The Last Time* can be seen as a response to the alienation that one experiences in our heavily mediatised culture and an attempt to reconnect with a certain social and environmental reality that is always lost in mainstream cinema,[5] but it also functions to question and interrogate spectators' perceptual choices in a reflexive way. In *The Society of the Spectacle* (1995; first published in 1967), Debord argued that mediated images alienate spectators from the real circumstances they represent and thus deny the possibility of creating meaning through action – through an active perceiving and embodying of space. He goes on to argue that the mediated spectacle that arises becomes a 'social relationship between people that is mediated by images' (Debord 1995: 12). This sense of the imposition of an image of social relations leading to the paralysis of active meaning-making on the part of the spectator, can be attributed to the mainstream institutions of cinema. Lyotard sees mainstream Hollywood as a capitalist machine that produces images of society alienating the spectator from the production of these images. He also argues that the social body represented in realist films becomes a 'region of de-responsibility at the whole which *ideo facto* is posed as responsible' (Lyotard 1989: 175). The arguments of both Debord and Lyotard rest on the fact that the audience is removed from the site of the production of the images they experience – both temporally and spatially. Whether sitting in front of a TV or a cinema screen, the subject's perception becomes fixed. Unable to interact with the images, the spectator's perception is restricted to whatever has already been montaged by the filmmaker/broadcaster. These arguments rest on the premise of a subject who is, to an extent, perceptually passive in relation to the spectacle presented. Cinematic pedipulation, as a mode of spectatorship, is more synonymous with activity and participation. It is a way of setting perception in motion that is unachievable during a conventional experience of film.

Conclusion

This chapter has analysed a cinematic piece that uses no cameras, narratives, actors nor montage in a traditional cinematic sense. *As If It Were The Last Time* is an interesting example of 'cinema' beyond the medium of film, both technologically, as a site-specific piece of audio theatre, and culturally, since it challenges and refashions many of the dominant conventions and expectations associated with cinema. Through its deconstructive strategies and emphasis on participatory experience it challenges the author-oriented design of canonical trajectories and the institutionalisation of meaning-making pertinent to so much of classical realist cinema. Arguably, *As If It Were The Last Time* offers its participants the opportunity to produce their own cinematic experience by means of drifting through a cityscape and juxtaposing cinematic components of narrative, music and suggested scenes with an active perception of the surroundings. This kind of activity suggests a way of decentralising the power that mainstream cinema has as a global institution to create perceptions of society and shifting it towards the pole of the spectator. Hollywood institutions and Western mainstream cinema more generally have for a long time dominated the global cultural landscape. Films have become a way in which to rewrite histories, (re)construct identities and ideologies, and to create images of society that adhere to specific aesthetic sensibilities. More importantly, however, films have become ways of constructing dreams and desires, thus becoming a cultural force which motivates economic activity. In the face of this mass spectacle, the spectator's ability to respond and participate as a free subject is contestable. In this context, *As If It Were The Last Time* creates an opportunity to re-think and revaluate the current cultural situation by recalibrating our mode of engagement in order to emphasise a more participatory, reflective spectatorship – even though it does this with specific focus on cinematic culture and points to a cultural shift that is much wider and global.

8
Landscapes and Aporias in Lars von Trier's *Dogville*

Dogville is unlike any of the other pieces analysed in this book in that it is not a live performance or a piece of theatre, but a film. Thus the balance between the dimension of the theatrical live performance and the cinematic becomes wholly contained within the film medium. There are no *ai*sthetic effects in *Dogville* as such and the post-cinematic is more of an aesthetic within the theatricalised film. Nonetheless *Dogville* shares many of the traits and concepts discussed in the context of the earlier pieces which relate to the foregrounding and reflexivity of the 'politics of perception'. *Dogville* can be said to exemplify MacCabe's category of a Brechtian film by drawing attention to the process of filmmaking, the use of distancing effects and by employing dialectics to engage the audience in its morally ambiguous themes. The striking feature of *Dogville* is that it is effectively a stage play filmed in a Dogme style cinematic fashion and montaged as a film. It is not a filmed play, however, nor is it a realist film. It is something in between, a theatrical film perhaps. Arguably the fact of the whole action taking place on a giant soundstage, with chalk lines demarcating invisible walls, props and furniture hanging on strings and actors miming actions that fill in for physical detail also creates a notion of an incomplete, deconstructed realist film. This is especially true when one considers the expectation of hyper-realism evoked by von Trier's Dogme 95 filming and editing stylistics.[1] Despite the fact that the theatrical elements remain an aesthetic in *Dogville*, the knowledge and experience of a theatrical event is often evoked to amplify the post-cinematic deconstructive devices used in the film. In that sense the interinvolvement of theatrical and cinematic space is part of the overall post-cinematic aesthetic adopted by von Trier.

The story takes place in America, in the quiet isolated town of Dogville, where the arrival of a stranger, Grace, a beautiful young fugitive from a gangster past, disturbs the secluded community. Grace (who is played by Nicole Kidman) is viewed with suspicion by the townsfolk. A young writer, Tom Edison Jr (played by Paul Bettany), decides to take care of her and make sure she is accepted by the local people. Tom, however, has an agenda of his own. He wishes to use Grace as an example, an illustration of a moral concern with tolerance and acceptance. He states: 'a greater attitude of openness and acceptance would be better for the country' (*Dogville* 2006). As Robert Sinnerbrink points out, 'the problem of *giving and receiving the gift*' (Sinnerbrink 2007) lies at the centre of the drama, where Grace and her contribution to the town are seen as a gift which inevitably tempts the townsfolk to demand and expect ever more from her. The question that arises is that of whether the community of Dogville is open to accepting a stranger in need, and if so, on what terms. Thus at the heart of the story lies the irreconcilability of moral demands and subjective needs. The moral obligation to help a stranger in need gradually leads to an escalation of exploitation that takes on different shapes and forms depending on the townsfolk and *their* needs in relation to Grace. The provocative libidinal economy of desire that is uncovered during the unfolding of the narrative leads to a drastic and tragic turn of events when Grace turns out to be the daughter of a Mafia don, and with the help of her father she decides upon the violent retribution which concludes the picture. The focus of this chapter will not be the political fable of *Dogville* as such but the intermedial aesthetics through which the fable is conveyed. These aesthetics deconstruct and challenge the expectations of realist cinema conventions and by doing so create a space of moral ambiguities and interpretative freedom. In *Dogville*, the interinvolvement of theatrical and cinematic modes of representation can be read from the angle of moral judgements. It will also be argued that the interinvolvement of theatrical and cinematic modes of representation in *Dogville* exposes the construction of culturally dominant cinematic representations which in turn carry moral and ideological implications. In order to explore this topic Jacques Derrida's theory of aporias will be used. It is a theory concerning moral judgements and the notion of justice. The concept of the 'politics of perception' will concern the more open mode of spectatorship which *Dogville* inspires, one that can make audiences more responsible/'response-able' for their choices and perceptions by exposing them to a contestable political allegory about the pitfalls of contemporary American liberal democracy. Finally it will be argued that the deconstruction of modes of cinematic representation and the emancipation of the spectator is a form of resistance against dominant American cinematic culture.

Dogville deconstructs and undermines a whole cinematic apparatus of American global cultural dominance in which realist cinema has been the main instrument. In many ways the realist cinema tradition, dating from early Westerns to contemporary Hollywood *is* America or what most people around the world understand as America. The aesthetics and conventions of realist film control the way in which America is perceived. To deconstruct these mechanisms, giving the spectator the freedom and power to interpret and make perceptual choices is thus not only a form of resistance against the cultural dominance of these tropes but also against the ideological and political perspectives that are defined and communicated through them.

First of all it is important to contextualise the political significance of *Dogville* by introducing some of the criticism surrounding the film. Since its appearance in 2003, the film has provoked a great deal of criticism and controversy concerning its violence – especially in relation to the female protagonist – its alleged anti-Americanism and its general nihilistic lack of 'humanism' (as criticised by the Cannes jury). Many commentators have taken the film as a direct criticism of American values, in particular those of liberal democracy. As Holger Römers argues, this is mainly due to the end credit sequence. He quotes Michael O'Sullivan as saying:

> Over a montage of archival photographs of impoverished U.S. citizens, director Lars von Trier [...] blasts David Bowie's song 'Young Americans'. It's his way, it seems, of hammering home the message that the town we just visited, and the bad behaviour of its residents [...] are meant to be taken as allegorical versions of our country and, by implication, us.
>
> (O'Sullivan quoted in Römers, 2004)

Römers points out that O'Sullivan's negative response to the film seems to arise from a very personal, subjective, potentially biased standpoint; he feels implicated and personally attacked by the film, especially when he stresses 'our country and, by implication, us'. Another reason for such criticism is that there appears to be a discrepancy between two 'realities' presented here, in particular the 'reality' of the photos at the end and the 'reality' of the town as it is represented in the film. According to Römers they each have a different ontological status: the photographs are documents from the times of the Great Depression selected from the famous Farm Security Administration[2] photograph collection, whereas the film is a moral fable set in a theatrical aesthetic.

However, O'Sullivan makes a clear link between one and the other, arguing for allegorical relevance, hence implicitly confusing the two. He also shifts the responsibility to von Trier for the interpretation he himself has made. This of course can be viewed as a defence mechanism against the feeling of guilt that arises from self-implication in the moral dilemma posited by the film. In addition, the use of words such as 'hammering' points to the fact that O'Sullivan claims the film to be exaggerated. A number of other critics have also pointed to the exaggerated nature of the film in relation to its subject matter. For example, critics have commented that the image of a woman as victim and Trier's 'apparent artistic delight in watching women suffer' (Peden 2005: 119) seemed to have hit a new low in his work after the victimisation of female protagonists in films such as *Breaking the Waves* (1996), *The Idiots* (1998) and *Dancer in the Dark* (1999). Roger Ebert accuses von Trier of approaching his audiences with 'the ideological subtlety of a raving prophet on a street corner' (Ebert 2004). A more articulate critique of the film's apparent anti-American attitude, however, is provided by Todd McCarthy, a well known film reviewer for *Variety* magazine:

> There is no escaping the fact that the entire point of *Dogville* is that von Trier has judged America, found it wanting and therefore deserving of immediate annihilation. This is, in short, his 'J'accuse!' directed toward an entire nation. [...] The identification with *Dogville* and the United States is total and unambiguous, even without the emphatically vulgar use of pointedly grim and grisly photographs of Depression-era have-nots and crime victims under the end credits, accompanied, as if it were needed, by David Bowie's 'Young Americans.' Through his contrived tale of one mistreated woman, who is devious herself, von Trier indicates as being unfit to inhabit the earth a country that has surely attracted, and given opportunity to, more people onto its shores than any other in the history of the world. Go figure.
>
> (McCarthy in Fibiger 2003)

This response is strikingly affective and does concern the violence of American-style democracy in relation to immigrants, or the *other*, which the film portrays through the outlaw character of Grace. *Dogville* was released shortly after the start of the Iraq War and into a climate of strong anti-American sentiments and criticism amongst European intellectual communities, which in turn could have spiked excessive defensive reactions from American commentators. It would be worth commenting upon the backdrop of the Iraq War but for the time being what is noteworthy is Robert Sinnerbrink's concluding judgement upon McCarthy. Even though Sinnerbrink's argument lies elsewhere, this quote is illustrative of what is most relevant to the argument here, namely the existence of a polarity or a perspectivist incompatibility at the heart of the film's post-cinematic and consequently 'post-political' nature:

> McCarthy's stridently defensive response is representative of a diffuse, inchoate, but also pronounced awareness of the political dimensions of *Dogville*, its violent critique of American, or more generally liberal democracy, an awareness that is articulated in *affective* rather than conceptual terms.
>
> (Sinnerbrink 2007)

Sinnerbrink points to a polarity between 'affective' and 'conceptual terms', suggesting that the overwhelmingly affective response is in this case less valid within academic discourse than a conceptual framework. The concept of the affect and affective response has often been problematised as an element of discursive and argumentative practice in academia; however, it is by no means an invalid spectator response. What is even more interesting is that Sinnerbrink describes McCarthy's response as 'diffuse' and 'inchoate'. For me it seems that a lot of the readings of *Dogville* point to a potential undecidability and disorientation which are the result of an amplification of perceptual choices contrived by the post-cinematic aesthetic of the film and the diffusion of an expected singular cinematic perspective. Through a unique interplay of theatrical staging and specific cinematic stylistics, von Trier attempts to emancipate the spectators, making them more aware of their role in producing meaning and allowing them to complete the film in their own minds. This emancipation undermines and dislodges the perspectivist aesthetic of classical realist cinema. Since constructing a perspective in most cases of classical realist film means constructing a specific ideology and worldview, *Dogville* effectively deconstructs this tradition. Arguably, *Dogville*, in a post-cinematic fashion, negotiates the agency of responsibility for the production of meaning, shifting from the director's responsibility to the 'response-ability' of the spectator. In consequence this intermedial deconstruction and spectator emancipation can be seen as a reaction and a form of resistance against the image of America sustained by culturally dominant cinematic aesthetics.

Beyond the luminous dust and shadow

What is immediately striking about *Dogville* is the insufficiency and incompleteness of the cinematic images it presents. *Dogville* takes place in a town that is represented only by a very theatrical, quasi-Brechtian set in which the whole town, with its streets, buildings, trees and orchards is demarcated in chalk on the floor of a gigantic soundstage (Figure 8.1).

It has thus been suggested that the setting in *Dogville* is visually missing while it is aurally present:

> [A]ll the sounds can be heard loud and clear: the opening and closing of the (non-existing) doors, footsteps on the gravel road, the singing of the birds, the sound of rain and wind, the barking of the dog Moses. This invites the spectators to create the town for themselves through hearing.
>
> (Laine 2006: 135)

Although Laine sees this as a creation of an in-between space, a contact between the film world and the world of the spectator out of which the cinematic emerges, I believe there is more at stake here than just stimulating the spectator's imaginative engagement. By seeing *Dogville* as an incomplete film, where the set is not missing, but is present as *an invisible*, a tension is established between a potential, expected realist representation and the regime of its specific aesthetic treatment. This of course is based on the assumption that the film stimulates expectations

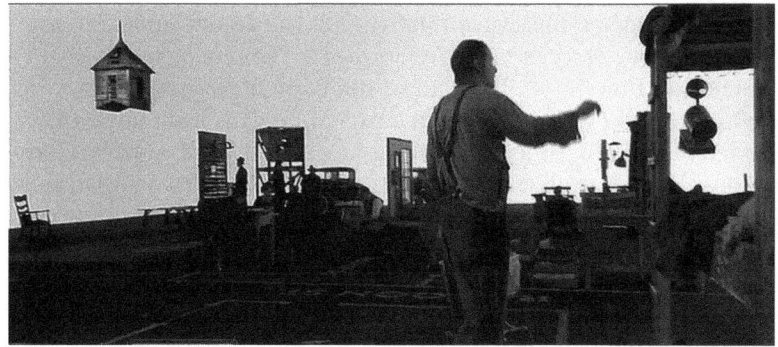

Figure 8.1   Enormous soundstage in Sweden where *Dogville* was filmed © Zentropa Entertainments

of realist representation from the spectator, through the Dogme 95 stylistic and also as a result of the fact that Dogme 95 itself addresses a long tradition of docu-drama stylistics and by extension realism in general. Jacques Rancière, in his book *The Emancipated Spectator*, argues against the notion of a passive spectator and claims that spectators have a choice as to how they wish to perceive an artwork. One of his arguments is that the spectator is emancipated when confronted with a tension between different regimes of representation at play. This tension he calls the 'pensiveness of the image' (Rancière 2009: 122). According to Rancière a pensive image is one where the pursuit of homogeneity between form and content has been abandoned. This may lead to an experience of indeterminacy, where the spectator is faced with a more open text, to use Roland Barthes's terminology.

It is worth explaining at this point how Rancière frames this notion of pensiveness. It is also important to state that while his analysis is mainly based on photography, it is also applicable to other media. One of the examples Rancière gives to illustrate his point is the photograph of Lewis Payne, a young man sentenced to death in 1865 for attempting to assassinate the US secretary of state (Figure 8.2).

Rancière states that the singularity of this particular photograph is based on 'three forms of indeterminacy' (Rancière 2009: 113), or three regimes of expression as he later calls it:

> The first involves its visual composition: the young man is seated in accordance with a highly pictorial arrangement, leaning slightly, on the border between a zone of light and a zone of shade. But we cannot know whether the positioning has been chosen by the photographer, or – if that is the case – whether he chose it out of a concern for visibility or an aesthetic reflex [...] The second indeterminacy concerns the work of time. The texture of the photograph bears the stamp of times past. By contrast, the body of the young man, his clothing, his posture and the intensity of his gaze are at home in our present, negating the temporal distance. The third indeterminacy concerns the attitude of the character. Even if we know that he is going to die and why, it is impossible for us to read the reasons for his assassination attempt, or his feelings about his imminent death, in his gaze.
>
> (Rancière 2009: 114)

All these indeterminacies amount to what Rancière calls an effect of the 'circulation, between the subject, the photographer and us, of the

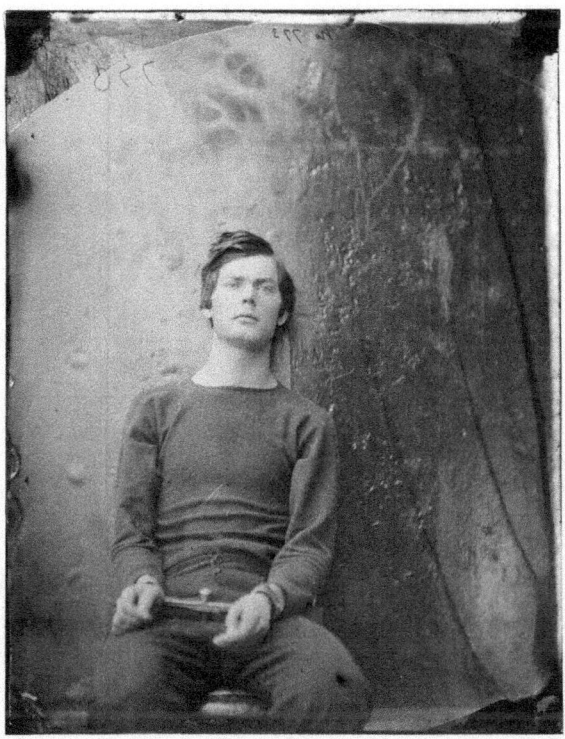

Figure 8.2 'Washington Navy Yard, D.C. Lewis Payne, in sweater, seated and manacled'. Photo: Alexander Gardner, 1865

intentional and the unintentional, the known and the unknown, the expressed and the unexpressed, the present and the past' (Rancière 2009: 115). Since Rancière talks about photography here this concept can easily be applied to the Farm Security Administration Photographs that are shown during the final credit sequence of *Dogville*. For instance, the specific social and historical context of the subjects in the photos comes into tension with the context of the *Dogville* fable. The Farm Security Administration was established in 1937, whilst *Dogville* is set during the Great Depression, anywhere between the late 1920s and the late 1930s. A tension also develops between the indiscernible attitudes of the subjects in the photos and those of the characters in the film. The uneasy stylistic mismatch between documentary photographs and the highly stylised theatrical film is another case in point. Finally von Trier's intention in putting the photos at the end of the film is unclear. Is this supposed to be a generalised statement about Americans or is it about humanity in general? Or is the reference specifically to the individuals shown in those photographs?

This notion of tension between different regimes of representation which creates an indeterminacy of reading or a more open text, emancipating the spectator, is not necessarily limited to the study of photography or static visual art but can also be applied to film and to the intermedial, post-cinematic stylistics of *Dogville*. The tension between the Dogme cinematic stylistic and the overtly theatricalised set can be seen as creating an indeterminate portrayal of events. For instance the cinematic realism evoked through period costumes, naturalistic acting and Dogme stylistics may clash with the minimalist theatrical set and its allegorical nature, thus potentially undermining the validity of the historical context of *Dogville*'s plot and foregrounding the 'politics of perception' at play.

Vesania: the mole and the eagle

A recurrent shot in the movie, which also serves as an introduction to the *Dogville* universe is the establishing 'God shot' (Figure 8.3).

This 'God shot' is an aerial view of a large floor plan sketched on the soundstage, with chalk lines on a dark background marking the location of houses and streets. The omniscient narrator tells us that the town is located at the edge of the Rocky Mountains, forlorn outskirts of the old American frontier, and the period is that of the Great Depression. The period tone is emphasised through the costumes, vintage cars and

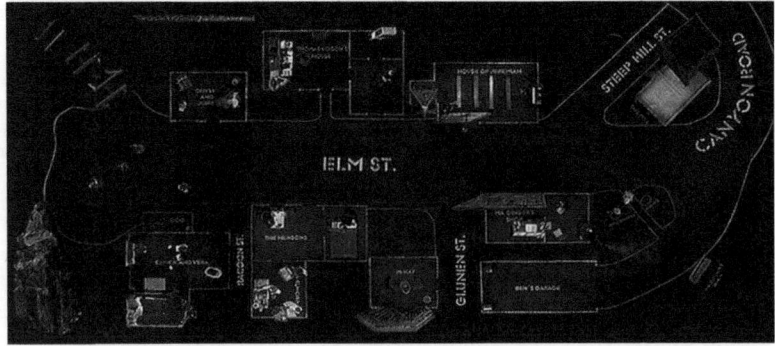

Figure 8.3   Dogville, the 'God shot' © Zentropa Entertainments

characters complaining about the harsh economic situation of the times they live in. As the camera descends, characters begin to appear in their blueprint houses and streets like players in a game. They perform the absent physical set through actions such as miming the opening of doors, the cleaning of windows, brushing invisible leaves off the porch and so on. In this ordered little world, the 'God shot' suggests a total perspective. The set looks like a game board, a finite space and a clearly observable environment wherein an intrigue is about to unfold. This theatricalisation is quasi-Brechtian in that it evokes an objective, almost experimental game-like 'reality', in which characters will be tested and conclusions will be drawn. As the narrator's speech comes to an end, the camera homes in on individuals, searching for a subject to identify with, the next vehicle for the progression of the narrative.

It is at this point that two specific regimes of representation clash. Hypothetically speaking, an image of a town shot in a realistic set-ting would tend to establish a perspective and a hierarchy of different components as a result of their various geometric, affective and cul-tural connotations. In this case, however, the boundaries of different components (buildings in this case) remain indeterminate due to a lack of contours and opaque surfaces. There is no way of masking or foregrounding as there would be in a realistic shot and the actions of characters are exposed, they can no longer be broken up through montage to produce salient individualised perspectives. The theatrical space of the soundstage conveyed in this shot enables the simultane-ous perception of an excess of action, which is quite different from the possibilities of perspectivist engagement offered by the more conven-tionally framed establishing shot that might be expected under a realist movie aesthetic. The excess of action taking place on stage calls for a re-framing of the way of looking that can accommodate the presented universe (Figure 8.4).

Gilles Deleuze, in his seminal work on cinema, states that normally 'the cinematic image contrasts with the theatrical image in that it goes from the outside to the inside, from the setting to the character, from nature to man' (Deleuze 1985: 156). From the opening shot *Dogville* evokes a tension between the theatrical and the cinematic image, emphasising this difference and evoking an oscillation between these two modes of representation. The theatrical is centred on the charac-ters' performances, working from the inside to the outside. The focus in traditional theatre is usually on the actor, who is the centre and the vehicle for a character's expression. This tends to focus the specta-tor's perception on the interior of the character, their thoughts and

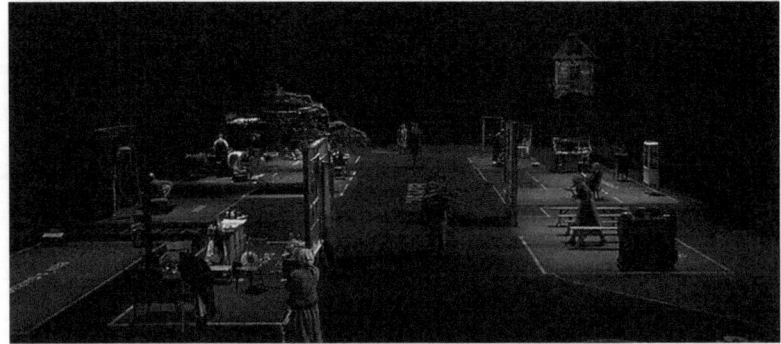

Figure 8.4   *Dogville*, houses without walls on Elm St © Zentropa Entertainments

observations. Only by revealing this interior does the actor create a world around them, the exterior to this interior. In classical cinema this process is inverted. The cinematic image starts with the outside, like the great landscapes in John Ford's Westerns. Only then does the camera home in on the characters, revealing the subjective thoughts and perceptions which comprise the inside. Hence this opening shot in *Dogville* also creates an oscillation between a focal mode of perception (character driven) and a dispersed mode of perception (environment driven). This is particularly interesting given that these initial shots essentially represent the community of Dogville. The oscillation and indeterminacy between these two perspectives is subsequently translated to a potential dialectic reading of the community suggested by the character of Tom. Tom's initial philosophical deliberations surrounding the nature of Dogville's community and the direction it should take in the future are set around the dialectic between an atomised unified social structure and a more dispersed and democratic system of individuals. As we are told early on, the atomised model has recently been dispersed and the community lacks a moral spine. The invisible walls of the mission house await a new preacher (atomised, embodiment of ideology) but meanwhile the space is used for community meetings (a democratic system that can never wholly agree on a solution). Thus the tension between the theatrical and cinematic regime of representation in the opening shots emphasises a dialectic tension between two ideological perspectives on how the community in Dogville is and should be constituted. This is where *Dogville* becomes an experiment in post-cinematic seeing, an experiment in what is politically at stake in post-cinematic perception.

What is particular to this aesthetic tension is the notion of simultaneity. The theatrical and cinematic become interinvolved in such a way as to produce an interesting perceptual effect similar to that which Lyotard defines as 'Vesania'. According to him, Vesania is the moment of estrangement of the viewer, an effect produced by a displacement of perspective:

> Vesania or 'systematic madness': the soul is transferred to a quite different standpoint, so to speak, and from it sees all objects differently. It is displaced from the sensorium communi that is required for the unity of life, to a point far removed from it – just as a mountainous landscape viewed from above calls for a quite different judgement when it is viewed from the plain [...] there would appear be a landscape whenever the mind is *transported* from one sensible matter to another, but retains the sensorial organisation appropriate to the first, or at least a memory of it.
>
> (Lyotard 1991: 182, emphasis added)

In this passage Lyotard points to an important notion that concerns all modes of perception, and that is the notion of judgement. Judgements are often the result of the function of a given perspective. Perspective here broadly indicating a system of organising data about a given set of circumstances in relation to a particular subject. Whether this concerns simple spatial awareness or complex deliberations upon morals and ethics, perspective can be seen as a function that an individual may use to generate knowledge and construct a worldview. This tension between the perspectives of the theatrical and cinematic aesthetics in *Dogville* arguably creates a heterogeneity of perspectives amplifying the indeterminacy of possible moral judgements and ideological representations in relation to the subject matter represented in the film.

In order to understand what is at stake in this heterogeneity of perspectives it is important to look at a key part of the concept of perspective, which is the implication of a human subject within a set of circumstances. This is crucial since character identification plays a key role in amplifying the indeterminacy of possible moral judgements and ideological representations in *Dogville*. As discussed in previous chapters, modes of inducing character identification in realist cinema are closely related to the construction of both an ideological and a moral perspective; this is also very relevant in understanding how *Dogville* deconstructs and complicates these realist notions of subjective engagement. Earlier this topic was approached through the concept of cinematic suture. Here the initial perspective is that of narrative structures and the 'libidinal economy' of *Dogville*, which will provide a basis for the later discussion of deconstructive post-cinematic strategies used in the film.

Seeing through invisible walls

In their article '*Dogville*: A Parable on Perversion' (2004), Adela Abella and Nathalie Zilkha read *Dogville* as a film structured around emotional manipulation. This effectively classifies the narrative structure of *Dogville* as belonging to the ramifications of the Situation-Action-Situation (SAS) formula.[3] However, *Dogville* jars this schema, offering a heterogeneity of perspectives and stimulating a more emancipated spectatorship. What is interesting is that this 'heterogeneity of perspectives' and simultaneity relates to the notion of perversion, which is one of the themes in *Dogville*.

Abella and Zilkha define the state of perversion as a simultaneity of two coexisting perspectives or 'versions of reality' (Abella and Zilkha 2004: 1519) which are not cohesive and are ultimately irresolvable. They see in the narrative of *Dogville*, a recurrent motif of two non-conflictual realities in the psychology of the majority of the key characters. They claim that '[t]he emphasis is placed on the simultaneous and non-conflictual presence in the subject's psychic reality of two incompatible versions of reality, maintained side by side through the splitting of the ego' (Abella and Zilkha 2004: 1519).

These two non-conflictual realities are evident in the attitude of the townsfolk towards Grace. On the one hand, they exploit her, causing her harm. These exploitations eventually escalate into serious abuse and violence towards Grace. On the other hand, they justify their behaviour, and deny the fact they are causing her harm, because they choose to perceive their actions as fair, an exchange of services for the protection they are offering her. This is epitomised in the character of Tom, who throughout the film develops and theorises the platonic relationship he has with Grace. Despite his apparent high moral standards he eventually rapes her.

This psychoanalytic approach to the notion of self-integrity is insightful in showing how the post-cinematic aesthetic creates a sense of moral instability. On the one hand, perversion consists of 'the denial of separation between the self and the object with a view to avoiding the experience of loss' (ibid.), hence an avoiding of a sense of incompatibility of the self and its environment. In the case of *Dogville* this could be interpreted as the townsfolk's denial of the fact that they are causing Grace to suffer as they do not want to lose their morally acceptable self-image and consequently change their behaviour towards her, which yields them benefits. On the other hand, perversion consists of idealism and notions of ideological totality since it is 'also the denial of the finitude of life and its limits with the aim of maintaining idealisation' (Abella and Zilkha 2004: 1519). For example Tom's character denies the ends to which his actions lead in order to persist with an idealised moral image of himself and the notion of a rather idealised platonic relationship with Grace. Reading *Dogville* as an illustration of the problem of perversion shows both the masochistic character of the protagonist Grace and the provoked sadism of the townsfolk in relation to her. But this can also be applied to the spectators, as they become implicated and left in a position of undecidability with no possibilities for closure.

These two uncompromising realities within the film are intertwined in a libidinal economy of denial. The townsfolk are clearly handicapped in one way or another yet they all claim to be self-sufficient. As Grace offers herself in order to satisfy their 'futile desire' (Abella and Zilkha 2004: 1522) she also participates in their game of denial, which leads to a game of seduction. Both Grace and the townspeople deny the fact that they are beginning to exploit her. Grace often remarks that she is happy to take on more work and that she isn't tired despite the clear signs that the workload is becoming a strain for her. This subtle complicity opens 'the floodgates to a limitless greed' (ibid.) leading to 'abject exploitation, rape, slavery and torture' (ibid.). This results in a vicious circle that may be irritating for the audience, but could be explained by Grace's presumed fear of being found out by the gangsters in pursuit of her: 'the more the innocent victim submits masochistically, the more her torturers feel encouraged and driven to go beyond all conceivable limits' (ibid.).

The other perspective on reality arrives with the gangsters, when we learn that Grace endured the torture by her own choice in order to arouse sadism in the town community. Once the exploitation has reached its peak, the roles are reversed. Her masochism (self-implication) and omnipotent narcissism (belief in idealistic ego and moral superiority) at the beginning of the film changes to sadism (the destruction of the village) and a new moral perspective (making the world a better place) towards the end. This final perspectival twist undermines the spectator's previously established position of moral superiority. Spectators become victims of the deliberate obscuring of elements that are normally essential for creating a cohesive singular perspective on a story. When the other side is revealed, that of her gangster family background, Grace's moral position loses integrity.

Dogville certainly exhibits von Trier's substantial capacity for manipulation but his intermedial aesthetic allows more breathing space than would seem to be the case, hence perceptual choices have to be made – and can be made – throughout. Intermedial strategies in *Dogville* become key in conveying the heterogeneity of perspectives implicit in Grace's situation and the moral ambiguities implicit in the identification with this character.

A good example of this is a striking scene where Grace is being raped by Chuck (Stellan Skarsgard) in Chuck's house. The camera moves out from a mid-shot of the two characters into a long shot and an extreme long shot. The apparently private, concealed space of the house is merged with that of the town and the townsfolk, who are unaware of what is going on behind its invisible walls. A policeman arrives and hangs out a wanted poster for Grace, which immediately draws the attention of the townsfolk and generates suspicion as to Grace's identity and her possible links with the criminal world. Thus we are presented with two perspectives in one shot: Grace the victim, Grace the criminal (Figure 8.5).

Despite the sympathies we may have towards Grace at this point, this image creates an ambiguity. A spectator does not feel necessarily drawn into taking Grace's perspective as would likely have been the case with a perspectivist film. In a perspectivist mode of filming, which is usually associated with the classical realist tradition, saliency can be achieved in a number of ways, for instance through montage and editing, shot composition, the use of lighting, framing or the use of opaque elements of set to conceal or reveal certain aspects of the image. In the above scene a sense of what Lehmann calls 'simultaneity' (Lehmann 2006: 87) arises. Part of it has to do with the fact that von Trier chooses not to cut

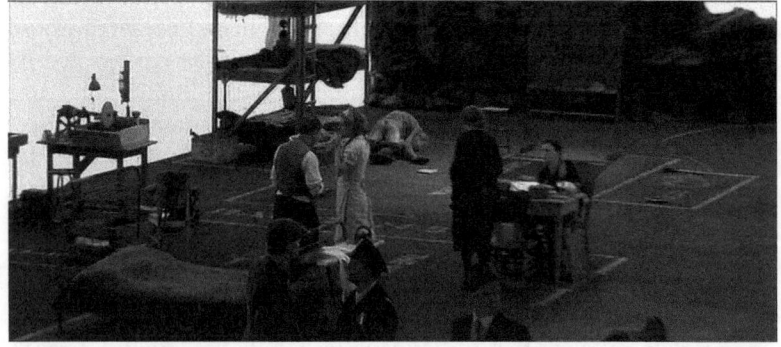

Figure 8.5   *Dogville,* rape scene © Zentropa Entertainments

between the two actions taking place, instead he uses the depth of field to compose them all in one shot. Arguably this gives more freedom of choice for the spectator, allowing them to do part of the editing, almost as if they were in a theatre. Bazin claimed that the depth of field had this reality-function: 'the viewer had to organize his perception himself in the image instead of receiving it readymade' and that 'the gain in reality could be achieved only through an "excess of theatricality"' (Bazin in Deleuze 1985). Bazin is referring to the shot compositions in *Citizen Kane* but the effect is similar here.

What further amplifies this effect is the interinvolvement of the theatrical and the cinematic aesthetic. Even though *Dogville* is a film, and all elements of the piece are contained within that medium, the tension between the theatrical and the cinematic plays a key role here. The cinematic Dogme 95 stylistic may evoke a reading that is akin to von Trier's hyper-realism whilst the theatrical may evoke the notion of a Brechtian play. It is not only a clash of aesthetics at play here, but also a cultural awareness that cinema and theatre have distinct means of creating illusionistic representations. Such readings obviously assume that the spectator has an awareness of these stylistics and von Trier purposefully plays upon them here. One of the striking features of *Dogville* that exemplifies this clash is the lack of walls in the town, or rather their invisible presence.

If one were to read the film in consonance with the Dogme stylistic, the absence of walls would be literal, a result of its documentary agenda. From a theatrical perspective the absence of walls may simply come across as metaphorical. The experience of *Dogville* can oscillate between the two. It is the tension and the oscillation between these two modes of expression that become interesting when related to the morally ambiguous ways of perceiving characters and situations in the film. Sets and walls in both theatre and film can serve as framing devices that can separate different events but also guide the perceptions that characters and spectators may have of an event, especially when it comes to the aesthetics of realism. To understand this better let us take a quick look at one of the potential film intertexts of *Dogville*, Arthur Penn's 1967 movie, *Bonnie and Clyde*. One of the reasons why audiences identify so strongly with Bonnie and Clyde, despite their criminal identity, is because they are represented as individuals. Most of the people they kill are shown for no more than a few seconds and are quickly edited out. We do not get the background story of their victims nor any substantial context to form a stronger subjective attitude, as we do in the case of the two protagonists. What we see mostly in the film is the title characters' reactions to events, and through that we are encouraged to assume their perspective. Furthermore Bonnie and Clyde spend most of their time in hiding and the spectators 'hang out' with them. The outside world is closed off from them as are the effects and consequences of their crimes. This isolation induces a specific perception and a worldview that comes with it. In other words, there is a potential relationship between 'walls' and worldview or ideology.

This relationship is made fluid in *Dogville* as a result of the tension between the two modes of expression. In the rape scene we even see the townsfolk looking toward the place where Grace is being raped, but they do not react nor acknowledge the event, even though as actors they are all in the same physical space. From a theatrical perspective this can be explained by the existence of walls that are there metaphorically. The cinematic realist perspective may imply that they deliberately choose not to see certain things. In this sense, through theatricalisation, *Dogville* exemplifies a post-cinematic reaction to realist cinema's power to frame and construct cohesive ideological worldviews. Perhaps it is the invisible habit of ideological construction or perspectivist viewing that realist cinema has induced in Western culture that is being uncovered and made visible here. Thus the perceptual choices that spectators make at these ambiguous moments may cause them to reflect upon the political and ideological implications of such perceptions in ways that may have been less feasible during the experience of a perspectivist and politically singular realist film. In that sense I believe *Dogville* poses wider philosophical and political questions by foregrounding the 'politics of perception'. These questions concern the ideological frameworks through which we have become accustomed to perceive movies but also concern the way in which these perceptual habits influence the way we perceive our day-to-day reality and culture as a whole. There are also questions concerning the institutions that propagate these perceptual habits and frameworks, and their political agendas, which use the power of realist cinema as a machine for the dissemination of ideology. These issues will be addressed in more detail below. Before that I would like to explore another distinct post-cinematic feature of *Dogville* which is the deconstruction of a unique and potentially beautifully dangerous property of realist cinema: the affective image.

Affective aporias

This section looks in more depth at the notion of 'affect' in *Dogville* and investigates how it arises out of the interinvolvement of the theatrical and cinematic aesthetic. Since the notion of affective engagement is key in the identification processes of realist cinema and consequently in the construction of moral perspectives, this section will be insightful in terms of how the intermedial deconstruction of *Dogville* can emancipate the spectator and foreground alternative moral perspectives. In his article, 'Grace and Violence: Questioning Politics and Desire in Lars von Trier's *Dogville*', Robert Sinnerbrink indicates the way in which the theatricalisation of cinematic conventions in *Dogville* induces a state of aporia in the spectator. He makes a series of points which set the specific stylistic strategy of *Dogville* in opposition to mainstream Hollywood aesthetics; essentially, he perceives the theatrical component as a key factor in destabilising a potentially mainstream cinematic experience. The first point he makes is in relation to *Dogville's* theatricalising aesthetic as a reaction against and an interruption of the illusory consistent and harmonising Hollywood aesthetic:

> [It opens] up the affective experience of an impasse, an *aporia*, a tragic irreconcilability, all of which contribute to the aesthetic reconstitution of (cinematic) experience in response to the hegemony of Hollywood, the audiovisual or culture industry aspect of American global hegemony.
>
> (Sinnerbrink 2007)

Sinnerbrink's second point relates to the way in which von Trier 'appropriates generic conventions of Hollywood – particularly the melodrama' – refashioning them into what Sinnerbrink calls a 'philosophical melodrama' (ibid.). The third point, however, is about the recuperation and amplification of affect. He cites Žižek's (2001: 59) response to the film:

> Slavoj Žižek remarks, it is as though von Trier requires the form of independent art cinema in order to screen and transmit the 'forbidden' content of affectively charged, emotionally excessive melodrama, along with its philosophical and political accompaniments.
>
> (Sinnerbrink 2007)

While Sinnerbrink looks at the tension between the two stylistics from the point of view of what a theatrical aesthetic can do to a cinematic experience, his argument suggests some further interesting aspects of von Trier's post-cinematic strategy for *Dogville*. Among these is his claim that the interruptions of the illusory mainstream film aesthetic amplify affect in an excessive manner.

In classical realist film affect has played a crucial role in the apprehension of the cinematic image. Eisenstein defined affect as the shock of the image and according to Deleuze it '[was] the very form of communication of movement in images' (Deleuze 1985: 153). According to Deleuze's interpretation of Eisenstein, the shock and thought of the image were coupled, '[t]he cinematographic image must have a shock effect on thought, and force thought to think itself as much as thinking the whole' (ibid.). Thus the aesthetic forms postulated by Eisenstein rest upon a harmonisation, a coupling of affect and thought. Realist films usually provide audiences with a wealth of stimuli that eventually ends up being 'read'. By this I mean that the influx of information conveyed by a film ends up being filtered, distilled and reduced into specific frameworks of meaning, potentially far less complex and simplistic mental structures, albeit more organised, than the original complex sensorial stimuli. This reduction of shock into thought requires aesthetic operations on the part of the filmmaker but also specific perceptual skills on the part of the spectator. Learning how to perceive, or how to cope with this influx of information and the specificity of the film language is what is at stake in learning how to become a critical film viewer. The affective, sensible structures of film support and enhance meaning, but there is also Lyotard's 'libidinal normalization', beyond which certain boundaries of affect are not to be exceeded due to their potentially 'dangerous' implications, be these moral, political or concerning the representation of social relationships.

Affect in *Dogville* is often amplified specifically in order to trigger these potentially controversial implications and it is done so by means of a rupture of the aforementioned coupling. This rupture, uncoupling or disengagement – sometimes only momentary – produces the excess of an affective charge. This excessive affective charge has the potential to destabilise the sense-making frame, leaving the spectator unable to conceptually grasp what has happened. This experience of being vulnerable or caught off guard may in fact emancipate the spectator, prompting a more active engagement and awareness in the process of making perceptual choices.

Two structurally parallel scenes in *Dogville* can be used to demonstrate the way in which this amplification of the affect works. One is the scene in which Grace's hard-earned figurines of dwarves are smashed by Chuck's wife as a punishment for Grace having hit one of her children. The other is where Grace chooses to destroy the village, killing all of its inhabitants in order to rid the world of all the evil implicit in *Dogville*. This murder scene structurally echoes and is analogous to the smashing of Grace's dwarves. One of the most affect-laden moments in this second scene is when Grace forces Chuck's wife to watch all of her seven children, including a baby, being shot – a diabolic revenge for a punishment once effectuated upon her.

I will first consider the dwarf figurine scene, where Grace is being punished for having hit one of Chuck's children. The audience may feel that this is undeserved retribution since the child perversely provoked Grace into hitting him in order to fulfil his teenage sexual fantasy, but the mother is extremely partial and intolerant in her judgement. Thus, she destroys the Seven Dwarves figurines that Grace worked very hard to collect and which are a token of her effort and dedication towards the village community. She is forced to watch her efforts literally turning into shards. One of the reasons why this scene carries such an affective charge is that Grace is forced to witness the destruction. This notion of being forced to witness or being exposed without any means of turning away or escape is amplified by the whole concept of a town without walls.

As noted earlier, the invisible walls in *Dogville* could be read as being in a state of tension, depending on whether they are viewed through a cinematic or a theatrical stylistic. This sense of instability is also evoked by von Trier's filming methodologies. Most of the action is filmed with a steady-camera which von Trier himself holds. The frame becomes destabilised, always in movement, and the camera work becomes a performance in itself because it becomes an embodiment of the director. Von Trier transgresses the cinematic and theatrical space because cinematically the camera evokes a Dogme stylistic, but theatrically von Trier articulates himself as a present camera's-eye witness on the soundstage, moving between the actors and actively responding to their performance. The tension between the cinematic and the theatrical in this scene denies the possibility of a stable stylistic to which to escape or from which to seek comfort, instead one is exposed to an uncomfortable visibility, which constitutes the crux of the drama. The relationship between affect and thought, the emotions expressed and the sense-making frame of the represented situation are uncoupled. In a classical realist scenario this coupling tends to be transparent, but the disorientation and the subtle confusion inherent in the stylistic tension renders it as opaque. This opaqueness separates the two components of affect and thought, making them more pronounced in their own terms. The affect is more fully abstracted from the thought and is intensified in the process. The thought component is liberated from the affect and hence it can be more freely reflected upon.

This scene also functions on a metaphorical level in an analogy with the story of Snow White and the Seven Dwarves. In Disney's film, Snow White, like Grace, is also a fugitive from a dysfunctional family situation, given a haven in the small community of the seven dwarves who demand that she does their housekeeping in return for her protection. However, in Disney's film Snow White is trapped within an ideological framework that constructs her role as a submissive and naive female who can only be saved by a male hero and finally returned to her beloved father. Von Trier undoubtedly plays with these schemata here, but subverts them in a shocking manner.

The final scene inverts the dynamics of the dwarves scene; roles are reversed and the proportions of the punishment massively amplified. Here, Grace is the executioner and devises the plan to murder all seven children, including the baby. Their mother is forced to watch as the gangsters gun them down, with Grace saying that if she manages to hold back her tears the killing will stop.

We see close-ups of the mother and her children in order to reinforce a sense of identification, but what is striking about this scene is the witnessing. The mother tries to cover her eyes in order not to see, but Grace tells the gangsters to force her to watch. The notion of invisible walls is dramatised again here. What makes this scene strangely ambiguous is its obvious relation to the dwarves scene and the perverse conclusion of this dialectic which equates the destruction of dwarf figurines to the killing of human beings. An audience who had been led into sentiments of revenge through having identified more with Grace throughout the film might feel that they were being put into a morally uncomfortable position here, watching humans being killed in the cause of a private moral integrity that Grace is attempting to accomplish. There is an equation here which is reinforced by the stylistic tension. As a result of this aporetic tension there is no clear sense of hierarchy of affect. Emotions delivered by the performers are not framed within a more homogeneous cinematic stylistic that would potentially provide a moral stability to the action. Instead the heterogeneous stylistic de-hierarchises these affective moments, allowing for a potential paradoxical reading that figurines are as valuable as human beings. The affect-laden images become detached from the sense-making frames of their respective representation, foregrounding both the affect and thought.

So far I have looked at the way in which the stylistic tensions in *Dogville* deconstruct realist cinematic conventions and open the opportunity to challenge the expectations and viewing habits associated with them. The following two sections of this chapter will explore what is philosophically and politically at stake in these tensions created by the interinvolvement of the theatrical and the cinematic. They will look in detail at the intermedial strategies in *Dogville* and the ways in which they foreground the moral dilemmas that lie behind perceptual choices inherent in the 'politics of perception' of spectating and shed some light on the relationship between the post-political and the post-cinematic in *Dogville*.

The paradox of idealism

Dogville represents a community where the moral law is ultimately absent. There is no general figure representative of law, such as a pastor or a mayor, who might be able to impose a moral framework upon the townspeople. Despite their initial appearance as God-fearing folk, the people take many liberties, such as lying to the policeman, when it comes to adhering to a moral code. Ultimately this lack of moral law is reinforced by the fact that *Dogville* does not offer a narrative closure in a classical sense, instead it ends with an ambiguity, a state of aporia. *Dogville* becomes more of an open text, a process of meaning-in-the-making where different parties make their own interpretation of reality, be they characters in the film or spectators. What becomes central in *Dogville* is the notion of judgement and the impossibility of infinite justice. Judgement is a question of unfolding, a 'genre of becoming' (Lukács in Lattek 2006: 102), and once the decisive point is reached law is entirely undermined. To quote Derrida: 'justice as law is never exercised without a decision that cuts, that divides' (Derrida in Lattek 2006: 102). Thus the film puts the spectator in an undecidable position where they have to grapple with a judgement that undermines the totality of moral law. In his reading of *Dogville* Michael Lattek explains this by summing up Derrida's argument:

> (1) Freedom and responsibility are requirements for justice. To be just or to be a judge, one has to perform a 'reinstituting act of interpretation' thus creating and destroying the law all the time. (2) The second aporia has already been mentioned and is only recalled as the dividing nature of justice or the decision that cuts, which is always haunted by the ghost of the undecidable. (3) Justice has an immediate urgency to it that Derrida compares to the Greek usage of the word horizon meaning 'both the opening and the limit that defines an infinite progress or a period of waiting'.
>
> (Lattek 2006: 109)

Lattek then elaborates on the notion that one must assume one's own responsibility to 'think in terms of justice' (Lattek 2006: 111). As soon as this happens one betrays the idea of universal justice since that becomes a thought of singularity. Thus we end up with a paradox which causes the second aporia of the undecidable. Derrida claims that this experience of the undecidable is key for decisions to be taken and law brought through action, usually accompanied by some sort of violence to enforce it. At the end of the film the spectator is confronted with Grace's dilemma. She has sacrificed herself for her ideals but has in the final analysis misjudged the townsfolk, giving them too much credit for moral behaviour and inciting evil action. The townsfolk's dilemma sprang from the divide between their sense of what constitutes ethical behaviour towards Grace and their desire for her and the benefits of exploitation. They have solved the paradox by enforcing their private laws or rights and denying empathy and identification with their victim, which leads to the point of Grace being violently raped.

What is interesting here is that the moment of the second aporia relates to the stylistic tensions in the film. The impossibility of any reconciliation between two conflictual perspectives, or modes of seeing, leads to the emancipation of the spectator, who is prompted to make a choice as to how they wish to perceive this paradox. Some of the most evocative moments of this are the 'God shot' scenes, when Grace looks at the town as if from the side. The lighting undergoes changes and a narrator explains her thoughts and dilemmas. This shows the cinematic apparatus in action, which attempts to modify the physical appearances of space in order to induce a perspective.

Through its post-cinematic strategy and the resultant aporetic tensions, *Dogville* conveys the fact that these moral paradoxes are beyond definite resolution in that they also seem to incite a quasi-Brechtian dynamic of opening up the possibility for change. This links with Derrida's notion that justice is an impossible concept, something that is receding into the future and always in a state of coming about:

> 'The impossible' is not a simple logical contradiction, like x and *not-x*, but the tension, the paralysis, the aporia, of having to push against and beyond the limits of the horizon, *passage à frontières*. To desire the impossible is to strain against the constraints of the foreseeable and possible, to *open* the horizon of possibility to what it cannot foresee or foretell.
>
> (Caputo cited in Cornell 1992: 15)

Caputo claims that Derrida's approach here is essentially *inventionalist.* Derrida claims and defends deconstruction as a process of development and progress. He specifically claims that deconstruction can be used to improve or perfect institutions and their laws. The dismantling of a construct opens the opportunity for something completely new to arise. The construct is not abandoned but re-assembled or re-invented. What is even more crucial is that Derrida calls this experience of aporia a 'voyage', a type of traversal without 'guardrails' (Derrida 1997: 134), which pushes against the limits of perception and 'tries to go where it cannot go' (ibid.). In this sense *Dogville* could be said to explore the limits of realist representability of the moral law in its totality. The moral perspective that in a classical realist film may be constructed as singular is being deconstructed here. As a result the spectator is given space to re-assemble and re-invent their own moral perspective, potentially becoming more aware and reflexive of the perceptual choices they make. This sense of deconstructive and aporetic moments results from the narrative and representational dimensions of the film but is essentially reinforced through the interinvolvement of theatre and film aesthetics.

Another way in which *Dogville* creates this sense of perspectivist undecidability and aporia, is through the use of the Farm Security Administration photos in the final credit sequence of the film, which, as representations of 'real' people, have a different ontological status to the characters in the film with whom they are being juxtaposed. In that sense it could be argued that the final credit sequence carves a representational space which is beyond the ontological limits of the film (Figure 8.6).

The photographs are portraits of people from towns and villages that have been struck by hardship. Sinnerbrink – arguing that these photos have a different ontological status from the rest of the film and ground it in a historio-political time-space – commented that it shows all those excluded from the 'liberal democratic image of America' (Sinnerbrink 2007). He also claims that the spectator becomes self-complicit and is left with a notion of ambivalence and democracy as conditioned by desire:

> We should be careful, therefore, not to succumb to the temptation to read the film as a straightforward political or moral allegory. On the contrary, *Dogville* is akin to a Nietzschean genealogy of morals, an ambivalent unmasking of the economy of desire and will to power that sustains the moral, social, and political order.
>
> (Sinnerbrink 2007)

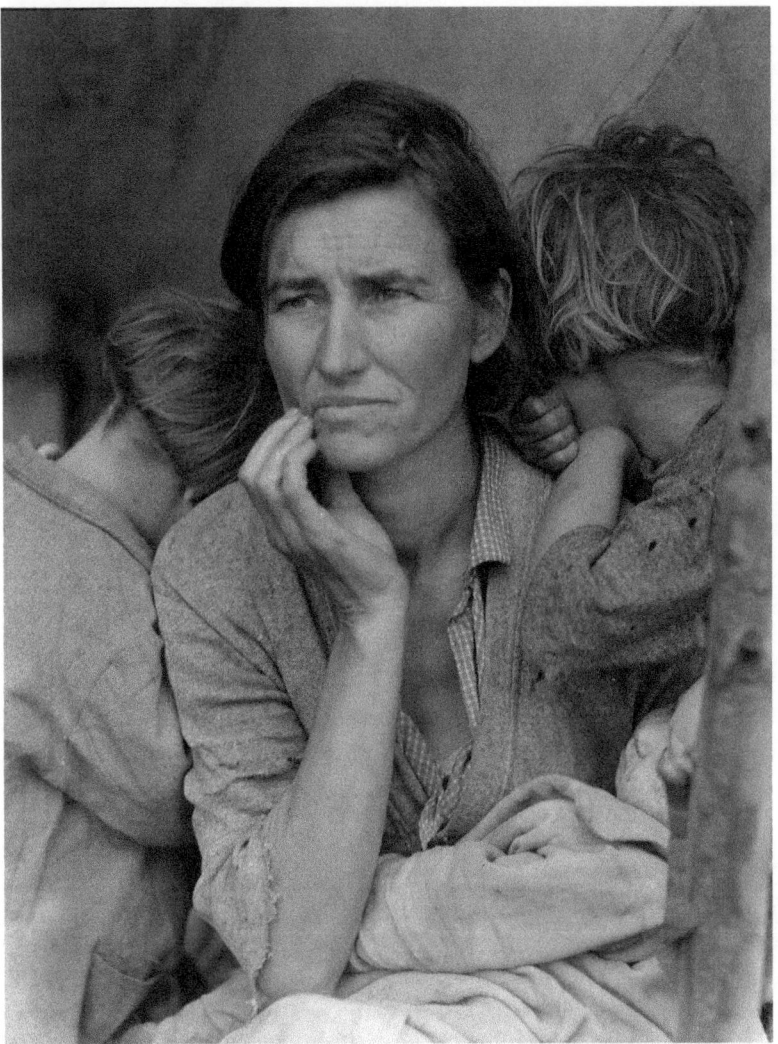

Figure 8.6   Migrant mother, California 1936. Photo: Dorothea Lange

The final credit sequence, often cited as a proof of the film's anti-American attitude, can also reveal more about the role of those undecidable moments within the film. In his article, '"Colorado Death Trip": The Surrealist Recontextualization of Farm Security Administration Photos in *Dogville*', Holger Römers argues against the view that the final credit sequence is simply an analogy. He claims that it recontextualises the photographs within the context of the violence portrayed in *Dogville*, creating a surrealist grotesque, wherein 'real' people are recontextualised in a 'surrealistic pandemonium of rape and massacre' (Römers 2004: 5). What is interesting here is not so much the aspect of recontextualisation as the tension between these two perspectives, between the metaphorical world of *Dogville* and the specific historical reality of the photographs. Lyotard once talked about landscape paintings in a museum being pulled out of their context, re-framed and recontextualised through the act of viewing. Similarly here, von Trier provokes by creating a gap between the metaphorical world of *Dogville* and the historical reality of the photographs. It is then that the emancipated spectator makes a connection potentially based on the morally informed perceptual choices made during the film. This is because these choices will affect the way in which spectators perceive and relate to the characters in the film. They are also able to choose how far they wish to associate real people with an allegorical, politically charged fable, and the choice that is made will stem from the moral position taken on the foregrounded dilemmas that I have discussed so far.

Conclusion: post-political?

With the focus on this emancipating stylistic tension, I would now like to move on and explore the political implications of *Dogville* and what its post-cinematic intermedial aesthetic can tell us about the potential relation between aesthetics and the politics of deconstructing culturally dominant realist aesthetics. To start off the discussion it might be interesting to highlight an opposition of views on this matter concerning Jacques Rancière's and Sinnerbrink's approach. In his article 'The Ethical Turn of Aesthetics and Politics' Rancière sees *Dogville* as exemplifying the 'ethical turn', a turn towards ethics that is essentially abandoning what he calls the 'old term of morals'. This latter term according to him is 'the distinction between fact and law, what is and what ought to be' (Rancière 2006: 2). Ethics on the other hand is what Rancière criticises as 'the dissolution of the norm into the fact – the identification of all forms of discourse and practice under the same indistinct point of view' (ibid.). Rancière locates the dramaturgy of *Dogville* in the light of this shift towards the indistinction of fact and law. He contrasts it with Brecht's *Saint Joan of the Stockyards*, whose story according to him has been transposed into *Dogville*. Whether *Dogville* is a re-write of Brecht's work is arguable. It definitely plays with a Brechtian theatrical aesthetic on a formal level, as was argued earlier, but story-wise it deals with a very different world. Brecht's play is a critique of American capitalism through exploited workers in Chicago's suburbs, whilst von Trier's film explores Christian idealism and ideas of liberal democracy as constitutive of rural America. Rancière, however, contrasts the two to illustrate his point. He claims that in Brecht's play a conflictual drama is set up between two rights and morals, the right of the oppressed opposed to the right of the state whose oppression is represented by the strike-busting policemen. The division of these two rights he calls 'politics'. Politics is thus the act of division wherein mediation cannot occur. There can be no consensus between the two dissenting parties, hence a violent solution to the conflict is inevitable. He claims that the distinction between cause and effect, the fact and the law in Dogville, becomes conflated into one notion of evil. Evil no longer stems from an external system which can be understood and related to as in Brecht's play but is a mechanism which perpetually reproduces itself:

> Grace no longer represents the good soul mystified by her ignorance of the causes of evil. She is just the stranger, the excluded one who wants to be admitted into the community and who is subjected by the community before being rejected by it. Her disillusionment and her narrative of suffering no longer depend on any system of domination that could be understood and destroyed. They depend upon a form of evil that is the cause and the effect of its own reproduction. This is why the only fitting retribution is the radical cleansing exercised upon the community by a Lord and Father who is no one else but the king of thugs. 'Only violence helps where violence reigns' was the Brechtian lesson. Only evil repays evil, is the transformed formula, the one that is appropriate for consensual and humanitarian times. Let us translate this into the language of George W. Bush: only infinite justice is appropriate in the fight against the axis of evil.
> (Rancière 2006: 3)

Another important point in Rancière's argument is the notion of consensus. Where politics seek to divide the different rights of a 'people', consensus 'strives to reduce the people to the population' (Rancière 2006: 6). This somewhat provocative idea stems from a specific distinction that Rancière makes between people and population. In his thinking, people are not necessarily coupled with dissenting political groups or ideologies, but can be subdivided into representatives of different rights whose allegiances can shift and change over time, between a main current, opposition, alternative views and so on. Thus, 'people' are a differentiated mass that cannot be subdued by one totalising framework. However his term 'population' is precisely the opposite. It is a more singularly oriented mass where dissention does not occur. In such a state there is no place for the other which becomes either 'the sick, the retarded or the forsaken to whom the community must stretch its hand in order to re-establish the "social bond"' (Rancière 2007: 7) or the radical, alien delinquent who threatens to unsettle the 'social bond'. He then makes the broader claim that the small society of Dogville reflects the 'depoliticised national community' (ibid.), which he extends to the 'new international landscape' claiming that the ethical turn exemplified by *Dogville* is a global phenomenon.

This is where Sinnerbrink and Rancière part in their political commentary on *Dogville*. Sinnerbrink is more interested in the socio-political implications of the film and specifically in challenging Rancière's claims that *Dogville* is a timeless, post-political film removed from any concrete historical context, exemplifying the 'ethical turn'. Sinnerbrink criticises Rancière for reading *Dogville* as an experiment, a mechanism or quite simply a parable, where the key aspect is the impossibility of reconciliation of two realities. For Sinnerbrink, however, the evil has a cause and a political term and he attempts to prove three points which challenge Rancière's de-contextualised reading. One relates to the interjection of Grace who is an outsider and at the same time a moral figure who unveils the cruelty and brutality upon which the democratic system of the town's community is based. The second relates to the fact that her treatment and exploitation result from a libidinal economy that underlies and sustains the 'inequality and injustice in contemporary democracy' (Sinnerbrink 2007). The third claim is that the retributive ending is not, as Rancière argues, an exemplification of the end of politics in favour of an ideology and consensus, but an 'articulation of the deadlocks of contemporary liberal democracy' (ibid.).

Despite the extensive criticisms of Christian values that underlie the law as construct in Europe and America to this day, these claims still seem fundamentally generic. Sinnerbrink justifies this generic tendency in his argument by linking it with the global social reach of the Hollywood film industry that makes everyone concerned an 'honorary American':

> The film we have been watching thus indicts itself; moreover, it exposes our own economy of desire, our own complicity (as honorary Americans) with *Dogville*, even our own sado-masochistic

complicity with the violence the film depicts, especially in its destructive conclusion.

(Sinnerbrink 2007)

Sinnerbrink is clearly concerned about the power of cinema to induce and engrain ideology into the spectator's mind. Following on from this he also sees *Dogville* as negotiating that very power and reacting against it. Sinnerbrink admits at the end that the lesson learned from *Dogville* lies in the notion of ambivalence and aporias:

> The questions *Dogville* leaves us with are disturbing and unsettling. We are left hovering between the deadening nihilism of forced liberal democratic consensus, with its moral hypocrisy and social exploitation, and a violent destruction or passage à l'acte that would annihilate the corrupted democratic community while also cancelling itself. [...] It presents a diagnosis of the nihilistic dogmas of democracy, describing our social pathologies without prescribing a cure; an answer to the political question, what is to be done?
>
> (Sinnerbrink 2007)

The state in which one does not know what to do or how to move forward – 'not knowing where to go' (Derrida 1993: 12) – is indeed a state of aporia. However the philosophical implications of this state of aporia are much older than American democracy. Sinnerbrink leaves us with a problem. Derrida claims that the Greek word *problema* has at least two meanings, one being a projection, a task to be accomplished in the future, and another one being a protection, a shield cast ahead of us 'behind which one guards oneself in secret or in shelter in case of danger' (Derrida 1993: 12). Indeed, the contemplation of the state of aporia may often be used as a shield, a shelter for meditation. This is in fact what Sinnerbrink says the film offers, a philosophical meditation. But surely the film does more than that. Sinnerbrink rightly criticises Rancière for ignoring *Dogville*'s dimension of cinematic technique and theatricality, yet he himself does little to explore the relation between the post-political and the post-cinematic aesthetic. Also his final question: 'What can be done?', which implies the possibility of a real political action, results from not paying attention to what *Dogville* intrinsically is, namely a post-cinematic film.

By considering the film's post-cinematic aesthetic and its potential to emancipate the spectator, involving them in the play of 'politics of perception', a different question can be posed. Not 'What is to be done?' but what is our ability to respond to that question? Or in other words, what is our 'response-ability'? As has been argued in the previous chapters the 'politics of perception' is not about inciting specific political action or response; rather it is about interrogating and negotiating our freedom and possibility of response. It is essentially about giving the spectator greater freedom to manage and organise their perceptual responses in relation to the presented material. Thus it is also a challenging and questioning of one's perceptual choices and the foregrounding of the factors that are at stake in these choices. Therefore the foregrounding of a 'politics of perception' in *Dogville* can be seen as a post-cinematic reaction to the more passive, prescriptive and by nature perspectivist modes of spectatorship inherent in mainstream dominant cinematic cultures, precisely because it gives the spectators the 'response-ability' to manage and organise their perceptions as opposed to imposing a more rigid realist aesthetic structure that would do this for them. Going back to Lehmann's theatrical definition, the aesthetic of 'response-ability' can be defined as moving away from a:

> deceptively comforting duality of here and there, inside and outside [...] move the mutual implication of actors and spectators in the theatrical production of images into the centre and thus make visible the broken thread between personal experience and perception.
>
> (Lehmann 2006: 186)

Even though *Dogville* does not break the 'here and there', which Lehmann refers to in relation to mass media by positing the actors and spectators in the same physical space, it still blurs the distinction between *mise-en-scène* and *mise-en-cadre*. In other words the place of production of the cinematic image (the theatrical dimension of the studio set) and its reception on the framed screen (what it could potentially be if it was a realist film) reveal a rupture, the impossibility of coupling personal affective experience with a cinematic perception of the events. Watching *Dogville* can be like watching a film in the making, not on a narrative level, but on a formal aesthetic level.[4] 'Can be' because the range of varied and often contrasting responses to this film shows that different spectators perceive this film in different ways. I do believe however that these variances are a result of the film's formal undecidability and essentially exemplify the 'politics of perception' at play. This is because the formal undecidability is what reinforces the state of aporia which places the subject in a position where their ability to respond is put into question.

There are two conflictual strands at stake in the notion of 'response-ability'. One is responsibility as duty, an obligation to act, the notion of *problema* as projection. The second is a defensive stance, the *problema* as a shield, a protection, a questioning of the ability to act. *Dogville* explores these two strands of 'response-ability' in aesthetic terms. It is precisely an aesthetic question since it concerns the processing and organisation of sensible matter. As far as the medium and experience of film is concerned, again Eisenstein's model can be recalled. On one side of the polarity there is a shock, the involuntary emotional response to engage and empathise, on the other the formation of a concept and integration within the global themes of the film, which requires an external body of knowledge, the broadly termed 'cultural baggage'. The uncoupling of these two polarities leads to a question. Does a spectator suppress their immediate emotions in favour of an ideological programme or cultural training? After all injustice and justice are only temporary feelings that have to be submitted to law. Or – based on a subjective, affective experience – does one reconstruct their ideology? Perhaps, it is not so much the feeling of being an accomplice in the crime, or a masochist, as it is this aesthetic deadlock and the failure to represent and solve the problem in a satisfactory way that fuels some of the angry responses cited at the start of this chapter. If the medium of cinema in a classical sense can provide cultural training and couple our responses with a representable ideological and moral framework, then *Dogville* exposes the gap, the rupture within moral representation. Thus some of the highly negative responses to *Dogville* can be explained by the fact it ruptured and wounded the American cinematic tradition, not in representational terms but by formally wounding cinema itself. As we have observed, American culture defines itself through mainstream Hollywood, both nationally and globally. An attack on the cinematic nature of this definition, its imperial global dominance and the political identity stemming from it, through a profound, perceptual wound of undecidability, can be read as a direct attack on America itself.

Dogville's multi-perspectival intermedial strategy is very different from a more classical approach to bringing together two separate ideological perspectives. In the mainstream, Clint Eastwood came up with the idea of making two films about the first American invasion on Japanese soil, namely that on the island of Iwo Jima. One film represents the American perspective, it is called *Flags of our Fathers* (2006), and the other shows events from the Japanese perspective, *Letters from Iwo Jima* (2006). How just and fair Eastwood has been is a broad topic beyond the scope of this book. What is interesting, however, is the ambition to offer an experience that would be unachievable with one film. Given the plurality of ideological perspectives and worldviews of the characters represented in each of the films, this objective would be unachievable even with a thousand films. The 'experiment' is certainly interesting and somewhat compelling but it is limited to the classical representative medium, and consequently more acceptable and less controversial for the American public. *Dogville* creates moments of aporia, which in a classical film could only be achieved through a shift of perspective structurally created by the filmmaker, either through montage or editing, a change in narrative mode, or even relying on visual effects such as superimposition. For example, a twist at the end which makes the viewer recall the whole film in a different perspective (*The Sixth Sense* (1999)), a cut to a different character and his take on reality (the last scene in *Silence of the Lambs* (1991)) or, as in the case of Eastwood's films, a feeling of aporia experienced in retrospect after seeing the two films. However, this is very different from the immediate effect of having a clash of two perspectives in one shot and a single virtual physical space created by theatricalisation. This is because the process of shifting in the conventional examples above is meant to be conclusive and finite aesthetically and structurally, and not aporetic. In *Dogville* the shifting and oscillation between two modes of perception, the theatrical and the cinematic, are foregrounded to a much greater extent than in classically representational movies and often held in simultaneity.

This is perhaps where Rancière's critique of *Dogville* somewhat misses the point, not least in light of his own theories of the emancipated spectator and his thoughts on the relationship between aesthetics and politics. Rancière criticises *Dogville* from a purely thematic and illustrative standpoint, failing to acknowledge the political potential of the various aesthetic disruptions caused by the formal, post-cinematic strategies adopted in the film. This is not what one might anticipate since Rancière has often contested the notion that art can be seen as carrying specific political messages – a direct effect of the meaning-making narrative structures. He has claimed that the political potential of art lies in the 'disruption of a given organization of the relation between the sensible presentation and forms of meaning' (Rancière in Dasgupta 2008: 74). He gives the example of Brecht's estrangement techniques which can act as a disruption to the 'scenery of the sensible' (Rancière in Dasgupta 2008: 74). It is 'this disturbing element', he says, which 'must lead to the awareness that there is something wrong with the social order' (ibid.). The aesthetic disruption in *Dogville* – but also the aporetic uncertainties that come with it – could be interpreted as leading to an awareness of a particular political situation, thus foregrounding the 'politics of perception'. By negotiating the notion of 'response-ability', it would even be plausible to say that *Dogville* potentially emancipates and inspires a certain attitude of political mobilisation. Perhaps not in the context of the fable but by highlighting the fact that there might be something wrong in the way dominant cinematic aesthetics control and induce moral, ideological and political perspectives. Rancière then argues that the role of art should not so much be in constituting political subjects as in the 'reframing of the field of subjectivity as an impersonal field' (Rancière in Dasgupta 2008: 75). Again this is something that can be extensively argued for *Dogville*. It seems that in his critique of *Dogville*, Rancière has omitted his very own line of enquiry, albeit one that was developed in more substance in his later work *The Emancipated Spectator* (2009). Rancière insightfully concluded his point about the undecidability inherent in the aesthetic regimes of art, stating that 'artists create objects that escape their will' (Rancière in Dasgupta 2008: 74). This is certainly true of the post-cinematic pieces analysed in this book, where not only the 'politics of perception' become foregrounded and more open to interpretation but also the uncertainties behind the political intentions of their authors. Perhaps it was these uncertainties behind the 'political intentions' of *Dogville* and the consequent opening up of these question for the interpretation of the audience that were the cause of much of the controversy with which the film was received. Because such 'unstable grounds', which inspire the audience to re-frame their perceptions, may suggest that there is something very wrong not only with the social order of things but also with the way we have been culturally trained to perceive the world.

9
Conclusion

The aim of this book was to set out to define the concept of post-cinematic theatre and performance within the broader field of multimedia and intermedial works. It has been defined as a form of intermedial practice that addresses a heightened cultural awareness of dominant cinematic codes and conventions, namely those of realist cinema, and has been explored through the analysis of a selection of post-cinematic works, dating from the late 1980s to the present day, a number of which are still being performed and developed. The analysis has considered what is at stake in the interinvolvement of theatrical and cinematic modes of representation, arguing that this type of theatre has the potential to deconstruct films and investigate the perceptual habits and expectations associated with cinematic experiences. Moreover, it has been shown that this interinvolvement leads to a greater perceptual freedom for the audience, which has been associated with Lehmann's concept of a 'politics of perception', and that it foregrounds the political and ideological factors underlying forms of perception.

An array of post-structuralist theories have been used in order to theorise the experience of these deconstructions. For instance, the second chapter considered the 'politics of perception' in Robert Lepage's *Elsinore* and *The Anderson Project* with a particular focus on the concepts of 'décalage' and 'mediaphors' and their function as a deconstructive aesthetic prompting the audience to assume a more reflexive, 'writerly' role in the construction of meaning. The chapter explored the relationship between Lepage's décalage and Sergei Eisenstein's theory of classical film montage and cinematic metaphor and supplemented the argument with reference to Colin MacCabe's discursive critique of meta-discourses in realist cinema. The chapter argued that Lepage's works reveal a post-cinematic aesthetic that stimulates the audience to become more active in the process of meaning-making and exemplifies what Lehmann calls the aesthetic of 'response-ability' or the 'politics of perception'.

The discussion in Chapter 3 centred around the notion that post-cinematic theatre has the potential to go beyond the 'pleasure'-bound representations that Lyotard locates in mainstream classical cinema, by playing upon the tension between pleasure and what he defines as *jouissance* (divergent libidinal pleasure). Where film has failed for Lyotard – due to its ontological limits – post-cinematic theatre maintains the potential to explore the 'boundless' enjoyment of *jouissance*. This experience of *jouissance* can have a key role in deconstructing the prescribed pleasures of film and become revealing of enjoyment beyond the standard social and cultural ramifications. By foregrounding this tension between pleasure and *jouissance* and by shifting the emphasis of this polarity towards the pole of *jouissance*, the case studies can be seen to negotiate the 'politics of perception' behind representations of pleasure in film culture. Specifically this concerned the deconstruction of the perception of heteronormative pleasures in Station House Opera's *Roadmetal Sweetbread*. In the same company's *A Mare's Nest*, it was argued that to an extent it is the audience itself that performs and embodies what could be called the cinematic apparatus, making the piece an exploration of the *jouissance* of a wandering perception. By allowing this freedom to the audience, the piece explores enjoyment beyond a fixed and structured perspectivist spectator position. The fourth chapter, on the work of the Wooster Group, extended the theoretical context of the previous chapter. It discussed the concept of pleasure in mainstream cinema and the opportunity for post-cinematic performance to move beyond this aesthetic framework and recuperate the experience of *jouissance* in reference to *House/Lights* and *Hamlet*. The chapter also looked at the way in which the spectator's experience and the emotional journey can be framed as the main point of focus and content of the piece.

In Katie Mitchell's *Wunschkonzert* the discussion moved to an examination of the ways in which the interinvolvement of the theatrical and cinematic modes of representation explored the ethical considerations of constructing filmic and cinematic representations. It also considered the ethical dimension of revealing and staging this process theatrically. Specifically this concerned the ethical issues behind representing and eliciting identification with a story about suicide. By looking at the piece from a representational perspective, it could be said that the *Wunschkonzert* brings forward questions about how suicide ought to be perceived and represented. This raised questions of the relationship between ethics and morality, affective engagement and critical engagement, but also between the notions of goodness and the perception of truth.

Analysis of Imitating the Dog's *Hotel Methuselah* enabled an exploration of the disorienting aspects of the processes underlying post-cinematic performance which stimulate the audience to reconstruct a narrative from the disconnected elements conveyed by the spectacle. This chapter referenced Lyotard's theory of the disorienting landscape. *Hotel Methuselah* had been performed during the heated debates surrounding the Iraq war, and the formal interplay of cinema and theatre in this piece questioned representations of war trauma. At the time, there were many arguments in the media about the political apathy surrounding these debates. *Hotel Methuselah* could be said to provoke its spectators to be more active and reflexive of how they perceive the issue of war in the media and cinema, and the political implications of their perceptions. By emancipating the spectator through these formal strategies the piece negotiated the 'politics of perception'.

Chapter 7 looked at Duncan Speakman's *As If It Were The Last Time*. The piece was analysed through the prism of Peter Greenaway's four 'tyrannies' in order to explore the ways in which the post-cinematic aesthetics of this particular soundwalk re-fashion and deconstruct culturally dominant conventions of realist cinema. The chapter argued that this kind of audio-theatre offers a categorically different degree of participation and audience emancipation from the pieces analysed earlier, whilst still embedding itself heavily within cinematic culture. The chapter used intermedial theory, mainly stemming from Gabriella Giannachi's and Steve Benford's research on 'mixed-reality performances', supported by site-specific performance theory and Michel Chion's concept of 'acousmatization', in order to explore the 'politics of perception' arising from the post-cinematic aesthetic of the piece. The chapter concluded with an exploration of the relationship between the 'politics of perception' and neo-situationist philosophy, namely Guy Debord's concept of *dérive*, and the insights that this offered into the site-specific soundwalk character of the piece.

Chapter 8 explored the 'politics of perception' in relation to moral judgements through an analysis of the intermedial aesthetics of Lars von Trier's film *Dogville*. These aesthetics expose the construction of cinematic representations which in turn potentially carry moral and ideological implications. The political fable of *Dogville* is centred on the conflicts between incomer Grace and the townsfolk of Dogville. Both can be perceived as either victims or criminals, depending upon what angle is taken by the spectator. Grace is an outlaw on the run, a victim of circumstance but also the daughter of a ruthless mafia boss. The townsfolk are victims of the Great Depression, simple folk following their own ways, but also cynical, exploitative and perverse individuals. Derrida's theory of aporias concerning moral judgements and the notion of justice are used to demonstrate what is at stake in making perceptual choices in *Dogville*. The politics behind these choices relate directly to how the freedom of individuals can be integrated into a community. This is an abstract concept and hence *Dogville* can be read as a political allegory. As pointed out before, it can concern the freedom that a liberal democratic state gives to its minorities and also the tensions and conflicts resulting from social injustice. It can refer to the right of highly technologically and economically developed societies to oppress, occupy or even annihilate 'lesser' societies that are perceived as threatening or containing desirable resources. Again the concept of the 'politics of perception' is not necessarily specific to a certain political issue or representation of political content. Its foregrounding is essentially a stimulation of the audience to take charge and become more responsible/'response-able' about their choices and perceptions. And this is achieved by challenging the cinematic codes of representation that are designed to create a more perspectivist experience. Finally I argued that this deconstruction and emancipation of the spectator is a form of resistance against dominant American cinematic culture. By effectuating this intermedial deconstruction *Dogville* undermined a whole cinematic apparatus of American global cultural dominance, where realist cinema has been the main instrument.

On the whole, the pieces analysed here use intermedial strategies to engage the audience in a deconstructive, reflexive process which breaks the powerful spell of cinematic illusion. The book has postulated that cinematised culture affects our perceptions of reality and art by calibrating our senses and affectivity through aesthetic structures. Cinematic culture effectively casts a sophisticated spell, a sensible superstructure like Guy Debord's all engulfing spectacle, reaching out into our higher order consciousness, but also into the more immediate affective unconscious strata through which it shocks us and compels us to settle on particular representations of reality. This book has highlighted the institutional character of this spell and the mass social reach of the ideological and political manipulations it can effectuate. By breaking this spell, which to a great extent stems from the classical realist tradition, post-cinematic theatre and film stimulates a heightened awareness of cinematic culture and its modus operandi and also negotiates a certain political freedom of perception.

I would like to finish by briefly looking at what the emergence of post-cinematic performances suggests about the politics of cinema – more specifically the institutional control of cultural production – from the theatre-maker's standpoint. There is a relationship between the advent of the digital and post-cinema in general. Key to this over the last decade or so is that the technology of filmmaking and editing has become very cheap and very widely accessible. From a technical point of view, achieving near Hollywood standards in filmmaking and visual effects is feasible, albeit laborious, for anyone with home technology. There are also numerous internet communities and forums through which professional filmmaking skills are being disseminated and made widely accessible; with time and skill it is possible for anyone to develop a proficient basis in that area. Thus the knowledge and resources to achieve professional standards no longer lie exclusively with Hollywood studios and institutions. In response to this, mainstream cinema has introduced a variety of technological nuances such as 3D films, face capture and extensive CGI, things that are still very difficult to replicate and achieve with mere film technology. As far as the post-cinematic age is concerned, there is not only greater freedom for the spectator but also for the independent theatre/filmmaker. This freedom can be perceived as a reaction against the dominant institutionalised culture of mainstream cinema in which case it can be seen to exemplify some of the tenets of liberal democracy, akin to the freedom often attributed to YouTube where everyone has the means to broadcast their videos and opinions. But one has to ask whether these modes of expression are not already replicating the modes of representation instilled through domi-nant cultures. This problematic can be addressed in all the case studies in this book, for instance in the case of *Hotel Methuselah* which so heav-ily relies on film noir traditions. Yet the 'politics of perception' is not about specific messages but about forms through which these messages can be conveyed. The post-cinematic pieces analysed in this book use intermedial strategies and interinvolve film and theatre in order to chal-lenge our perceptions and expectations of culturally dominant forms of cinematic representation. As far as the works discussed in this book are concerned, the potential for the experience of that elusive freedom, the newness of perceptual experience, lies precisely in the intermedial juxtaposition of cinema and theatre.

By unsettling the audience's modes of perception and negotiat-ing space for experiences beyond dominant cultural frameworks, post-cinematic theatre and performance has the potential to foreground our sense of a 'politics of perception'. In an increasingly visual culture, cinema as an institution with its culture of spectatorship and popular modes of representation, which infiltrate into most media, plays a key role in how audiences perceive reality and define themselves as social and political beings. Thus post-cinematic theatre has the potential, not so much to challenge the concept of the cinematic as to establish a dialogical relationship with cinematic means of conveying cultural knowledge. Instrumental to this is the spectator's emancipation which allows for this reflective stance to become more pronounced. And thus perhaps the main value of post-cinema lies not in original artistic forms of conveying and interrogating knowledge but in inspiring the audience to test their limits to perceive and cognise our heavily cinematised world.

Notes

1 The Post-Cinematic Landscape

1. A distinction between film and cinema will be made and addressed in this book. Generally speaking film is the medium and the main technology of cinema. Cinema, however, is a cultural phenomenon and an art form.
2. This will be returned to below, with reference to Stephen Heath's and Colin MacCabe's theory of a Brechtian film.
3. A good recent film reference here would be the German film, *The Life of Others* (2006), which offered a representational political perspective on life in the former East Germany.
4. A concept that explores the complex relationship between what is heard and what is seen.
5. 'Remediation' is a term coined by Jay David Bolter and Richard Grusin in their book *Remediation* (1999). It was used to address the way in which the '[new media] refashion older media' (Bolter and Grusin 1999: 15) by framing and absorbing them. In that sense YouTube and TV for instance remediate film that may initially have been intended to be experienced in cinema.
6. This is similar to the way in which the advent of digital technologies allowed practitioners to create intermedial platforms that opened up new opportunities to explore film, thus potentially inspiring more reflexive and critical attitudes towards cinema culture.
7. *Mise-en-cadre* is the cinematic counterpart of the *mise-en-scène*. It means all that is included in the frame of a shot.
8. In Münsterberg's case the spectator is treated as an undifferentiated universal individual. Eisenstein is more careful in his writings in that respect, yet for a substantial part of his research, he argues for a transcendental aesthetic of montage.
9. 'If you stare long into the abyss, the abyss stares back into you.'
10. First published in *Cinethique*, 1970.
11. Clayfield focuses his analysis on works such as the DVD version of Chris Nolan's *Memento* (2001) (not the standard cinematic experience of it), independent sector projects like Simon Pumell's *Bodysong* (2003), and praxis-based research projects in the video art sector by Lev Manovich and Adrian Miles.
12. The 'interactive audience participation' to which Clayfield refers is a problematic term. However it essentially points at an attempt to break with aesthetics of passivity that have been culturally associated with mainstream realist cinema.
13. Such interpretations of these terms may lead to a conclusion that they operate upon a bifurcation between 'drama and not drama' (Bottoms 2009: 67). Stephen Bottoms criticises Lehmann in these terms in his article 'When Authorizing the Audience'. To support his claim that Lehmann bifurcates theatre into two exclusive terms – dramatic and postdramatic – Bottoms

offers the following quote: 'the adjective "postdramatic" denotes a theatre that feels bound to operate beyond drama, at a time "after" the authority of the dramatic paradigm in theatre' (Lehmann in Bottoms 2009: 67). He does not quote the sentences that follow, however, which contextualise and qualify the latter quote more substantially:

> What it does not mean is an abstract negation and mere looking away from the tradition of drama. 'After' drama means that it lives on as a structure – however weakened and exhausted – of the 'normal' theatre: as an expectation of large parts of its audience, as a foundation for many of its means of representation, as a quasi automatically working norm of its drama-turgy.
>
> (Lehmann 2006: 27)

14. The very title, wherein film is called the 'photoplay', already suggests the strong influence that theatre had on film at the time, or at least the way in which early film theory was trying to conceptualise film literarily, as a photographed play.

2   Décalage and Mediaphors in Robert Lepage's *Elsinore* and *The Andersen Project*

1. Wolfgang Iser (1978) argued in his reader-response theory that one of the key preoccupations of classical text is the management and organisation of gaps.
2. Films achieve an image of movement through montage of still images. So how can static artforms such as sculpture and painting also achieve this? One could draw a distinction between the potential of a photographic portrait and a painted portrait to convey an image of movement. Arguably a photographic portrait does register movement since the shutter speed has a time interval. But in many cases this interval will be extremely small, around 1/30–1/60 of a second for studio portraits; not a period in which a lot registers, especially if the model is told to keep still. An artist will make various sketches or even take photographs registering different points in time and may continue to work on a subject for weeks or months, effectively inscribing movement. Even if the content is the same, achieving an image of movement in a painted portrait will be much more effective than in a standard photographic portrait. Hence, the popular statement about great painted portraits is that 'they come alive when one looks at them'.
3. Given the 'hypermedial' nature of theatre it is difficult to define which technologies should be called extra-theatrical. We can assume, however, that cinematic cultural constructs and the technologies that are proper to them (cameras, screens and so on) can be seen as extra-theatrical elements. This is as far as cinematic culture can be defined as extra-theatrical.
4. These concepts will be explored in more detail in subsequent chapters.
5. This is a very old technique initially developed by Max Fleischer in 1917 as a way of transforming live action footage into cartoon animations.

3 Acinematic Montage in *Roadmetal Sweetbread* and *A Mare's Nest*

1. Abjection can be understood here as the rejection of that which interferes with symbolic signification within the cinematic image. This may include any movement that is not immediately readable or referring to an order of representation.
2. Film as the organic body of cinematographical movements.
3. An interesting way to look at this is when we consider the difference in temporality of film and theatre. The physical unit of time within a film is finite, since in theory and as far as our perceptual capacities are concerned the interval between each frame is always the same, invariant. The change in movement in film is framed by a finite time base and therefore all images of movement are divisible by its frame rate. There is no finite, discrete time base or frame rate in theatre as such. Unlike in film there is no 'ultimate' time base unit to which images can be synchronised, because the interval is not a constant. Hence movement in theatre can be perceived as being endlessly divisible. Even though specific moments within a theatrical performance can be accentuated and therefore perceived as synchronised or rhythmic, there is no constant interval between them to which they would be ultimately reducible. The change in movement is not reducible to a finite time interval, instead it is subjected to differential change. Hence one could say that theatre enables us to perceive the differentiation of change. This is why theatrical presence can sometimes be related to physical concepts such as entropy and chaos theory in the case of Beckett's minimalist theatre, or the Deleuzian concept of 'differential presence' where the perceptual process itself is constantly susceptible to change.
4. This sequence is made up of a site-specific recording and varies depending on where the piece is performed.
5. A classic technique of achieving the *impression* of chance in montage for both cinema (Eisenstein) and theatre (Meyerhold) is recoil. For example if there are three episodes representing the breakdown of a relationship between a couple – absence of wife, fantasy about betrayal and a fight in a hotel room – they can be directed with varying degrees of intensity. If they are then montaged in an ascending order of intensity the general idea of an increasingly deteriorating relationship and the specific illustration become obvious and therefore predictable, hence not very chance like. Instead, the recoil method suggests rearranging the order so that it is less predictable, nonetheless the overall concept of increasing intensity is still clear. For example one could have the medium intensity event first (fantasy about betrayal), followed by the low intensity event (absence of wife) and finally the high intensity one (fight in a hotel room). The general increase in tension is still implicit but not obvious from the material, hence it gives an impression of chance.
6. The reason for this is that the murderer is concealed and so is their gaze. The mother is backlit in that shot sequence plus the cuts are too fast for any kind of substantial perception of their gaze to develop. Hence identification with Marion dominates the sequence.

4 Guilty Pleasures and Intermedial Archaeologies in the Wooster Group's *House/Lights* and *Hamlet*

1. A term used by Andrew Quick in his essay 'The Space Between: Disorienting Landscape in the Photographic Works of Willie Doherty' (2005), derived from Lyotard's essay 'Scapeland' (1988). This concept will be explored in more depth in Chapter 6.
2. The methodology that the Wooster Group uses can be seen as a construction of the operators that Lyotard talks about.

5 The Ethics of Perception in *Wunschkonzert*

1. This philosophical approach could be defined as psychism. It also finds confirmations and affinities within neuro-scientific theories such as that of mirror-neurons as a mechanism for non-semiotic, pre-linguistic affective communication.
2. *Superego* (the ideal, 'raw model' dimension of the psyche). *Ego* (rational decision-making dimension). *Id* (the dimension of the unconscious drives).
3. This is obviously a transcendental approach that partially evades historical and cultural specificity.
4. There is – as outlined earlier – a distinction here again between ethics and morality. Hamlet still feels pity and has sentiments of remorse when he decides to avenge his father; he even accepts Claudius's apologies. One could argue that he still feels that killing a human being is unethical no matter the cause. Yet he is convinced of the moral rectitude of his plan.

6 Disorienting Landscapes in *Hotel Methuselah*

1. In many ways Lyotard's and Lehmann's thinking has affinities with Roland Barthes's claim that some texts are more 'readerly' than others, even though all texts can be considered 'readerly' and 'writerly' to varying degrees. 'Readerly' texts make no special demands on the reader to produce their own meaning. They situate their subject matter within culturally dominant systems of representation, and become 'like a cupboard where meanings are shelved, stacked, [and] safeguarded' (Barthes 1974: 200).
2. Eisenstein makes a very convincing comparison between parallel montage techniques used by David Griffith and narrative structures employed in Charles Dickens's *Oliver Twist*. For reference see 'Dickens, Griffith and Ourselves' (Eisenstein 1996: 193–240).
3. Gilles Deleuze puts forward an argument in *Cinema 1* based on Bergson's theory of movement, that one of the essential differences between the movement in film and the movement in reality is that movement on film happens between frames. It is always an illusion happening between still images – 'immobile sections'. In reality movement is a qualitative change of the real, one that always carries the possibility of the unpredictable.

4. In traditional theatre the logical and eventual progressions of a piece, the rhythm and pace, are dictated and controlled by the performers. The *live* movements define the space and the narratives within it.
5. Deleuze defines a 'state of things' as 'a determinate of space-time, spatio-temporal coordinates, objects and people, real connections between these givens' (Deleuze 1986: 100).
6. The 'common region' is a term used in cognitive psychology to define a tendency to group elements together that belong to a common region or designated area.
7. An augmented chord made up of a tonic, a third and an augmented fifth, for example: (C, E, G#)

7 Pedipulating '*Footage*' in Duncan Speakman's *As If It Were The Last Time*

1. Eisenstein often dismisses artistic strategies which attempt to break an imaginary unity of the subject and hence compromise a unified singular perceptual trajectory. This was evident from his essay on Laocoön and also explains his objection to futurism, cubism and any artwork where the unity of the subject and perspective is compromised. For instance, he critiques works such as Balla's 'Man with Six Legs in Six Positions' as being 'primitive' (Eisenstein 1949: 50).
2. Following this cinematic culture, people at home may choose to simulate a similar environment when watching movies – for instance, by means of a home cinema set-up.
3. For instance a metropolis may be represented as a busy and fast-paced cityscape. Such imagery reinforces a dominant contemporary political standpoint: that which is fast, busy and massive in scale supports the concept of productivity and progress in a capitalist society. The proliferation of such cinematic constructs may in turn influence perceptual habits with which audiences approach the real world.
4. We have explored these modes through Colin MacCabe's theories in Chapter 2 on Lepage's work.
5. This is because regardless of how a movie may represent reality, it will always select particular movements, intensities and images in order to form a fixed representation of reality.

8 Landscapes and Aporias in Lars von Trier's *Dogville*

1. *Dogville* is by no means a pure Dogme 95 film although some of its stylistics have affinities with the ten points of 'The Chastity Vow', which defines the stylistic reaction against Hollywood mainstream elaborated by Lars von Trier and Thomas Vinterberg. It is arguable that *The Idiots* is the 'purest' Dogme 95 film von Trier ever made. Ever since, his style has gone astray, yet it still uses and explores a lot of the assumptions stated in those ten points. In fact in his later films, such as *Dancer in the Dark*, von Trier juxtaposes the Dogme

95 thesis and 1950s Hollywood musical conventions, in order to explore the aesthetic tension between the two for dramatic purposes. The use of Dogme 95 in *Dogville* is juxtaposed against theatrical conventions, melodramatic fable devices and the gangster movie genre. The ten points of 'The Chastity Vow' are as follows:

1. Shooting must be done on location. Props and sets must not be brought in (if a particular prop is necessary for the story, a location must be chosen where this prop is to be found).
2. The sound must never be produced apart from the images or vice versa. (Music must not be used unless it occurs where the scene is being shot.)
3. The camera must be hand-held. Any movement or immobility attainable in the hand is permitted. (The film must not take place where the camera is standing; shooting must take place where the film takes place.)
4. The film must be in colour. Special lighting is not acceptable. (If there is too little light for exposure the scene must be cut or a single lamp be attached to the camera.)
5. Optical work and filters are forbidden.
6. The film must not contain superficial action. (Murders, weapons, etc. must not occur.)
7. Temporal and geographical alienation are forbidden. (That is to say that the film takes place here and now.)
8. Genre movies are not acceptable.
9. The film format must be Academy 35 mm.
10. The director must not be credited.

2. The Farm Security Administration was created in 1937 to assist poor American farmers during the Dust Bowl and the Great Depression years. It had a special photographic section led by Roy Emerson Stryker, which created 77,000 black-and-white documentary photographs depicting the most affected farmers and their difficult living conditions.
3. The realist tradition that can be seen in Westerns such as those of John Ford, according to Deleuze, rests in short on the Situation-Action-Situation or Action-Situation-Action (SAS or ASA) formula where the sensory-motor linkage between the situation and action is crucial.
4. *Dogville* is not a film about making a film like *Adaptation* (2002) or making a media production out of someone's life, like *The Truman Show* (1998). It is an unfinished film.

Bibliography

Abella, A. and N. Zilkha (2004) 'Dogville: A Parable on Perversion', *International Journal of Psychoanalysis*, 85: 1519–26.

Albersmeier, F.-J. (ed.) (1995), *Theorie des Films*, Stuttgart: Reclam.

Arfara, K. (2008) 'Review Essay: The Wooster Group: Hamlet, or the Tragic of the Surface', *Performance Research: A Journal of the Performing Arts*, 13(1): 134–7.

Aristotle (1940) *Aristotle's Art of Poetry: A Greek View of Poetry and Drama*, Oxford: The Clarendon Press.

Auslander, P. (1992) *Presence and Resistance: Postmodernism and Cultural Politics in Contemporary American Performance*, Ann Arbor: University of Michigan Press.

Auslander, P. (1999) *Liveness*, London: Routledge.

Balázs, B. (1938) 'Zur Kunstphilosophie des Films', in F.-J. Albersmeier (ed.), *Theorie des Films*, Stuttgart: Reclam, pp. 204–26.

Balázs, B. (1972 [1952]) *Theory of the Film; Character and Growth of a New Art*, New York: Arno Press.

Balázs, B. (1975 [1959]) 'Theory of the Film', in D. Talbot (ed.), *Film: An Anthology*, Berkeley and London: University of California Press, pp. 201–15.

Barthes, R. (1974) *S/Z: An Essay*, New York: Hill and Wang.

Baudrillard, J. (1988) *The Ecstasy of Communication*, New York: Automedia.

Baudrillard, J. (1994 [1981]) *Simulacra and Simulation*, Ann Arbor: University of Michigan Press.

Baudrillard, J. (2000) *The Vital Illusion*, New York: Columbia University Press.

Baudry, J.-L. (1985 [1970]) 'Ideological Effects of the Basic Cinematographic Apparatus', in B. Nichols (trans. and ed.), *Movies and Methods Volume II*, Berkeley and Los Angeles: California University Press, pp. 531–42.

Bay-Cheng, S., C. Kattenbelt, A. Lavender and R. Nelson (eds) (2010) *Mapping Intermediality in Performance*, Amsterdam: Amsterdam University Press.

Bazin, A. (2005) 'Theater and Cinema', in R. Knopf (ed.), *Film and Theater: A Comparative Anthology*, Binghampton, NY: Vail Ballou Press, pp. 110–33.

Bennigton, G. *(1988) Lyotard: Writing the Event*, Manchester: Manchester University Press.

Benjamin, A. (ed.) (1989) *The Lyotard Reader*, Oxford: Blackwell.

Bergson, H. (1911) *Creative Evolution*, London: Macmillan and Co.

Blau, H. (1982) *Take Up the Bodies: Theater at the Vanishing Point*, Urbana: University of Illinois Press.

Bleeker, M. (2008) *Visuality in the Theatre: The Locus of Looking*, Basingstoke: Palgrave Macmillan.

Boenisch, P. (2006) 'Aesthetic Art to Aisthetic Act: Theatre, Media, Intermedial Performance', in F. Chapple and C. Kattenbelt (eds), *Intermediality in Theatre and Performance*, Amsterdam: Rodopi, pp. 103–16.

Bolter, J. and D. Grusin (1999) *Remediation: Understanding New Media*, Cambridge, MA: MIT Press.

Bordwell, D. and Noël Carroll (1996) *Post-Theory: Reconstructing Film Studies*, Madison: University of Wisconsin Press.

Bordwell, D. (1999) *A Case for Cognitivism*, available online at http://qmplus. qmul.ac.uk/pluginfile.php/13140/mod_resource/content/1/david%20bord well%20-%20a%20case%20for%20cognitivism.pdf (accessed 25 June 2014).

Bottoms, S. (2009) 'When Authorizing the Audience: The Conceptual Drama of Tim Crouch', *Performance Research*, 14(1): 65–76.

Brooks, P. and A. Quick (dir.) (2006) *Hotel Methuselah*, Lancaster: Nuffield Theatre.

Burnett, R. (2004) *How Images Think*, Cambridge, MA: MIT Press.

Callens, J. (2009) 'The Wooster Group's Hamlet, According to the True, Original Copies', *Theatre Journal*, 61(4): 539–61.

Cameron, J. (2009) (dir.) *Avatar*. Twentieth Century Fox and Lightstorm Entertainment.

Carroll, N. (1998) *A Philosophy of Mass Art*, Oxford: Oxford University Press.

Chapple, F. and C. Kattenbelt (eds) (2006a) *Intermediality in Theatre and Performance*, Amsterdam: Radopi.

Chapple, F. and C. Kattenbelt (2006b) 'Key Issues in Intermediality in Theatre and Performance', in F. Chapple and C. Kattenbelt (eds), *Intermediality in Theatre and Performance*, Amsterdam: Rodopi, pp. 11–26.

Childs, N. and J. Walwin (eds) (1998) *A Split Second of Paradise*, London: Rivers Oram.

Chion, M. (1994) *Audio-Vision: Sound on Screen*, New York: Columbia University Press.

Christiansen, R. (1996) 'High-tech Tricks Take Center Stage In Lepage's Glitzy "Elsinore"', *Chicago Tribune*, available online at http://articles.chicagotribune. com/1996-02-17/news/9602170197_1_hamlet-scenes-jamboree (accessed 16 June 2014).

Clayfield, M. (2005) *A Cinema Exploded: Notes on the Development of Some Post-Cinematic Forms*, available online at http://umintermediai501.blogspot. co.uk/2010/05/cinema-exploded-notes-on-development-of.html (accessed 25 June 2014).

Connor, S. (1989) *Postmodernist Culture: An Introduction to Theories of the Contemporary*, Oxford: Blackwell.

Cornell, D. (1992) *The Philosophy of the Limit*, New York: Routledge.

CREW (2010) *CREW online*, available online at http://www.crewonline.org/art/ projects/4 (accessed 13 June 2010).

Crohn Schmidtt, N. (1990) *Actors and Onlookers: Theatre and Twentieth-Century Scientific Views of Nature*, Evanston, IL: Northwestern University Press.

Cull, L. (2009) (ed.) *Deleuze and Performance*, Edinburgh: Edinburgh University Press.

Cull, L. (2011) *Theatres of Immanence*, Basingstoke: Palgrave Macmillan.

Dasgupta, S. (2008) 'Art is going Elsewhere, and Politics Has to Catch It. An Interview with Jacques Rancière', *Krisis: Journal for Contemporary Philosophy*, 1: 70–6.

Davies, A. (1988) *Filming Shakespeare's Plays*, Cambridge: Cambridge University Press.

Davies-Crook, S. (2011) 'Duncan Speakman: "Our Broken Voice"', *Dazed Digital*, available online at http://www.dazeddigital.com/artsandculture/article/10495/ 1/duncan-speakman-our-broken-voice (accessed 16 June 2014).

Debord, G. (1956) 'Theory of the Dérive', in *Les Lèvres Nues #9*, trans. Ken Knabb, available online at http://www.cddc.vt.edu/sionline/si/theory.html (accessed 16 June 2014).

Debord, G. (1958) 'Definitions', *Internationale Situationniste*, 1 (Paris, June).

Debord, G. (1995) *The Society of the Spectacle*, trans. Donald Nicholson-Smith, New York: Zone.

Deleuze, G. (1983) *Cinema I*, trans. H.T. a. R. Galeta, London: Athlone Press.

Deleuze, G. (1985) *Cinema II*, trans. H.T. a. R. Galeta, London: Athlone Press.

Deleuze, G. (1986 [1983]) *Cinema I*, trans. Hugh Tomlinson and Barbara Habberjam, London: Athlone Press.

Deleuze, G. (1988) *Bergsonism*, New York: Zone Books.

Derrida, J. (1976) *Of Grammatology*, Baltimore: Johns Hopkins University Press.

Derrida, J. (1982) *Margins of Philosophy*, Chicago: University of Chicago Press.

Derrida, J. (1993) *Aporias: Dying – Awaiting (one another at) the 'limits of truth' (mourir – s'attendre aux 'limite')*, trans. Thomas Dutoit, Stanford: Stanford University Press.

Derrida, J. (1997) *Deconstruction in a Nutshell: A Conversation with Jacques Derrida*, ed. J. Caputo, New York: Fordham University Press.

Dixon, S. (2007) *Digital Performance: A History of New Media in Theatre, Dance, Performance Art and Installation*, Cambridge, MA: MIT Press.

Dundjerovic, A. (2007) *The Theatricality of Robert Lepage*, Canada: McGill-Queen's University Press.

Eastwood, C. (2006) (dir.) *Flags of our Fathers*, Warner Bros. Entertainment Inc. and Dreamworks LLC.

Eastwood, C. (2006) (dir.) *Letters from Iwo Jima*, Warner Bros. Entertainment Inc. and Dreamworks LLC.

Ebert, R. (2004) '*Dogville*', *Chicago Sun Times*, 9 April, available online at http://rogerebert.suntimes.com/apps/pbcs.dll/article?AID=/20040409/REVIEWS/404090303/1023 (accessed 16 June 2014).

Eisenstein, S. (1947) *The Film Sense*, London: Faber and Faber.

Eisenstein, S. (1949) *Film Form*, London: Dennis Dobson.

Eisenstein, S. (1951) *Film Form: Essays in Film Theory*, London: Dobson.

Eisenstein, S. (1989) 'Montage and Architecture', *assemblage10* (December): 111–31.

Eisenstein, S. (1991a) *Selected Works: Volume 2: Towards a Theory of Montage*, ed. Michael Glenny and Richard Taylor, London: British Film Institute.

Eisenstein, S. (1991b) 'Laocoön', in *Selected Works: Volume 2: Towards a Theory of Montage*, ed. Michael Glenny and Richard Taylor, London: British Film Institute, pp. 139–81.

Eisenstein, S. (1996) *Selected Works: Volume 3: Writings, 1934–47*, ed. Naum Kleiman and Richard Taylor, London: British Film Institute.

Eisenstein, S. (2005) 'Through Theatre to Cinema', in R. Knopf (ed.), *Film and Theater: A Comparative Anthology*, Binghampton, NY: Vail Ballou Press, pp. 239–50.

Ezra, E. and S. Harris (eds) (2000) *France in Focus: Film and National Identity*, Oxford: Berg.

Fibiger, B. (2003) 'A Dog Not Yet Buried – Or *Dogville* as a Political Manifesto', *A Danish Journal of Film Studies*, 16, Special Issue 'Film and Politics' (December), available online at http://pov.imv.au.dk/Issue_16/section_1/artc7A.html (accessed 25 June 2014).

Forman, R. (1976) 'How to Write a Play', *Performing Arts Journal I*, 2: 84–92.

Freud, S. (1997) *On Sexuality*, Harmondsworth: Pelican Books.

Fuchs, E. (2002) *Land/scape/theatre*, Ann Arbor: University of Michigan Press.

Gadamer, H.-G. (1993) *Truth and Method*, London: Sheed & Ward.

Giannachi, G. and S. Benford (2011) *Performing Mixed Reality*, Cambridge, MA: MIT Press.

Giannachi, G. and N. Stewart (eds) (2005) *Performing Nature: Explorations in Ecology and the Arts*, Oxford: Peter Lang.

Giesekam, G. (2007) *Staging the Screen: The Use of Film and Video in Theatre*, Basingstoke and New York: Palgrave Macmillan.

Goldberg, R. (1979) *Performance Art: From Futurism to the Present*, London and New York: Thames and Hudson.

Goulish, M. (2000) *39 Microlectures: In Proximity of Performance*, London: Routledge.

Greenaway, P. (2010) 'New Possibilities: Cinema Is Dead, Long Live Cinema', lecture presented by the Townsend Center for the Humanities, https://www.youtube.com/watch?v=u6yC41ZxqYs (accessed 23 June 2014).

Foster, H. (1985) *Recordings: Art, Spectacle, Cultural Politics*, Port Townsend: Bay Press.

Habermas, J. (1990) *Moral Consciousness and Communicative Action*, trans. C. Lenhardt and S.W. Nicholsen, Cambridge, MA: MIT Press.

Hassan, I. and S. Hassan (eds) (1983) *Innovation/Renovation: New Perspectives on the Humanities*, Madison: University of Wisconsin Press.

Heath, S. (1992) 'Lessons from Brecht', in F. Mulhern (ed.), *Contemporary Marxist Literary Criticism*, New York: Longman, pp. 230–57.

Hébert, C. and I. Perelli-Contos (2001) *'La face cachée' du théâtre de l'image*, Paris: Harmattan.

Heilpern, J. (1997) 'Elsinore: Robert Lepage's Bad Day at the Office', *New York Observer*, available online at http://observer.com/1997/10/elsinore-robert-lepages-bad-day-at-the-office/ (accessed 16 June 2014).

Heim, W. (2006) 'Navigating Voices', in G. Giannachi and N. Stewart (eds), *Performing Nature: Explorations in Ecology and the Arts*, Bern: Peter Lang, pp. 199–216.

Herzog, W. (2010) 'On the Absolute, the Sublime, and Ecstatic Truth', trans. Moira Weigel, *Arion* 17(3), available online at http://www.bu.edu/arion/on-the-absolute-the-sublime-and-ecstatic-truth (accessed 16 June 2014).

Humphrey, N. (2006) *Seeing Red: A Study in Consciousness*, Cambridge, MA: Belknap Press.

iCinema (2013) Website, http://www.icinema.unsw.edu.au/.

Innes, C. (2005) 'Puppets and Machines of the Mind: Robert Lepage and the Modernist Heritage', *Theatre Research International*, 2 (July 2005): 124–38.

Iser, W. (1974) *The Implied Reader: Patterns of Communication in Prose Fiction from Bunyan to Beckett*, Baltimore and London: Johns Hopkins University Press.

Iser, W. (1978) *The Act of Reading: A Theory of Aesthetic Response*, London: Routledge & Kegan Paul.

Jameson, F. (1984) 'The Politics of Theory: Ideological Positions in the Postmodern Debate', *New German Critique*, 32: 53–65.

Jones, A. (2001) 'Conspiracy on Stage, Screen and in the Audience', *Birmingham Post*, 5 February.

Jones, J. (2002) 'Review of Mare's Nest', *Live Art Magazine*, 38.

Jones, R.E. (1992) *Towards a New Theatre: The Lectures of Robert Edmond Jones*, New York: Limelight Editions.

Kant, I. (1952) *The Critique of Judgement*, trans. J. C. Meredith, New York: Oxford University Press.

Kattenbelt, C. (2006) 'Theatre as the Art of the Performer and the Stage of Intermediality', in F. Chapple and C. Kattenbelt (eds), *Intermediality in Theatre and Performance*, Amsterdam: Rodopi, pp. 29–40.

Kaye, N. (1996) *Art into Theatre: Performance Interviews and Documents*, London: Routledge.

Kaye, N. (2000) *Site-Specific Art: Performance, Place and Documentation*, London: Routledge.

Kaye, N. (2007) *Multi-Media Video Installation Performance*, Oxford: Routledge.

Kelleher, J. (2009) *Theatre & Politics*, Basingstoke: Palgrave Macmillan.

Kent, S. (1998) 'An Act in Several Parts: The Work of Station House Opera', in N. Childs and J. Walwin (eds), *A Split Second of Paradise*, London: Rivers Oram, pp. 117–35.

Kirby, M. (1972) 'On Acting and Non-Acting', *Theatre Drama Review*, 16(1) (March): 3–15.

Klich, R. and E. Scheer (2012) *Multimedia Performance*, Basingstoke: Palgrave Macmillan.

Knopf, R. (ed.) (2005) *Film and Theatre: A Comparative Anthology*, Binghampton, NY: Vail Ballou Press.

Kristeva, J. (1982) *Powers of Horror: An Essay on Abjection*, trans. Leon S. Roudiez, New York: Columbia University Press.

Kuchenbuch, T. (2006) 'Theoretical Approaches to Theatre and Film Adaptation: A History', in F Chapple and C. Kattenbelt (eds), *Intermediality in Theatre and Performance*, Amsterdam: Rodopi, pp. 169–80.

Lacan, J. (1991) *The Seminar of Jacques Lacan: Book II: The Ego in Freud's Theory and in the Technique of Psychoanalysis 1954–1955*, New York: W.W. Norton & Company.

Laine, T. (2006) 'Lars Von Trier, *Dogville* and the Hodological Space of Cinema', *Studies in European Cinema*, 3(2): 129–41.

Lattek, M. (2006) 'A Reading of *Dogville*', *Anamesa: The Violence Issue*: 99–115.

Lavender, A. (2001) *Hamlet in Pieces*, London: Nick Hern Books.

Lehmann, H.-T. (2006) *Postdramatic Theatre*, trans. Karen Jürs-Munby, Oxford: Routledge.

Lepage, R. (2007) *Le Projet Andersen*, Quebec: Diffusion Dimedia.

Lévinas, E. (1969) *Totality and Infinity; An Essay on Exteriority*, The Hague: Nijhoff.

Lévinas, E. (1987) *Collected Philosophical Papers*, Dordrecht: Martinus Nijhoff.

Lévinas, E. (1998) *The Lévinas Reader*, Oxford: Blackwell.

Lyotard, J.-F. (1976) 'The Tooth, the Palm', *Sub-Stance*, 15: 105–10.

Lyotard, J.-F. (1979) *The Postmodern Condition: A Report on Knowledge*, Manchester: Manchester University Press.

Lyotard, J.-F. (1984) *The Postmodern Condition: A Report on Knowledge*, Minneapolis: University of Minnesota Press.

Lyotard, J.-F. (1989) 'Acinema', in Andrew Benjamin (ed.), *The Lyotard Reader*, Oxford: Blackwell, pp. 169–80.

Lyotard, J.-F. (1991) *Inhuman*, trans. Geoffrey Bennington and Rachel Bowlby, Cambridge: Polity Press.

MacCabe, C. (1974) 'Realism and the Cinema: Notes on Some Brechtian Theses', *Screen*, Summer, 15(2): 7.

MacCabe, C. (1985) *Theoretical Essays: Film, Literature, Linguistics*, Manchester: Manchester University Press.

Martin, S. (2005) *Andrei Tarkovsky*, Harpenden: Pocket Essentials.

McLuhan, M (1975) *Understanding Media: The Extensions of Man*, London: Routledge & Kegan.

Metz, C. (1982) *The Imaginary Signifier*, Bloomington: Indiana University Press.

Meyerowitz, P. (ed.) (1971) *Writings and Lectures 1909–1949*, London: Owen.

Myers, M. (2006) 'Homing Place: Performing Emplacement', PhD thesis, University of Plymouth.

Miller, J.-A. (1978) 'Suture (Elements of the Logic of the Signifier)', *Screen*, 71(4): 24–34.

Mitchell, K. (dir.) (2009) *Wunschkonzert*, Köln: Schauspiel Köln.

Mitry, J. (1990) *Esthétique et psychologie du cinéma*, Paris: Editions universitaires.

Mostra Live Cinema (2010) *Live Cinema*, available online at http://www.live cinema.com.br (accessed 16 June 2014).

Mulhern, F. (ed.) (1992) *Contemporary Marxist Literary Criticism*, New York: Longman.

Münsterberg, H. (2002) *Hugo Münsterberg on Film: The Photoplay: Psychological Studies and Other Writings*, New York: Routledge.

Nichols, B. (ed.) (1985) *Movies and Methods Volume II*, Berkeley and Los Angeles: University of California Press.

Nietzsche, F. (2003) *Beyond Good and Evil*, London: Penguin.

Palatini Bowers, J. (2002) 'The Composition that all the World Can See', in E. Fuchs (ed.), *Land/scape/theatre*, Michigan: University of Michigan Press, pp. 121–44.

Parker-Starbuck, J. (2011) *Cyborg Theatre: Corporeal/Technological Instersections in Multimedia Performance*, Basingstoke: Palgrave.

Pearson, M. (2010) *Site-Specific Performance*, Basingstoke: Palgrave Macmillan.

Peden, K. (2005) '"The Threepenny Shot" review of *Dogville* (2003) and *Inside Deep Throat* (2005)', *Critical Sense: A Journal of Political and Cultural Theory*, 13(1) (Spring 2005): 119–29.

Peperzak, A. (ed.) (1995) *Ethics as First Philosophy: The Significance of Emmanuel Lévinas for Philosophy, Literature, and Religion*, New York: Routledge.

Perrella, S. (1998) *Hypersurface Architecture*, London: Methuen.

Phelan, P. (1993) *Unmarked: The Politics of Performance*, London, New York: Routledge.

Place, J.A. and L. Peterson (1974) 'Some Visual Motifs of Film Noir', *Film Comment*, 10(1): 30–2.

Place, J.A. and L. Peterson (1996) 'Some Visual Motifs of Film Noir', in A. Silver and J. Ursini (eds), *Film Noir Reader*, New York: Limelight Editions, pp. 65–75.

Pluta, I. (2010) 'Robert Lepage and Ex Machina, *The Andersen Project* (2005)', in S. Bay-Cheng, C. Kattenbelt, A. Lavender and R. Nelson (eds), *Mapping Inter-mediality in Performance*, Amsterdam: Amsterdam University Press, pp. 191–7.

Quick, A. (2005) 'The Space Between: Disorienting Landscape in the Photographic Works of Willie Doherty', in G. Giannachi and N. Stewart (eds), *Performing Nature: Explorations in Ecology and the Arts*, Oxford: Peter Lang, pp. 147–64.

Quick, A. (ed.) (2006) *Hotel Methuselah: A Document, by Imitating the Dog*, theatre programme, Leeds.

Quick, A. (2007) *The Wooster Group Workbook*, New York: Routledge.

Quick, A. (2009) 'The Stay of Illusion', *Performance Research*, 14(1): 29–36.

Rancière, J. (2006) 'The Ethical Turn of Aesthetics and Politics', *Critical Horizons*, 7(1): 1–20.

Rancière, J. (2009) *The Emancipated Spectator*, London: Verso.

Rebellato, D. (2009) 'When We Talk of Horses: Or, What Do We See When We See a Play?', *Performance Research*, 14(1): 17–28.

Rees, A. (1999) *History of Experimental Film and Video: From The Canonical Avant-Garde to Contemporary British Practice*, London: British Film Institute.

Robinson-Riegler, G. (2004) *Cognitive Psychology: Applying the Science of the Mind*, Boston: Pearson Education.

Römers, H. (2004) '"Colorado Death Trip": The Surrealist Recontextualisation of Farm Security Administration Photos in *Dogville*', *Senses of Cinema*, available online at http://sensesofcinema.com/2005/feature-articles/dogville_farm_admin_photos/ (accessed 25 June 2014).

Rorrison, H. (1980) 'Piscator's Production of "Hoppla, Wir Leben", 1927', *Theatre Quarterly*, 10(37): 30–41.

Rosen, P. (ed.) (1986) *Narrative, Apparatus, Ideology: A Film Theory Reader*, New York: Columbia University Press.

Shakespeare, W. (1987) *Hamlet*, Oxford: Oxford University Press.

Shevtsova, M. (2013) 'A Conversation on the Wooster Group's *Hamlet*', *New Theatre Quarterly*, 29: 121–31.

Shuttleworth, I. (1996) 'Elsinore', *Financial Times*, available online at http://www.cix.co.uk/~shutters/reviews/96094.htm (accessed 25 June 2014).

Silver, A. and J. Ursini (eds) (1996) *Film Noir Reader*, New York: Limelight Editions.

Silverman, K. (1983) *The Subject of Semiotics*, New York: Oxford University Press.

Sinnerbrink, R. (2007) 'Grace and Violence: Questioning Politics and Desire in Lars von Trier's *Dogville*', *Scan Journal*, available online at http://scan.net.au/scan/journal/print.php?journal_id=94&j_id=11 (accessed 16 June 2014).

Sobchack, V.C. (1992) *The Address of the Eye: A Phenomenology of Film Experience*, Princeton, NJ: Princeton University Press.

Sontag, S. (1966) 'Film and Theatre', *Tulane Drama Review*, 11(1) (Autumn, 1966): 24–37.

Sontag, S. (2005) 'Film and Theater', in R. Knopf (ed.), *Film and Theater: A Comparative Anthology*, Binghampton, NY: Vail Ballou Press, pp. 134–51.

Speakman, D. (2009) *As If It Were The Last Time*, unpublished script.

Speakman, D. (2010) *wearecircumstance – as if it were the last time*, available online at http://wearecircumstance.com/as-if-it-were-the-last-time.html (accessed 25 June 2014).

Station House Opera (2004) *A Mare's Nest*, Lancaster: Nuffield Theatre.

Station House Opera (2006) *Roadmetal Sweetbread*, France: Nevers.

Stewart, K. (1996) *A Space on the Side of the Road: Cultural Poetics in an 'Other' America*, Princeton, NJ: Princeton University Press.

Svoboda, J. (1996) 'Laterna Magika', *TDR: Tulane Drama Review*, 11(1): 141–9.

Talbot, D. (ed.) (1959) *Film: An Anthology*, Berkeley: University of California Press.

Tallon, A. (1995) 'Nonintentional Affectivity, Affective Intentionality, and the Ethical in Lévinas's Philosophy', in A. Peperzak (ed.), *Ethics as First Philosophy: The Significance of Emmanuel Lévinas for Philosophy, Literature, and Religion*, New York: Routledge, pp. 107–22.

Taylor, G.R. (ed.) (1972) *The Turner Thesis Concerning the Role of the Frontier in American History,* Lexington, MA: D.C. Heath.

Thiele, R. (2008) '"Forensische Studien der Hoffnungslosigkeit" ("Forensic Studies of Hopelessness"), Katie Mitchell and Leo Warner in conversation with Rita Thiele', *Wunschkonzert* (programme notes), Köln, trans. Karen Jürs-Munby.

Toklas, Alice B. [Gertrude Stein] (1933) *The Autobiography of Alice B. Toklas,* New York: Harcourt Brace and Co.

Trier, L. von (dir.) (2005) *Dogville,* London: Icon Home Entertainment

Vanhoutte, K. (2010), 'Haunted Performance: Spectral Illusions Past and Present', paper presented at IFTR (International Federation for Theatre Research), *Cultures of Modernity,* Munich, Germany, 24–31 July, Ludwig-Maximillians Universität:, Munich.

Verstraete, P. (2010) 'The Listener's Response', *Performance Research: A Journal of Performing Arts,* 15(3): 88–94.

Wallis, B. (1984) *Art after Modernism: Rethinking Representation,* Boston, MA: David R. Godine.

Wolff, T. (1998) 'Elsinore', Performance Review, *Theatre Journal,* 50(2): 237–40.

Worthen, W.B. (2008) 'Hamlet at Ground Zero: The Wooster Group and the Archive of Performance', *Shakespeare Quarterly,* 59(3): 303–22.

Wynants, N. (2010), 'Techniques of the Spectacular: Immersive Viewing Apparatus and Performance', paper presented at the IFTR (International Federation for Theatre Research), *Cultures of Modernity,* Munich, Germany, 24–31 July, Ludwig-Maximillians Universität, Munich.

Wyschogrod, E. (1995) 'The Art in Ethics: Aesthetics, Objectivity, and Alterity in the Philosophy of Emmanuel Lévinas', in A. Peperzak (ed.), *Ethics as First Philosophy: The Significance of Emmanuel Lévinas for Philosophy, Literature, and Religion,* New York: Routledge, pp. 137–50.

Žižek, S. (2001) *The Fright of Real Tears: Krzysztof Kieślowski Between Theory and Post-Theory,* London: British Film Institute.

Žižek, S. (2012) *Less than Nothing: Hegel and the Shadow of Dialectical Materialism,* New York: Verso.

Index

Printed and bound by CPI Group (UK) Ltd, Croydon, CR0 4YY